The Bisexual Imaginary

The Bisexual Imaginary

Representation, Identity and Desire

Edited by BI ACADEMIC INTERVENTION:
Phoebe Davidson
Jo Eadie
Clare Hemmings
Ann Kaloski
Merl Storr

CASSELL

London and Washington

For a catalogue of related titles in our
Sexual Politics/Global Issues list please
write to us at the address below.

Cassell
Wellington House
125 Strand
London WC2R 0BB

PO Box 605
Herndon
VA 20172

First published 1997

British Library Cataloguing-in-Publication Data
A catalogue record for this book is available from the British Library.

ISBN 0-304-33744-7 (hardback)
    0-304-33745-5 (paperback)

Cover photograph, *Self-portrait with Dumb-bells: I Am in Training, Don't Kiss Me*
(1927) by Claude Cahun, reproduced with the permission of Jersey Museums Service.

Typeset by Ben Cracknell Studios
Printed and bound in Great Britain by Biddles Ltd, Guildford and King's Lynn

Contents

Acknowledgements

We would like to thank the many people who helped and supported us during the preparation of this collection. In particular we would like to thank Mary Maynard at the University of York for her advice on the perils of publication; Heloise Brown for painstakingly preparing the index; Paul Day for transcribing many hours of taped roundtable discussion; Diarmid Scrimshaw for his assistance with the scanning of images for Stephanie Device's photo-essays; and Cath Stowers for all her work in the early stages of this project. We would also like to thank the Centre for Women's Studies at the University of York for their generous support.

Claude Cahun's *Self-portrait* and *Self-portrait with Dumb-bells* are reproduced by kind permission of the Jersey Museum, and we would like to thank the Museum Curator, Louise Downie, for her assistance. Hannah Höch's *The Coquette I, Marlene* and *The Strong Men* are reproduced by kind permission of the Design and Artists Copyright Society.

The text for Stephanie Device's butch/femme sequence in 'Sometimes It's Hard to Be a Woman' is taken from Pat Califia, 'The Femme Poem', in Joan Nestle (ed.), *The Persistent Desire: A Femme-Butch Reader* (Boston: Alyson Publications, 1992). Copyright ©1992 by Joan Nestle. It is reprinted by permission of the publisher. The text for 'Etiquette for Ladies' is taken from *Routledge's Etiquette for Ladies* (author and date of publication unknown).

An earlier version of parts of Nick Selby's discussion of Allen Ginsberg appeared in his article 'Allen Ginsberg's "Howl": Sexuality and Popular Heroism in 50s America', *Revue Française d'Etudes Américaines*, 68 (1996). Extracts from the poems 'A Supermarket in California', 'America', 'Howl', and 'Footnote to Howl' are taken from Allen Ginsberg, *Collected Poems 1947–1980* (Viking, 1985) and are reprinted by permission of Penguin Books, London, and HarperCollins Publishers, Inc., New York. Copyright © 1955 by Allen Ginsberg. Copyright Renewed.

Bi Academic Intervention began in 1993 at the National Bisexual Conference in Nottingham, UK. It provides an active and interactive forum for academics, activists and researchers working on bisexuality and bisexual issues. Since its inception Bi Academic Intervention has held regular biannual day schools on bisexuality, and we would like to thank all the participants at these day schools. Their stimulating and sometimes challenging discussion of work in progress has been a major contribution, not just to individual essays offered here but to this collection and its project as a whole.

Notes on Contributors

KATE CHEDGZOY teaches in the Department of English and Comparative Literary Studies at the University of Warwick. She is the author of *Shakespeare's Queer Children: Sexual Politics and Contemporary Culture* (Manchester University Press, 1995), and is currently working on a project on intimacy and desire in early modern culture.

PHOEBE DAVIDSON has recently completed research on the history of female bisexuality. She has written numerous articles on bisexuality, some of which have been published in *Rouge*. She is about to embark on further training in Integrative Psychotherapy.

STEPHANIE DEVICE is a woman who takes photographs.

JO EADIE lectures in Film Studies at the University of Buckingham, and in English for the Open University. He has published widely on bisexuality, including articles in Joseph Bristow and Angelia R. Wilson (eds), *Activating Theory: Lesbian, Gay, Bisexual Politics* (Lawrence & Wishart, 1993) and Mark Simpson (ed.), *Antigay: Homosexuality and Its Discontents* (Cassell, 1995). He has been an activist, trainer and community worker within the bisexual community for five years and now writes for *Bi Community News*, the UK's monthly bisexual newsletter.

MARIAM FRASER wrote her thesis *Gestures Before Bodies, Masks Before Faces* on the discursive production of the self of Simone de Beauvoir and of bisexuality. She is a lecturer at Loughborough University.

CLARE HEMMINGS is a DPhil student with the Centre for Women's Studies, University of York. Her thesis is concerned with theorizing bisexual desire in relation to contemporary UK and US culture and theories. Her recent publications include: 'Resituating the Bisexual Body', in Joseph Bristow and Angelia R. Wilson (eds), *Activating Theory: Lesbian, Gay, Bisexual Politics* (Lawrence & Wishart, 1993); 'Locating Bisexual Identities', in David Bell and Gill Valentine (eds), *Mapping Desire: Geographies of Sexualities* (Routledge, 1995); 'From Lesbian Nation to Transgender Liberation: A Bisexual Feminist Perspective', *Journal of Gay, Lesbian, and Bisexual Identity*, 1, 1 (1996); 'Writing a Bisexual Genealogy – Mapping out the Territory; From Landmarks to Spaces', in Gordon Brent Ingram (ed.), *Queers in Space: Landscapes of Marginalized Sexualities* (forthcoming, 1997).

ANN KALOSKI is a lecturer and researcher at the Centre for Women's Studies, University of York, working on bisexuality and lesbian feminist writing. She is a co-founder of Bi Academic Intervention, and has presented papers and workshops on aspects of her work at local and national conferences in the UK, the USA and continental Europe. She is currently editing a book on women's friendship for Taylor & Francis.

SHARON MORRIS teaches photography, video and related studies at the Slade School of Fine Art, University College London, where she is conducting research into the relationships between words and images in unconscious structures. She is co-author of a chapter on 'Freud's Telescope Model', in Bernard Burgoyne (ed.), *Schemas and Diagrams in Psychoanalysis* (Rebus Press, 1997). Her poetry and photographs are published in *Coil*, 3 (1996) and Rachel Lever (ed.), *Her Mind's Eye* (Pyramid Press, 1996).

NICK SELBY is a lecturer in American Studies at the Unversity of Wales, Swansea. He has also taught at the University of Wisconsin, La Crosse, where he has spent time researching the work of Ginsberg. His research interests include Whitman, sexuality and The Beats, and American popular culture. His book *Ezra Pound, Fascism and American Poetics* is forthcoming in the Mellen Press American Studies series.

MERL STORR is a lecturer in Sociology at the University of East London, where she specializes in the history and sociology of gender and sexuality. She has previous publications on psychoanalysis, sexology and formations of sexual identity, including contributions to Joseph Bristow and Angelia R. Wilson (eds), *Activating Theory: Lesbian, Gay, Bisexual Politics* (Lawrence & Wishart, 1993) and Tim Jordan and Adam Lent (eds), *Storming the Millennium: New Political Movements* (Lawrence & Wishart, 1997). She is currently researching bisexuality and sexual dimorphism.

Introduction

'Tell me, Mr Strachey,' the military interrogator asked, ' what would you do if you saw a German soldier attempting to rape your sister?' Several of his sisters were in the gallery. Strachey briefly turned to look at them, consideringly, and then faced the board to give his answer. 'I should try to come between them,' he said.'[1]

Of all Lytton Strachey's splendidly notorious *bon mots*, this is one of the most notorious and – for our particular bisexual imaginary – one of the most splendid. Strachey's intervention – both literal and metaphorical (although it may be unclear which is which) – answers his interlocutor's question by refusing to answer it. The question, coming from the authoritative position of a military tribunal, attempts to put conscientious objector Strachey in the wrong, but Strachey's reply is even more 'wrong' than the questioner expects it to be: so wrong, in fact, that the question itself implodes under the weight of its own authority. What an intervention!

The Bloomsbury group, of which Strachey was a member, is well known as a site of modernist sexual experimentation. In fact many commentators have wanted to claim the group, or at any rate some of its members, as bisexual antecedents.[2] We do not intend to claim that Strachey was bisexual; nor are we especially interested in whether his friends were. Our intention in this collection is not to intervene in biographies but rather to make a series of interventions in a range of discourses which refuse the normative questions that those discourses usually ask about bisexuality. Sometimes our contributors refuse the questions altogether and ask their own instead; sometimes, like Strachey, they answer them in such a way that the questions themselves collapse.

What all the contributions have in common is a central concern with representation. We see representation as a key issue within emergent bisexual theory for a number of reasons. First, it is important because it is an area where so much intellectual work has been – and goes on being – done; in so far as Bi Academic Intervention is an *intervention*, one of whose goals is to carve a space for bisexual theory, we want to produce work which will impact upon and redirect an existing and important field. Second, it is important because of debates about bisexual invisibility. There is an ongoing concern within bisexual communities to make bisexuality visible in places where it has previously been marginalized, and the strategies and pitfalls of representation occupy a key place in this concern. But third, another goal of Bi Academic Intervention is to intervene *within* bisexual communities. We are uncomfortable with the assertion that bisexual visibility has been a constant absence, and is therefore now an unproblematic good, and want to ask: what are the different effects of images of bisexuality, and the different meanings that become invested in it? This enables us to ask whether images of bisexuality have in fact been visible in very marked ways, structuring debates – or indeed, in the case of psychoanalysis, founding an entire discipline – without having themselves been subject to serious scrutiny.

The notion of a 'representation' is a broad one – including visual and aural performances, scientific data and legal classifications, pornography and advertising, virtual reality and political debate. Commenting on the term, Gillian Beer suggests that:

> We currently favour the word 'representation' because it sustains a needed distance between experience and formulation. It recognises the fictive in our understanding. It allows a gap between how we see things, and how, potentially, they might be. It acknowledges the extent to which ideologies harden into objects and so sustain themselves as real presences in the world. The objects may be books, pictures, films, advertisements, fashion. Their encoding of assumptions and desires re-inforces as natural and permanent what may be temporary and learnt.[3]

It is therefore a term which opens a route into the fixities and naturalizations – but also the radical potentials – of all discursive fields. It is against 'natural and permanent' meanings of bisexuality, whether literary, medical, historical or artistic, that these chapters stake their claims.

We want in this introduction to identify key debates about representation. This will serve as a general introduction to issues for readers who may not be familiar with them; for those who are more familiar with these issues, it will suggest some of the distinctive ways in which bisexuality and representation come together. The term 'imaginary' has many resonances, especially with notions of representation, identity and identification. For cultural critics and theorists, 'imaginary' can be used in the sense of 'cultural imaginary', a repertoire of cultural images and meanings which may be called upon to make sense of the world(s) in which we live.[4] Psychoanalysts use 'imaginary' to refer to a psychic realm of narcissism and identification, in ways we shall discuss in more detail below.[5] Colloquially, of course, 'imaginary' means 'imagined' or 'unreal'. As such it is still commonly encountered by bisexuals as an insult, an attempt to dismiss bisexuality as an 'unreal' or deluded sexual identity; but it might also be used as a term for opening up new spaces of fantasy and play, or for imagining new possibilities. In this introduction, and in the chapters that follow, we shall be exploring the hitherto uncharted territories of 'the bisexual imaginary' in all of these senses – and perhaps in new ones.

The transmission of information

> *represent*: 1. stand for or correspond to. 2. be a specimen or example of, exemplify. 3. act as an embodiment of, symbolize; call up in the mind by description or portrayal or imagination; place a likeness of before the mind or senses. 4. serve or be meant as a likeness of. 5. state by way of expostulation or persuasion. 6. describe or depict as; declare or make out. 7. fill the place of, be a substitute for. (*Concise Oxford Dictionary*, 1990)

One of the resonances of the term 'representation' – and this is also one of its problems – is that it invokes the idea of political representation: that there is in some sense a link between a visual or textual representation of a community, and a party, a candidate or spokesperson, who is said to 'represent' that community.[6] The term seems to encapsulate a central problematic for any project to 'represent', visually or textually, a community or group which is also engaged in some form of politics: that which 'represents' bisexuality in an artistic or textual sense is also somehow supposed to 'represent' bisexuals to the world, to act as 'our' representative. One term which tends to recur when discussing representation is 'stereotypes', invariably regarded as A Bad Thing. Yet stereotypes are just a shorthand for passing on information: they become problematic for us only when we disagree with particular stereotypical representations, especially when we feel we have no power to affect dominant images of ourselves, or of those with whom we sympathize.

Structuralist and post-structuralist theories are useful here. Briefly, structuralism – after Ferdinand de Saussure – argues that all language is a system of signs. Each 'sign' is made up of 'the signifier' – an aural or graphic representation – and 'the signified' – a meaning. The connection between the two is arbitrary: for instance there is no reason why the marks d-o-g should invoke for readers a wolf-like pet, as is made clear by the fact that this connection only works for English speakers. Not only is the connection between signified and signifier arbitrary, but it is also relational; that is, each part in the system gains its meaning only from its *difference* from something else. So, d-o-g only attains its meaning through not being d-o-t or h-o-g.

This kind of reasoning, formulated within linguistics, has been taken up by other disciplines (first by anthropology, most famously by Lévi-Strauss,[7] and thereafter by other forms of cultural theory) which attribute similar systems of signs to wider cultural activities. Structuralist concerns have developed into post-structuralist concerns, which reformulate the notion of 'difference' by paying attention to the ways in which *power* is at stake in the production of meaning. For instance, who has the power to decide, and in what circumstances, what and how signifiers such as 'bisexual' mean? The question about stereotypes thus becomes less a matter of ditching them – even if this were possible – and more an analysis of the ways in which meanings accrue; and also – to take the analysis into more actively political realms – what strategies can be used to effect a more useful or enabling range of meanings.

An important aim of this book is to make explicit the workings behind the available meanings of bisexuality, to consider how the images which might constitute a bisexual imaginary are transmitted, and come to be formed, rather than to merely label such images 'bipositive' or 'biphobic', good or bad. From this a second, connected, aim of this collection – to offer more nuanced and differentiated representations of bisexuality – may be attempted.

The expectation that representations should 'represent' us in a political sense is anyway quite unrealistic. Given the diversity among and between bisexual communities and movements – a diversity those communities and movements themselves have been eager to celebrate – there is clearly no reason why any of us should expect any given image of bisexuality to represent 'us', rather than any other bisexual individuals or groups – or even, ultimately, to 'represent' any real-life bisexuals at all. It's now some twenty years since feminist and other movements began the (still incomplete) project to abandon the notion of 'positive images', of (politically) 'representative' (visual/textual) representations, which are based on 'a common misconception to see images as merely a reflection, good or bad, and compare "bad" images . . . to "good" images'.[8] Image-makers themselves have spoken of the 'burden' they bear in producing representations of groups which are under-represented in contemporary culture and which therefore tend to expect those representations to reflect them. In a discussion among lesbian and gay film-makers in *Queer Looks*, for example, Pratibha Parmar speaks of 'what it means to be identified as a gay or a lesbian film-maker. There are expectations from the particular constituency about what your identity is supposed to represent . . . [T]he burden of representation . . . is thrust upon you'; Isaac Julien similarly speaks of the limitations imposed on representations of black characters 'because of the barrenness of the repertoire of images'.[10] The repertoire of images of bisexuality is perhaps similarly barren, and the expectations placed on 'bisexual representations' similarly unrealistic.

Thus bisexuals also need to explore our own representations. How, for instance, do Madonna or David Bowie come to be treasured bisexual images? These celebrities do not, for most bisexuals, represent anything that we might be – they are wealthy, beautiful, famous, talented, glamorous, adored, and able to manipulate their image to an extent that very few of us are ever likely to attain. And yet they are potent and positive images for large numbers of bisexuals, for reasons that have nothing to do with their 'accuracy' and everything to do with affectivity and emotion. In a similar vein, we might look at how femme/butch identification amongst bisexuals has, until recently, been buried in the rush to denounce binary oppositions;[11] or at how the denial of the swinger – whose identification was essentially as a heterosexual who experimented purely for pleasure – has forestalled a serious bisexual exploration of the meanings, potentials and depth of swinging culture. In our desire to see ourselves positively, to like our own 'selves', we have often closed off and restricted meaning, attempting to stabilize rather than analyse.

Stuart Hall has pointed out that identity 'is always constructed through memory, fantasy, narrative and myth. Cultural identities are the points of identification, the unstable points of identification and suture, which are made within discourses of history and culture. Not an essence, but a positioning.'[12] Hence it may be that the most productive tension in representation is that those whom we use to represent us may have very little in common with us, but rather serve as resources with whose meaning we may negotiate. For just as we engage creatively with the images we receive from elsewhere, so our enemies are able to engage with our own 'positive' images. The notorious actions of US Senator Jesse Helms are an example of this kind of engagement. In 1989 Helms conducted a campaign that resulted in the banning of several exhibitions of photographer Robert Mapplethorpe's work and a savage cut in the federal funding of the National Endowment for the Arts, which had funded Mapplethorpe's retrospectives. Significant in this backlash was the increased visibility of Mapplethorpe's work – the circulation of his photographs in the Senate and in courts made them excessively visible in order to justify their suppression.[13] There is no image whose fidelity to, or ownership by, a community can guarantee its political uses. As we have already suggested, the point about images is not their content but how that content accumulates meaning – the different and changing contexts of images.

Representation is an arena packed with contradictory messages. The openness of the image makes it a treasure chest whose surfeit of meaning the reader never exhausts: for new social and political situations produce new ways of reading. To return to David Bowie: just as his power as a bisexual icon was seriously dented by his increasingly straight style, he appeared at the 1996 'Brit Awards' on British television, dressed queerly in suit and stylish stilettos, singing about the ambiguity of gender and sexuality.[14] Appropriating the recycled culture he helped to produce? Probably. Cashing in on the potent pink pound? Almost certainly. And yet the image of 'our David Bowie' was back: proud and acceptable. Now, in the mid-1990s, when bisexual is chic again,[15] Ziggy has grown up.

The consumer of images

While the now largely familiar objections to the investment in representational fidelity – or, more simplistically, to 'positive images' – are forceful, they do not simply erase the desire that so many people continue to feel for positive images or role models with which to identify. Sometimes this is couched in explicitly political terms: Loraine Hutchins and Lani Ka'ahumanu, for example, write that bisexuals 'must identify the obvious, reclaim our writers, poets, painters, and activists' and go on to compile a list of 'bisexual' figures including Anaïs Nin, James Baldwin, Langston Hughes, Bessie Smith, Djuna

Barnes and the ubiquitous Bloomsbury set.[16] At other times this desire is couched in more personal terms: *The Rocky Horror Picture Show*, for example, appears to have been formative for many bisexuals.[17] In either case, there is a strong sense in which, despite the arguments against 'positive images', the availability of images with which to identify continues to be important for the development of a sense of self, whether that 'self' be individual or collective.

Psychoanalysis has provided one way of making sense of the importance of images as points for identification with the idea of the 'mirror stage', developed by Jacques Lacan. According to Lacan, babies begin to develop the rudiments of a sense of self when they begin to be able to recognize their own reflections in a mirror. Until this point the baby's experience of itself has been chaotic and unformed: it has had no clear sense of boundary between itself and its environment, and its sense of its body has been a disunified, messy collection of sensations and impulses. The image of the baby in the mirror, by contrast, appears to be whole and unified, and in recognising that baby as a reflection of itself – that is, by identifying with that reflected image – the baby achieves its first sense of itself as unified, whole, a self-contained and individual being separate from the world. This is an intense, and intensely pleasurable, moment. However, as Lacan is at pains to stress, neither the pleasure nor the recognition is straightforward, since in fact the mirror stage is a moment not so much of recognition as of *mis*recognition: the baby in the mirror is an illusion, as its very unity, wholeness and self-containment attest; even as 'I' identify with, and take pleasure in, this image of an autonomous self, 'I' know that that self is not 'me' precisely because it is autonomous and 'I' am chaotic, disunified, fragmented. Moreover, the importance of the mirror stage in the construction of the self is even more radical than this account might suggest, since it does not merely develop the sense of self but actually constitutes the self as such. It is, strictly speaking, misleading to speak of the baby experiencing 'itself' before the mirror stage because, according to Lacan, before the mirror stage there really is no 'self' to experience. The mirror stage is what constitutes us as human subjects. Thus the mirror stage is simultaneously about identification and alienation: one needs an image in order to become a 'self', but that image is always an illusory one, and one's 'self' is therefore always precarious, based on an illusion and ultimately, as Lacan puts it, 'fictional'.[18]

This might allow us to make sense of the continuing need – not just on the part of bisexuals – for images with which to identify. If we constitute ourselves in the mirror stage as subjects through an image which is not us, we go on unconsciously using images that we encounter to form and structure our sense of 'self'. The irony of the image, though, is that, like the mirror, it never can really show who 'we' are, and never does: it always gives us a picture of ourselves as somewhere else, the wrong way round, more whole and perfect than we could ever really be. We narcissistically invest in finding that repetition of ourselves which will confirm who we are, but we are always both something less – less whole, less unified, less ideal – and something more – more complex, more contradictory, more unbounded – than any image we might find. Although the gaze at the mirror of representation is intended to confirm who I think I am, it will always also provoke the unnerving feeling that I am not who I thought I was after all.

What fuels this tension is the simultaneous stability of identity – produced and reproduced through concrete images, preserved in photo albums on the personal level, or perpetually reiterated in community publications like *Gay Times*, *The Pink Paper*, or *Bi Community News* which promote collective identities – and its instability. Identity is always unstable in (at least) two senses: on the one hand, as Jane Flax has argued, it is always a fragmentary process, formed through multiple identifications with multiple and even incompatible images and objects;[19] and on the other hand it is always an uncompleted process, inaugurated by an act of perception which is constantly repeated, producing what Julia Kristeva has called a 'subject-in-process'[20] whose identities are assumed only to be thrown into doubt. Diana Fuss describes the complicated stabilities and instabilities of identity and identification as follows:

> at the very same time that identification sets into motion the complicated dynamic of recognition and misrecognition that brings a sense of identity into being, it also immediately calls that identity into question. The astonishing capacity of identifications to reverse and disguise themselves, to multiply and contravene one another, to disappear and reappear years later, renders identity profoundly unstable and perpetually open to radical change. Identification is a process that keeps identity at a distance, that prevents identity from ever approximating the status of an ontological given, even as it makes possible an illusion of identity as immediate, secure and totalizable.[21]

The psychic realm where this endless work-in-progress of identity occurs is the realm that psychoanalysts following Lacan have called the *imaginary*. The imaginary in this sense is the realm of images and identifications, the space where identity is formed, deformed and reformed through the dialectic of identification and alienation, and where we are endlessly reconstituted as subjects in relation to both ourselves and others. It is thus a space of possibility and affirmation, but also of disorientation and confusion.

We might imagine the bisexual imaginary, then, as a space through which we move, unclear whether it is an art gallery or a museum or a series of peepshows, the figures who make their appearance there offering a welcome affirmation of who we are, or an unwelcome confirmation of who we hoped we were not. The structure of that imaginary space disorients who I am: changing the 'who' from pronoun to interrogative; subverting the 'I' by returning to its gaze images of others from elsewhere; undoing the 'am' by refusing to repeat its grammar of singularity. We want to offer in this book just such a space, passage through which will not reassure or comfort you, but will rather unsettle your familiar perceptions of sexuality while offering little reassurance in their place.

Representation and production

The previous sections have looked at the semiotics and psychic dynamics of representation: we must also consider the importance in any debate on representation of questions about how an image is made possible, and the centrality of such issues as the funding of work, the market for which it is produced, its intended audiences and its socio-economic contexts. One approach which insists on these issues is cultural materialism, which has gained a particular currency in studies of sexuality and representation through the work of Alan Sinfield and Jonathan Dollimore.[22] Cultural materialism, drawing on traditions of Marxist and other political forms of literary criticism, pays attention to the particularities of the socio-economic and historical contexts in which representations are produced and consumed, and insists that all representations, by virtue of their location in those contexts, have particular political projects and effects. Careful critical reading can reveal those hidden projects; and 'dissident' reading – reading a text against the grain by looking for the moments of awkwardness or silence which indicate that those projects are under particular strain – can make it possible to open up new projects, and to create new effects, for representations which have hitherto been read as conservative. Thus cultural materialists insist on seeing art not as some rarefied practice divorced from socio-economic realities but as cultural *production*, with all the materialist and political force of that term. Sinfield summarizes cultural materialism thus: 'Traditionally, critics read for coherence; cultural materialists read for incoherence . . . we believe that every representation, with its appeal for recognition – It is like *this*, isn't it? – is political. But we think the politics should be up for discussion.'[23]

While cultural materialism, as this quotation suggests, is concerned to recognize the forces and conflicts that are played out through images – the example Sinfield gives in this context is how traditional, conservative readings of Shakespeare's *Macbeth* can be contested by readings which point out that Scotland is no less violent and disordered a place under its 'legitimate' rulers than it is under the eponymous usurper[24] – it is also concerned to register the socio-economic conflicts which support, hinder or inflect cultural production. Cultural materialism is a useful way of recognising that images do not simply have effects, but themselves *are* effects of wider conflicts: where resources go; who has access to materials; how, once accessed, those materials may be used; how, once used, they may – or may not – be disseminated; how, once disseminated, the contexts of their production affect the audience's understanding of them and the debates through which they are made meaningful.

Thus cultural materialism has made representation a vital issue by locating it simultaneously as a product of historical and socio-economic conflicts and as a mode by which those conflicts are enacted. This obviously marks an important shift away from the idea that meaning resides in the object perceived or in the way the viewer perceives it, towards a more socially and historically situated focus on the uses to which representations are put. In this sense this collection seeks to provide a context where the – sometimes controversial – choices of Shakespeare, Cahun, lesbian coming-out fiction, *The Hunger* and others as features of a bisexual imaginary can be made to engage with conflicts and debates which are alive for us.

While to some extent, as the above discussion of Hutchins and Ka'ahumanu's 'reclaiming' has indicated, bisexual writers and activists have been – and perhaps will always be – engaged in reclaiming or rewriting straight, lesbian and gay figures as bisexual, it is important to acknowledge that this happens not because it is an accurate reworking of history but rather because it reflects a particular moment in the relationship between bisexuality and other sexualities. Karl Marx, in a key text for cultural materialism, writes that people make their own history but not in conditions of their own choosing;[25] Alan Sinfield has rewritten this as 'we construct, in culture, the identities that we want – though not in conditions of our own choosing'.[26] If bisexuals in the 1990s are busily and successfully constructing a sense of bisexual identity and community, we are necessarily doing so in the context of a sexual culture where bisexuality as such has in many ways been elided. For this reason bisexuals have found it important to mark our existence in places where we may have been concealed, and it has become a particularly current bisexual mode of visibility to be constantly rewriting what has already been written by others. This leaves much of the work on bisexual 'visibility' open to accusations of essentialism – of falsely claiming that historical and cultural figures were 'really' bisexual, regardless of the historical, cultural or biographical inappropriateness of using that term in particular cases. At the heart of this problem is the question of what it is that we are 'reclaiming' – a question again of representation, but here of how we are to represent the past in ways that are both respectful of it and relevant to us. The reclamation of famous 'bisexuals' can never be historically faithful, given the relatively recent appearance of the concept as such and the myriad diverse ways in which individuals may experience and name their own sexual preferences. At the same time, it has already become a staple of lesbian and gay studies to map currents of 'homosexual' desire found in 'heterosexual' spaces, not least through the kinds of dissident reading of mainstream texts advocated by cultural materialism itself. One of the questions that this collection asks, then, is: how can we write about bisexuality without necessarily writing an (imaginary) bisexual into the picture? How, for example, might one offer a distinctively bisexual reading of *Giovanni's Room* or *Another Country* without claiming that either James Baldwin himself or his fictional creations 'were' bisexual? How might the music and lyrics of Ma Rainey and Bessie Smith be acknowledged as part of a bisexual imaginary without positing real-life, 'authentic' bisexual experience at their source? How, ultimately, can we imagine bisexuality in ways that recognize, precisely, that we are constructing and interrogating a bisexual imaginary rather than discovering an eternal, essential bisexual Truth?

Irony

We want to end this introduction with irony, and to suggest ways in which irony is a particular – though by no means exclusive – bisexual approach to representation. Postmodernism's founding tenet, that we are in a media-rich culture so saturated with images that all we can do to make them anew is to recycle and ironize them, has a particular resonance for bisexuals. There is still a poverty of images of bisexuality, and the recycling which generates contemporary bisexual imaginaries is often a quotation from other imaginaries – lesbian, gay, straight, swinging. Nevertheless, bisexuals currently have an unfashionable investment in the authenticity of their emotions which places us in a secluded spot on a map of contemporary sexualities.[27] While there is an increasing amount of deconstructive thinking around lesbian identity (as in Laura Doan's collection *The Lesbian Postmodern*) and gay masculinity (as in Eve Kosofsky Sedgwick's *Epistemology of the Closet*),[28] there is little or no irony in even recently published works on bisexuality, and instead, as we've already suggested, there is an impetus to make visible a stable bi identity. This suggests that bisexuals have still not achieved that level of saturation and stability which allows us to surrender to ironic play, nor reached a level of power where ironic representation can be risked.

On the other hand, in developing this 'authentic' sense of self, bisexuals do seem to have been adept in utilizing irony in particular ways. Take three examples: the San Francisco bisexual magazine *Anything That Moves*, the popularity of *The Rocky Horror Picture Show* and *Star Trek*[29] amongst bisexuals, and the shaping of the self at bisexual spaces such as the UK's annual bisexual conference. *Anything That Moves* plays on both biphobic and bi-positive discourses. Here bisexuals are able to take a common insult and make it 'mean' differently: it's a joke, pleasurable and playful for many bisexuals, but open to abuse, misunderstanding or even incomprehension from outside. One could similarly point to the peculiarly bisexual materiality of the displays of Trekkers (or Trekkies) and *Rocky Horror* aficionados, who make themselves 'real' through playing with transient – and alien – identities. Alongside the third example – where conference participants act out an image of bisexuality through wearing stylized clothes, taking part in the traditional group hug, facilitating the repetition of the discourses of diversity, rebellion and pleasure – it can be argued that the performance of a developing bisexual imaginary is double-edged. While group identification is clearly often experienced as a homecoming by many participants, there is also a strong sense of 'simulated ignorance', of knowing the silliness of it all and being able to enjoy the surrender and the risk. These are all examples of what could be termed an 'ironic authenticity': an acting out of the self which is conscious of its own status as performance – but no less real for all that.

Such an identity is 'on the edge' of authenticity and of artificiality. It's an identity which inhabits discourses (heterosexuality, homosexuality) where it is not recognized, an identity which says one thing and means another (to those in the know). Bisexual identities are, in short, formed through an ironic imaginary. Although all meanings, as we suggested earlier in this introduction, are contradictory and open to manipulation and play, bisexuality, like irony, necessarily partakes of the pleasures and problematics of partiality and of vacillation: it can never be *one* thing. The bisexual imaginary is both iconic (setting up an image) and ironic (destabilizing that image), without having to choose between the two.

Notes

1. Marjorie Garber, *Vice Versa* (London: Hamish Hamilton, 1996), p. 106.
2. See e.g. *ibid.*, esp. pp. 105–11.
3. Gillian Beer, 'Representing Woman', in Catherine Belsey and Jane Moore (eds), *The Feminist Reader* (London: Macmillan, 1989), pp. 63–4.
4. A key text here is Roland Barthes, *Mythologies*, trans. Annette Lavers (London: Paladin, 1973).
5. A key text here is Jacques Lacan, *Ecrits: A Selection*, trans. Alan Sheridan (London: Routledge, 1989).
6. Cf. Raymond Williams, *Keywords* (London: Fontana, 1988), pp. 266–9.
7. See e.g. Claude Lévi-Strauss, *Structural Anthropology*, trans. Claire Jakobson and Brooke Grundfest Schoepf (London: Allen Lane, 1968).
8. Griselda Pollock, 'What's Wrong with "Images of Women"?', in Roszika Parker and Griselda Pollock (eds), *Framing Feminism* (London: Pandora, 1987), p. 133.
9. Joy Chamberlain *et al.*, 'Filling the Lack in Everyone Is Quite Hard Work Really . . .', in Martha Gever, Joy Chamberlain, Isaac Julien, Stuart Marshall and Pratibha Parmar (eds), *Queer Looks* (London: Routledge, 1993), pp. 49–51.
10. *Ibid.*, p. 60.
11. See e.g. Robin Sweeney, 'Too Butch to Be Bi', in Naomi Tucker (ed.), *Bisexual Politics* (New York and London: Hawthorn Press, 1995).
12. Stuart Hall, 'Cultural Identity and Diaspora', in Jonathan Rutherford (ed.), *Identity* (London: Lawrence & Wishart, 1990), p. 226.
13. See Linda Williams, 'Second Thoughts on *Hard Core*: American Obscenity Law and the Scapegoating of Deviance', in Pamela Church Gibson and Roman Gibson (eds), *Dirty Looks: Women, Pornography, Power* (London: BFI Publishing, 1993).
14. *The Brit Awards*, BBC TV, March 1996.
15. Bisexuality went through a period of 'chic' in the 1970s similar to its 1990s chic, with high-profile articles appearing in the US periodicals *Newsweek* and *Time* in May 1974, and Janet Bode's feminist book on bisexual women, *View from Another Closet*, appearing in 1976. See Janet Bode, *View from Another Closet* (New York: Hawthorn Books, 1976), pp. 26–9, on attitudes of the day towards bisexuality; cf. Marjorie Garber, *Vice Versa*, pp. 18–20.
16. Loraine Hutchins and Lani Ka'ahumanu (eds), *Bi Any Other Name* (Boston: Alyson Press, 1991), pp. 128–9.
17. See e.g. Christopher Alexander, 'Affirmation', in Loraine Hutchins and Lani Ka'ahumanu (eds), *Bi Any Other Name*; Elizabeth Reba Weise, 'Bisexuality, *The Rocky Horror Picture Show*, and Me', *ibid.*
18. Jacques Lacan, *Ecrits*, p. 2.
19. See Jane Flax, *Thinking Fragments* (Berkeley: University of California Press, 1990).

20. See Julia Kristeva, *Revolution in Poetic Language*, trans. Margaret Waller (New York: Columbia University Press, 1984).
21. Diana Fuss, *Identification Papers* (London: Routledge, 1995), p. 2.
22. See e.g. Jonathan Dollimore, *Sexual Dissidence* (Oxford: Oxford University Press, 1991); Alan Sinfield, *Cultural Politics – Queer Reading* (London: Routledge, 1994).
23. Alan Sinfield, *Cultural Politics*, p. 38.
24. *Ibid.*
25. Karl Marx, 'The Eighteenth Brumaire of Louis Bonaparte', in Karl Marx and Friedrich Engels, *Collected Works. Volume 11* (London: Lawrence & Wishart, 1979), p. 103.
26. Alan Sinfield, *The Wilde Century* (London: Cassell, 1994), p. 21.
27. In this we are, perhaps, joined by many transsexuals, who, like bisexuals, are constantly pushed into a position where wholeness and stability need to be emphasized over ambivalence and hybridity.
28. Laura Doan (ed.), *The Lesbian Postmodern* (New York: Columbia University Press, 1994); Eve Kosofsky Sedgwick, *Epistemology of the Closet* (Hemel Hempstead: Harvester Wheatsheaf, 1991).
29. The level of science fiction fandom in bisexual communities is arguably a subcultural phenomenon in its own right. See e.g. Bernadette Lynn Bodsky, 'A Couple-three', in Kevin Lano and Claire Parry (eds) *Breaking the Barriers to Desire* (Nottingham: Five Leaves Publications, 1995); Marjorie Garber, *Vice Versa*, pp. 32–3; Liz Highleyman, 'Identity and Ideas', in Naomi Tucker (ed.), *Bisexual Politics*, p. 79.

ONE

Histories and Genealogies

I

Bisexual Theoretical Perspectives: Emergent and Contingent Relationships

Clare Hemmings

Introduction

My aim in this chapter is to explore some of the ways in which bisexuality has been and is being theorized in the USA and the UK, and to propose a way of theorizing bisexuality in conjunction with and contingent upon other desires, behaviours and identities, rather than as a separate, discrete identity. This way of theorizing bisexuality moves away from an approach that sees bisexual history as bonded to the emergence of bisexual identities or individuals, developing instead a 'bisexual perspective' that examines the importance of constructions and understandings of bisexuality in the formation and maintenance of sexual identity generally. Bisexual history is not a separate or separable phenomenon, is not only dependent upon identity politics, or chronological narratives of self that result in a bisexual identity. A bisexual perspective is a way of looking, rather than a thing to be looked for. In this context, the bisexual I/eye does not see itself reflected back in the object of its gaze, but foregrounds bisexuality in its various forms and functions, whatever the final form of the object. The 'final form' I address here is lesbian community in the late 1980s and early 1990s, in Northampton, Massachusetts, USA. The bisexual perspective I introduce highlights the importance of bisexuality in the formation and maintenance of that community.[1] The earlier part of the chapter briefly examines the growth of contemporary bisexual theory in the UK and the USA, and some of the difficulties of theorizing bisexuality when it has such a multitude of different – and often contradictory – meanings. The later part outlines the 'bisexual perspective' approach, and examines its effectiveness in relation to the above case study.

The growth of bisexual theory

To date there has not been a vast amount of bisexual theory that is not based on psychology, psychoanalysis, or sexual identity politics. When three influential works on bisexuality were published in the space of three years between 1975 and 1978 – Margaret Mead's often referenced 'Bisexuality: What's It All About?', Charlotte Wolff's *Bisexuality – a Study* and Fritz Klein's *The Bisexual Option*[2] – a virtual silence about bisexuality was broken, a silence that had lasted since Kinsey's findings in the late 1940s and early 1950s that 37 per cent of American males had had at least one incidence of homosexual contact to orgasm, and his development of the 'Kinsey Scale'.[3] Before Kinsey bisexuality was represented and produced in fictional works such as Virginia Woolf's *Orlando* and Radclyffe Hall's *Well of Loneliness,* or in sexological works such as Wilhelm Stekel's *Bisexual Love.*[4] After the late 1970s, bisexuality seemed to disappear once again as a public subject of discussion. Apart from the occasional article, there was almost no writing on bisexuality as a viable personal and political concern and choice, pretty much until the early 1990s. In the last few years, in the USA and the UK, there has been an 'explosion' of bisexual writing, and more particularly of bisexual anthologies.[5]

The lack of publications in the 1980s does not mean, of course, that no activism around issues of bisexuality was taking place. In fact, the steady growth of bisexual groups and local conferences in both the USA and the UK throughout the 1980s could be said to have been the driving force behind much of the writing in recent anthologies on bisexuality.[6] This recent interest is heartening, but interest in bisexual theory is still scarce. When I began working on bisexual theory in 1991 there were no undergraduate or graduate courses on bisexuality in the UK or the USA – Robyn Ochs's US course, 'Contexts and Constructs of Identity: Bisexuality', at Tufts in 1992, was the first course to offer bisexuality as its core topic.[7] That year also saw the publication of Elizabeth Däumer's article in *Hypatia* on bisexuality and lesbian ethics, which, as the first publication to theorize bisexuality in relation to queer theory and feminist theory, swiftly became one of the most influential articles for British bisexual theorists.[8] In the UK in 1992 a few bisexual writers, researchers and academics met up at the 11th National Bisexual conference in Nottingham, and formed the national network for research on bisexuality, Bi Academic Intervention.

Bisexual non-fiction writing has in the main been based on personal narrative, and politically, rather than explicitly theoretically, focused.[9] Many of the more theoretical pieces in bisexual anthologies, from *Bi Any Other Name* on, have been dismissed by mainstream queer or lesbian and gay academia on the grounds of not being theoretically rigorous enough.[10] In part I think this is because they do not use the accepted queer/critical theoretical canon (Freud, Lacan, Foucault, Butler, Sedgwick) and because they sometimes (but certainly not always) emphasize identity as well as behaviour, a position which is still highly unfashionable.[11] While lesbian and gay studies appear to have taken off in both the USA and the UK, 'bisexual studies' is a long way from being a reality.[12] It is only since 1995 that bisexual theorizing has emerged as a serious academic field of enquiry in its own right. As well as this volume, some examples of this increased theoretical interest and activity are a US bisexual and queer theory collection *Representing Bisexuality* (edited by Maria Pramaggiore and others) that is in the pipeline, and a discussion on bisexuality and sexual fluidity on the Queer Studies internet list in February 1995 that moved beyond the usual 'should we or shouldn't we include them' kind of debate.[13] Bisexual writers are also increasingly being asked to submit their work to anthologies that are not specifically bi-focused, but which consider a bisexual perspective to be a useful and necessary one.[14]

Marjorie Garber's epic *Vice Versa: Bisexuality and the Eroticism of Everyday Life* was published in summer 1995.[15] Garber's work is unlikely to change many queer scholars' minds about the importance of bisexual theory to sexuality studies. *Vice Versa* is extremely well referenced, engaging in tone and pleasurable to read, but could scarcely be considered theoretically rigorous – Garber uses different bisexual meanings interchangeably, and presents bisexuality as the 'answer' to restrictive notions of sexuality and society generally. Yet, given Garber's reputation – established after the publication of *Vested Interests* – and the large number of positive early reviews, it seems likely that *Vice Versa* will appear on student reading-lists and clear some space for a consideration of bisexual theory, if not within lesbian/gay/queer studies, then quite probably within cultural studies and film studies.[16]

Minefields of meaning

Part of the problem with bisexual theorizing has been working out what that task might involve.[17] Eve Kosofsky Sedgwick asks a similar question:

> Could we ask, about a concept like bisexuality that is gaining new currency, NOT so much 'What does it *really* mean?' or 'Who owns it and are they good or bad?', but 'What does it *do*?' – what does it make happen? – what (in the ways that it is being or *could be* used) does it make easier or harder for people of various kinds to accomplish and think?[18]

Sedgwick's line of questioning is useful in that it moves us away from absolute definition and possession towards looking at bisexuality as taking meaning through its function (and, one might also suggest, functioning according to particular meanings). How is bisexuality being used (and hence meaned) at present? Might it be used (and meaned) differently?

So many definitions of bisexuality proliferate in twentieth-century western UK and US culture that distinguishing one meaning from another, or working out what kind of bisexuality is meant at a given point, is a mammoth task in itself. Malcolm Bowie's definition provides the three most common definitions of bisexuality:

> **bisexuality**   This term has at least three current meanings, and these can easily produce confusion. As used by Darwin and his contemporaries it presented an exclusively biological notion, synonymous with hermaphroditism, and referred to the presence within an organism of male and female characteristics. This meaning persists. Secondly, bisexuality denotes the co-presence in the human individual of 'feminine' and 'masculine' psychological characteristics. Thirdly, and most commonly, it is used of the propensity of certain individuals to be sexually attracted to both men and women.[19]

As I indicated earlier, in 1928 *Orlando* and *The Well of Loneliness* represented and reproduced all three meanings of bisexuality, which are still current in much the same form today. I would also add to Bowie's definition that these three are not discrete, but reinforce one another. This is particularly true of the relationship between bisexuality as androgyny and bisexuality as potential. In a recent class I taught on bisexuality, a number of students' arguments that 'we're all bisexual really' were validated by examples of increasing acceptance of androgyny in nightclubs. Since one could not tell whether the desired person was male or female, and since that person was desired even so, these students concluded that this was bisexual desire (whether or not their actual sexual behaviour was still defined by same- or opposite-sex object-choices).[20] Bisexuality was being seen as pervasive, as allowing desire for either sex to 'surface', and as inclusive of and allowing for heterosexual and homosexual desires, behaviours and identities. It is precisely the individual's supposed androgyny that maintains the concept of bisexuality as potential, and makes it difficult to see bisexuality as an adult sexual identity (associated with particular acts and choices) in the same sense as heterosexuality or lesbian and gay identity.[21]

There are a number of related difficulties embedded in the structure of sexual identity that make the notion of bisexuality *as* adult sexual identity endlessly problematic. It is not structurally consistent in terms of the mutually determining object-choice and gendered subject position, or in terms of chronology. First, the sex or gender of sexual partner does not equal bisexuality. Because of this lack of consistency, the gender of the bisexual is also impossible to 'assign correctly' in order for masculinity and femininity to be seen as the only possible sexual complements. It is possible to attempt such reassignment with lesbian or gay male sexuality through terms such as 'mannish woman' and 'effeminate man', and their correlate 'opposite' object-choices. If one's own gendered subject position determines and is determined by 'opposite' object-choices, a bisexual's inconsistent object-choice (structurally at least) throws her or his own gendered position into question. A 'sometimes mannish bisexual woman'? It doesn't have quite the same ring to it. Again, the only way of producing bisexuality through this structure is as hermaphrodite, as androgyne or as the potential that precedes adult sexual choice.

Second, in terms of chronology, bisexuality does not structurally display the requisite consistency of object-choice over time. The present can be validated only by the anticipated future, which can be validated only by a past that is retrospectively given meaning according to the present. The actual events of the past are less important than the retrospective meaning they are given. One is allowed 'mistakes' as long as they are seen as mistakes, or as an interruption to the narrative of one's true sexual identity. This makes the structure of sexual identity and desire highly precarious, because it makes sense only if and when it is repeated, and so is always anticipating that moment of repetition, always failing to consolidate its permanence. As a consequence, bisexuality is frequently understood in terms of behaviour alone. Kinsey's ground-breaking work, for example, showed that a large number of United States men and women *behave* bisexually to some degree, but it saw that behaviour only as indicative of one's relative proximity to the oppositional poles of heterosexuality and homosexuality.[22] This production of bisexuality as sexual behaviour rather than identity partly informs more recent understandings of bisexuality as *only* sexual, and therefore as apolitical.[23]

Bisexual responses

Against these 'minefields of meaning', contemporary bisexual theory nearly always seeks to validate or produce bisexuality as a separate identity or position. It does this in what I identify as three central ways. First, bisexual theory frequently adopts identity and visibility tropes and narratives to advance notions of a 'separate bisexuality', one that may be linked to other identities and communities, but is discrete in and of itself. One way this is achieved is through the use of the terms 'monosexism' and 'monosexuality', which distinguish between bisexuals on the one hand and lesbians, gay men and heterosexuals (monosexuals) on the other. The pressure to decide in favour of one sex/gender or another (monosexism) is seen as one cause of bisexual oppression (biphobia). Another way of presenting bisexual identity as separate is through bisexual coming-out narratives that provide evidence of internal continuity to the experience of 'being bisexual'.[24] The problem with the understandable attempts to validate bisexuality as an authentic adult sexual identity is that similar models of identity are used (in which bisexual identity is impossible, as outlined above). Bisexuality becomes separated off from lesbian, gay and straight identity, from lesbian, gay and straight history.

Second, bisexual theory relies on the construction of bisexuality as more authentic than lesbian, gay or straight sexualities, as a way of validating bisexual identity. Once you start looking, bisexuality is everywhere. Bisexuals have been erased from history, wrongly represented and politically decried, not because bisexuality is rare but because it is everywhere repressed.[25] In fact, Garber goes so far as to insist that sexuality and bisexuality are synonymous, and, further, that '[b]isexuality is that upon the repression of which society depends for its laws, codes, boundaries, social organization – everything that defines "civilization" as we know it'.[26] The difference between Freud and Garber is that Freud does not advocate the 'unrepression' of bisexuality, whereas Garber does. Freud does not mind the unfairness, does not envision a world beyond taboo; Garber wants everyone to have equal access to all the possible sexual and erotic pleasures that bisexuality (sexuality) purportedly offers. Yet Garber's use of slightly updated Freudian under-standings of bisexuality does not actually advance the case for an acceptance of bisexual identity. It remains possible for Edmund White, in his review of *Vice Versa*, to confess that 'I denied the authenticity of my earlier heterosexual feelings in the light of my later homosexual identity. After reading "Vice Versa," I find myself willing to reinterpret the narrative of my own personal history', without having to claim a bisexual identity as a reflection of his true sexual self.[27] The assertion of bisexuality as underlying potential explains White's ability to move *from* heterosexuality *into* homosexuality. At no point does he have to consider taking on a bisexual identity. It is precisely this understanding of bisexuality as generalized sexuality that has prevented it being seen as a valid political and sexual identity.

The third way that bisexuality is advanced as 'separate' from other sexual identities is by positioning it as 'beyond', or as 'critical outside'. In particular, the latter position owes much to queer theory. It seeks less to explain or define bisexuality than it does to position bisexuality as a critical edge, as a tool that highlights structural problems within sexual identity formation in the first place. Elizabeth Däumer proposes that:

> we assume bisexuality, not as an identity that integrates heterosexual and homosexual orientations, but as an epistemological as well as ethical vantage point from which we can examine and deconstruct the bipolar framework of gender and sexuality in which, as feminists and lesbian feminists, we are still too deeply rooted.[28]

It is as if bisexuality were produced through a framework other than the stated 'bipolar' one of 'sexuality and gender'. In a similar vein to Däumer, my own work on the bisexual woman as 'double agent' within both heterosexual and lesbian communities presents bisexuality as if it transfers knowledge (and is therefore most knowledgeable), rather than being produced by knowledge, embedded within the structures of sexual identity.[29] The notion of bisexuality as 'outside', is, of course, absolutely produced through existing structures of sexual identity. Heterosexuality and homosexuality are meaningful in their contemporary forms only because bisexuality is produced as potential, as before and beyond sexual identity formation. The queer perspective, though, sees this position as *deconstructive* of identity, as a conscious positioning from which to look, rather than a pre-conscious one from which to emerge. Yet the aim is still to delineate the unique, separate insights bisexuality itself has to offer us (even as critical position), rather than critically evaluating bisexual emergence, its enmeshed relationship with 'other', at times inseparable, desires and identities, to build up a complex history, not just of bisexuality (though clearly that is one aim) but of the always contingent relationship of desire and identity.

Bisexual perspective

My project here is threefold. First, I am interested in theorizing bisexuality as *not* separate, *not* discrete. Because of bisexual presence (sometimes overt, sometimes not) in what are assumed to be gay, lesbian or straight spaces, bisexual history is partly lesbian and gay history, and vice versa. This sense of partiality is pertinent to the study of bisexuality in very specific ways, given that bisexuals have commonly occupied gay, lesbian or straight spaces and assign meaning to their desire in spaces that rarely reflect their named identity. Bisexuals come to think of themselves as bisexual almost exclusively in lesbian, gay or straight spaces.[30] I want to look at how bisexuality expresses itself in relation to those other terms (and in particular lesbianism), how its history is marked by its presence in those different communities.

Second, I aim to elucidate the ways in which the notion of a 'bisexual perspective' that I opened with can be useful for making sense of particular contexts. If bisexuality is not separate or discrete, it may also be influential even where bisexuals are not present. It is informative of other sexual identities, their production and perpetuation. It is informative of the ways we understand, name and express desire. Third, I want to highlight the knowledges of bisexuality produced in the margins of dominant discourse. Foucault argues that we 'release' subjugated knowledges, analyse and connect them, creating the genealogy that is at odds with 'history'.[31] Jana Sawicki describes this method as being 'designed to facilitate an "insurrection of subjugated knowledges"'.[32] I want to make the marginal bisexuality central. This third part of the project feels the most risky, as the potential for privileging bisexuality as the most subversive position looms large here. Yet in making bisexuality temporarily central my goal is to show how bisexuality is always produced within discursive forces and power-relations, is not repressed or hidden, free to emerge only when the forces that erase it have been surpassed. That risk – of repeating the production of bisexuality as 'outside' – is part of the project, in a way. To repeat that gesture, as I inevitably will do, is one of the markers of bisexual history, an emergent bisexual subjectivity.

Let me be clear that I do not think that identity narratives are a 'bad' thing as such. As someone who calls herself bisexual, I attach a narrative of self to that term, make sense of my experiences through that identity. Narratives are what enable us to make sense of our sexual selves in a hostile world. In fact, my need for this 're-imagining' is precisely *because* of a lack of a clear bisexual narrative, a lack of spaces where my sexuality is 'read as' bisexual.[33] We need stories – desperately. My purpose is to consider ways that bisexual stories and histories can be written so as to emphasize that familiar sense of partiality bisexuals commonly experience, rather than looking for narratives that emphasize only individual and community consistency and identity. Bisexual identity narratives do not make sense of the discontinuities and misrepresentations that make up my/bisexual life, and are part of my/bisexual history. If I tell my own past as internally consistent – I always knew I was bisexual; I always found both men and women attractive; once I came out as bisexual I found my identity (which had always been there) and community – that tells part of the story. But the time I have spent in the lesbian community, my three years as a lesbian separatist, the times where I am 'read as' something else, the always partial sense of 'homecoming', these things have in large part determined my present sense of self as bisexual, determine what it means to me to be bisexual, not just whether or not I am bisexual (see notes 30 and 33).

Northampton

I want to look at extracts from a case study of the relationship between lesbianism and women's bisexuality from work conducted in Northampton, Massachusetts, USA, as emerging through debates about the inclusion of the term 'bisexual' in the local annual Lesbian and Gay Pride March, between 1989 and 1992.[34] British readers may have seen the short documentary about Northampton on BBC2's *Gaytime TV* (13 June 1996). My aim in the case study is to show how a bisexual genealogy of desire makes sense of merged, indistinct desires and identities and the relationships between them, and illustrates the process of bisexual theory I am interested in within one particular context. More specifically, this work problematizes the assumed separation between sexual identities, by looking at the mechanisms used to maintain a sense of difference between lesbians and bisexual women, and by emphasizing the ways in which bisexual women's and lesbians' desires and experiences often undermine these attempts at separation.

Northampton, Massachusetts, has been home to one of the largest lesbian communities in the USA since the early 1970s, with the establishment of lesbian-feminist houses and co-ops. In the 1980s the lesbian influence on the town of Northampton itself became more firmly established, mainly through the growth of local lesbian businesses and cultural events. Lesbian-owned businesses, mostly bookshops, craftshops, lingerie shops, restaurants and bars proliferated, and, as a result, other stores began to target the burgeoning lesbian market. Culturally, the town offers lesbian music, lesbian dances, lesbian films (at the local arts cinemas), lesbian theatre, book-readings, academic papers and more. When you consider that Northampton itself has a population of only 30,000, this is staggering.

Yet, Northampton is not the totally safe lesbian haven that the tabloids would have us believe.[35] Since the 1970s the lesbian community has periodically been the target of homophobic violence.[36] More recently the failure of the Domestic Partnership Ordinance to pass the town referendum in November 1995 indicates that homophobia can be mobilized when right-wing factions feel that the town's lesbians and gay men have stepped over the line. As the report in the British daily newspaper *The Guardian* suggested the day before, 'a dream of sorts' was on trial: 'By Wednesday morning, [lesbians] will know if their safe haven is still safe.'[37] The failure of the Ordinance – by only 87 votes (4,770 to 4,683) – signals less that the haven is no longer safe, but more that lesbian safety in Northampton is always only partial, contingent and precarious.[38]

One might expect – in a town so full of lesbians and gay men, with so much to offer in the way of consumerism and community – that Northampton would be home to a thriving bisexual community, or, at the very least, a network of active, 'out' bisexuals. In 1995, however, there was only a small bisexual women's support group (with a core of six or seven people), a monthly bisexual women's brunch and scant community resources on bisexuality. A bisexual women's group had been more active a few years previous, but had fizzled out after the controversy surrounding the inclusion of bisexuals in the Lesbian, Gay (and Bisexual) Pride March. The Valley Bisexual Network, based in Amherst (one of the neighbouring towns), had over 150 members during the controversy, but it disbanded in 1992, coinciding with the arrival of a Queer Nation activists' group.[39] A bisexual women's support group had been formed by newcomers to Northampton in autumn 1993. This group had collapsed some six months later owing to internal conflicts over confidentiality and 'race'/ethnicity that had proved irresolvable.

Yet the evidence is contradictory. The personals ads in the local papers are full of 'bi women', 'bi femmes' or dykes 'seeking bi experience with non-sexist man'. Such bisexual desire, however, is not translating itself into group identification. If a lesbian community, a lesbian identity and lesbian desire do not allow for a strong bisexual communty, identity, desire, what does this suggest about the nature *of* that 'lesbian' signifier? Does it already include bisexual, so that there is no need for it to be named, stated as 'other' to lesbian? Or does it seek to exclude bisexual, to make it other, to serve as one relational factor (among many) that mark out the space of 'lesbian'? Issues of what is included in the term 'lesbian' run throughout the debates about the inclusion of the term 'bisexual' in the Lesbian and Gay Pride March.

Pride March controversy

The name of the annual Lesbian and Gay Pride March was changed to include the term 'bisexual' by the 1989 Pride March Committee. In 1990 the name was changed back, following a community meeting where a clear majority supported the original name. The debates surrounding these changes split the queer community in Northampton between, on the one hand, lesbians who saw the inclusion of the term 'bisexual' as signifying a move away from lesbian visibility and politics, a watering down of lesbian and gay community,[40] and on the other, bisexuals and their allies, who argued that the lesbian and gay community was and always had been their community: 'I say to . . . all the . . . people who still don't get why I and other bisexuals insist on "attaching" ourselves to the lesbian community: I do so because it *is* my community.'[41]

The debates about the inclusion of the term 'bisexual' in the Northampton Pride March and Committee emerged as a result of conflict within the lesbian and gay community, not outside it. Bisexuals wanted to see themselves represented in name as well as in terms of the work that they had put in in previous years of the March. The creation of their own bisexual community was not always an issue for bisexuals in the beginning. The majority of people arguing against changing the name of the march did so on the basis of 'group unity inclusion'.[42] The desire for 'naming' within the lesbian and gay community does of course signal a move towards separate identity and separate representation. As the arguments escalated, the concept of a separate bisexual community swiftly emerged. Yet although the debates were 'resolved' with the decision to include 'Bisexual' in 1992, and 'Transgender' in 1993, these terms did not finally signify communities of the same name.

My concern in the rest of this chapter is with the relationship between desire and identity in lesbianism and bisexuality, as evidenced through the Pride March controversy. This relationship is most clearly articulated through the language and rhetoric of visibility. Lesbians and bisexual women strive to 'see themselves', make or confirm identities of themselves through their images, recognize themselves as whole.

Visibility and identity

The increased visibility afforded bisexuals by the inclusion of their name in the Pride March is seen as *erasing* lesbian visibility. The association of bisexuality with the sexual accounts to some extent for this view that bisexual visibility equals lesbian invisibility, in that the visibility of the lesbian community as a *political* community is seen to be eliminated.[43] But what are more fundamentally at stake are the boundaries of lesbian identity itself and the supposedly discrete nature of 'lesbian difference'. In those terms, bisexual visibility *as part of* the lesbian community *does* mean the disappearance of 'lesbian visibility' and identity, *as* discrete or, at least, as self-evident.

The rhetoric of 'visibility' assumes not only a separation between terms (lesbian can be *seen, sees itself,* as different from bisexual), but also a reflexive relationship between individual lesbians or bisexuals that vouchsafes who you are (and hence reinforces that difference). 'Visibility' appears to function as a way of creating and maintaining self, as much as it is a way of obtaining external political validation. The dynamic of this visibility is that community reflects the individual, and individuals can see themselves reflected in both community and other similarly formed selves.[44] In this respect, visibility appears less to function as a way of presenting sexual identity to the world than to be about producing and confirming what constitutes that self. Instead of the identity residing in self, it is the reflection that carries the weight of identity, as well as being the site of the undoing of identity – the self and reflection (wherein lies identity) are obviously not the same, and the reflection is not singular (it includes environment, other people, etc.), even though the self can be recognized.

Lesbianism is, of course, always 'contested turf'. In this context what is interesting is the ways in which lesbianism both marks itself out as separate from and resistant to the 'bisexual threat', while simultaneously presenting an unassailable 'lesbian ethos' (and lesbian community). Two questions come to mind: in what does this 'lesbian difference' consist?; and, perhaps also by way of answering it, how is it articulated? One way of reading how the assumption of 'lesbian difference' functions is precisely to look at how the debates around bisexual inclusion or exclusion are constructed around relationships with and to men and masculinity.[45]

Privilege and passing

In one of their letters, at an early stage in the 'bisexual inclusion' debates, Elisabeth Brook and Sarah Dreher remark that at the first meeting of the 1990 Pride March Steering Committee, after pointing out that lesbian and gay issues differ from bisexual issues 'because bisexuals continue to enjoy heterosexual privilege', they were greeted with the response that they could 'pass' if they 'dressed differently'.[46] Dreher and Brook continue by saying that 'Mrs. Seigel [a prominent bisexual figure during the controversy] announced that she could speak for the Lesbian community "because I have always felt like a man in a woman's body." And so on. The horror continued.'[47]

The 'bisexual voice' in Dreher's and Brook's letter is seen to confirm the accusations of heterosexual privilege through association with three positions set up as the absolute antithesis of lesbian desire and identity: first, marriage to a man (and changing your name to your husband's); second, 'passing' as heterosexual, rather than being 'out and proud' as a lesbian ('passing' also carries connotations of passing as a man, and accessing heterosexual privilege in that way); third, personally identifying as a man in a woman's body, as transsexual. The final insult is that what appear in Dreher's and Brook's text as examples of bisexual difference from lesbianism are used by bisexuals as reasons for being able to speak for the lesbian community. At no point is there any discussion of different forms of these three positions, or even a presentation of why it is that they are considered so dreadful. The facts are assumed to speak for themselves, can only be seen in terms of 'horror'.

What a lesbian is is marked by what it indubitably is not, though the term is assumed to be self-referential and in need of no elaboration. The equation that is set up is: lesbian equals lesbian. This is considered to be self-evidential (as well as self-reflexive). Yet a whole range of related terms are signified through this equation – woman equals woman; man equals man; straight equals straight – as well as their hierarchical relationships to one another – man/woman; straight/gay.[48] The bisexual equals bisexual equation can be signified, but where it stands in hierarchical relation is more problematic – straight/bisexual?; bisexual/gay, lesbian? A single hierarchical, dualistic relationship cannot account for bisexuality, and in the two most obvious possible relationships 'bisexual' changes its hierarchical position, in which case it cannot be said to be defined by its hierarchical position alone. Where it is in opposition to 'straight', it must be really 'lesbian'; where in opposition to 'lesbian', it must be really 'straight'.

The lesbian equals lesbian equation also signifies particular sexual practices. Yet the specific *acts* signified are never actually spoken or written of explicitly. In fact, to begin to mention specificities is to suggest and highlight the ways in which the lesbian equals lesbian equation is not self-evidential. You then have to ask more precisely which acts, and which behaviours, really do signify 'lesbian' (which is, of course, to disrupt the whole functioning of the equation). Bet Power's letter to *Gay Community News* can be read as a response to the assumption that lesbian and transsexual are mutually exclusive terms. Power asserts that many of the lesbians were unhappy with the decision to revert to the former name of 'Lesbian and Gay Pride' precisely because of transvestite or transsexual feelings, behaviours and experiences.[49] Power contends that ' "[f]eeling like a man in a woman's body" is no horror, contrary to Ms. Dreher and Ms. Brook – it is simply a fact of life for another brave and proud group of newly-emerging oppressed people'.[50] What were assumed by Dreher and Brook to be incontrovertible absences from lesbian identity begin to emerge as not so incontrovertible after all.

'Lesbians don't fuck men'[51]

Probably the central assumption signified in the lesbian equals lesbian equation is that lesbian does not equal sex with men.[52] You can see this dynamic in Elisabeth Brook's letter in *Sojourner*, 'Lesbians Don't Fuck Men'. In it, Brook poses her questions – 'How can you call yourself a lesbian when you have sex with men? How can you have sex with men when you believe yourself to be a lesbian?' – in disbelieving terms.[53] For Brook, women who have sex with women and men are bisexuals: 'period'.[54] The relationship between sexual behaviour and identity is a self-reflexive one. And yet, in asking the question, Brook is forced to discuss lesbians who do have sex with men, even though this is supposed to be an impossibility. Once the central presupposition of the lesbian equals lesbian equation collapses, a space is created to ask the question in a different way. Greta Christina, for example, is able to enquire: 'Is a lesbian: a woman who only fucks other women?'[55] Here the incredulity of Brook's question is replaced by another rhetorical turn of phrase, only Christina's assumes the answer 'no'. Christina answers the question by saying:

> That would include bi women who're monogamously involved with other women. A woman who doesn't fuck men? That would include celibate straight women. A woman who would never get seriously involved with men? Rules out lesbians who've been married in the past. A woman who never has sexual thoughts about men? That excludes dykes who are into heavy and complex gender play, who get off on gay men's porn, or who are maybe just curious. Do you have to be 100% directed at women and away from men in thought, feeling, word, and deed from birth to qualify as a 'real' lesbian? That would rule out all but about two women on the planet. I hope they can find each other.[56]

Suddenly a whole range of practices, identities, experiences and histories are presented as not covered by the separation of 'lesbian' from sex with men, and as forming a part of almost every lesbian's erotic life.

Brook tries to manoeuvre around this inconsistency with reference to oppression and guilt. She says: 'Occasionally a lesbian may find herself having sex with a man because she is tired of fighting a homophobic society, because she is tired of hiding, because of her own internalized self-hatred or homophobia. But this is not bisexuality, this is pain.'[57] Lesbians do not have sex with men, then. Or, more precisely, a lesbian who finds herself having sex with a man (notice the passivity implied – a lesbian would never choose this sexual behaviour) can remain a lesbian in Brook's terms only if she is a 'guilty lesbian', a 'lesbian in pain'. There are good conscionable lesbians, and bad, guilty lesbians (bad in the sense of not displaying the requisite lesbian behaviour; bad at being lesbian, as well as bad, not good). The lapsed lesbian can re-enter the equation (which has become lesbian equals (good) lesbian) only by purging herself of her (non, or bad lesbian) error: '[t]he lesbians I know who find themselves attracted to men are disturbed by this, expend a lot of time and energy soul-searching, and try to get down to the root of the problem.'[58]

Colleen Urban argues similarly that to include bisexual women in the word 'lesbian' is threatening, 'because it does not recognize that there are women out there whose primary emotional, social, sexual, and spiritual connections are with women, exclusively'.[59] Like Brook, Urban's emphasis on the fact that some lesbians are exclusively committed to women does not put a final barrier between bisexuals and lesbians, but between 'complete lesbians' and lesbians and bisexuals who might have commitments to men (sexual or otherwise). The meaning of 'lesbian' has shifted, then, to being more to do with how you understand your relationship to sex with men than with not having sex with men at all, or with not finding men attractive. The lesbian equals lesbian equation now stands as an equation for 'ideal lesbianism', which has to be defined in relation to other forms of lesbianism, as well as other identities, and specific sexual practices. The 'lesbian difference' that seemed so incontrovertible, and was thought to reside at the heart of the lesbian community, becomes figured less as a marker of unequivocal difference than as a strategic distinction.

Static reflections

The self-referential equation of sexual identity cannot admit variation in time as well as in form. The reflection that confirms your identity only ever reflects who you are now, not who you might become, or even who you have been. It is a reflection that feeds off the object it confirms in an endless, but static, circle. In Lacanian terms, the image is 'empty':[60] it is wholly dependent on someone looking in the mirror and finding – or looking to find – confirmation of themselves. This is why it needs to be endlessly repeated, projected back into the past (this is who you always were) and endlessly into the future (this is your true self, and always will be). Separation, self-reflection, stasis: three aspects of sexual identity manifested through the visibility discourse in operation here. The 'Stay Out: Stay Proud' theme of the 1990 March is, ironically, motivated by fear. Stop changing. Let me see who you really are (so that I can see who I really am). In relation to the 'Claiming Our Identity: Protecting Our Lives' theme of the 1991 March, Brook 'encourages as many people as possible to "come out," or reveal their sexual identity'.[61] Ordinarily, this invocation would be read as asking people to 'reveal' the pre-existent truth of who they are. But in relation to the visibility discourse her comment reads as asking people to become who they are through revealing it (and seeing it reflected back). Particularly interesting about the visibility discourse here is the way it confirms identity as surface, rather than depth, as endlessly recreated and sustained, rather than as innate. There are no gaps between how one is seen, how one sees oneself, and the truth of how one is. What you see is what you get: representation equals truth.

Shifting desire and identity

I want to look at one example of how an individual's experience complicates this assumed relationship between representation and truth, and desire and identity. In her article 'On Bisexuals in the Lesbian Community', Sharon Gonsalves speaks of the difficulty of 'loss of our community'[62] for her personally, 'and for other lesbians who have come out as bisexual' (p. 7). Gonsalves is not speaking here of bisexual women who have finally realized their consistent bisexuality now that they have 'come out' as bisexual, or of bisexual women who were previously hiding in the lesbian community, masquerading as lesbians. Gonsalves presents herself as a lesbian who has taken a bisexual identity. This subtle but important distinction is underscored later in the same paragraph, when Gonsalves tells us, '[a]lthough being seen with a man may make me look like a straight woman (and afford me heterosexual privilege), I feel like a lesbian who's seeing a man'(p. 7). Gonsalves experiences her desire as lesbian even though she is in a relationship with a man. Or, more accurately, Gonsalves experiences her desire as lesbian and is in a relationship with a man. The two are not presented as mutually exclusive.

One might expect Gonsalves to continue to identify as a lesbian, then, but one who (occasionally) has sex with men: her lesbian desire relating to a lesbian identity still. After all, Gonsalves herself sees the lesbian community as 'a place where I belong' (p. 7). and she acknowledges that in some instances she does 'come out' as lesbian. Yet among lesbians Gonsalves feels 'like an imposter', 'invisible', and 'dishonest' if she is unable to come out as bisexual. The same visibility arguments that I have discussed above are employed by Gonsalves to lend credibility to her assertion that 'I am bisexual all the time, not straight among straights and gay among gays' (p. 8). *As* a bisexual, Gonsalves feels that she needs to be seen as bisexual, in order for her 'true self' to be acknowledged, understood and appreciated – '[g]etting rid of labels makes our differences invisible' (p. 8). The label 'bisexual' allows Gonsalves to be read as who she is.

And yet Gonsalves's own story is much more complex and contradictory than her 'pride-in-self-identity' story initially suggests. Gonsalves is suggesting that her 'bisexual self' is best represented sometimes by the term 'lesbian' (for example in some straight contexts), and at other times by the term 'bisexual' (for example in some lesbian contexts). The 'self' referred to is bisexual ('I am bisexual all the time'), but this is not necessarily signified by the corresponding identity label 'bisexual'. Although she stresses the importance of 'coming out', Gonsalves's narrative suggests that proclaimed identity does not necessarily equal self-identity, though that self-identity is perceived as constant.

It is already problematic that Gonsalves's lesbian desire may be directed to a man or a woman. More problematic still is that fact that the 'end result' of Gonsalves's desire is not lesbian identity but bisexual identity. It is usually assumed that desire and identity are of the same type. Desire leads to identity, which in turn explains desire: lesbian desire leads to lesbian identity; bisexual desire leads to bisexual identity. What Gonsalves is suggesting is that, for her, lesbian desire leads to bisexual identity. Gonsalves elaborates:

> As . . . a lesbian, I've learned a lot about myself; the patriarchy; ways male and female children are socialized; and about . . . oppression. . . I've also learned what relationships can and cannot be. I relate to individuals, not penises or breasts. I am capable of loving men and women, and they are capable of loving me. (p. 8)

Gonsalves's bisexual identity does not stand in contradiction to her lesbian desire. It grows from it, and from her experience of it. The problem comes in terms of the retrospective validation of her desire. Bisexual identity is not structurally seen to validate the lesbian desire that has led to it; lesbian identity cannot validate lesbian desire directed to men and women. Gonsalves is forced to find an alternative community – the 'hasbian community' (for bisexual women who were previously lesbians) – to provide the continuity in her narrative. Where lesbian community is deemed to allow lesbian identity to flow from lesbian desire, and to support that identity, closing the gaps between desire, identity and community, reducing the likelihood of 'misrecognition', Gonsalves's 'hasbian community' is self-consciously constructed to meet the needs of those for whom the disjuncture between desire and community has resulted in a bisexual identity.

Reading identity

By adopting the same terms of visibility and (self-)representation, Gonsalves domesticates the threat that the disjuncture between desire and identity poses. Yet even where bisexual and lesbian identities are consciously separated in Gonsalves's own narrative, her experience is unsettling. While representation may equal truth, it is not a deep truth, a truth that resonates with self, but a truth produced by the representation. In this respect, Gonsalves is lesbian when she states this, and is 'read' accordingly; she is bisexual when she states this and is 'read' accordingly. There is not a single image to account for Gonsalves's desires, and to 'produce' her identity. Rather, Gonsalves's identity is, effectively, produced by others' readings of her self-representation. There is not even only one mirror. Gonsalves's attempt to standardize her sexual narrative through the term 'hasbian' ignores the fact that one reason some lesbians are unwilling to include bisexual women in the lesbian community is because they know that to do so is, in effect, to change the meaning of 'lesbian' to the point where its internal variance can no longer be denied.

The seemingly paranoid fear expressed by some Northampton lesbians that the inclusion of bisexual women in the lesbian community, or the acknowledgement that some lesbians have sex with men, signals the demise of lesbian identity, is, perhaps, not so far from the truth. One lesbian comments that

> Claiming that lesbians sleep with men and calling themselves 'bi-dykes' oppresses lesbians as surely as straight male pornography. . . . Armed with heterosexual privilege and statistical distortions, bi's [*sic*] try to redefine 'lesbian' in their own image. Bi's [*sic*] are getting a lot of support for this. . . . If only it weren't for those damned uncooperative lesbians.[63]

Since the self is supposed to reside in the image reflected back to oneself and to the world, bisexual inclusion does change not only the meaning of but the very form of that image (and therefore that self). It is not just the threat of 'statistical distortion', but visual, virtual, and representative distortion that the author does not wish to 'co-operate' with. Jo Eadie suggests that

> Coming out appeals to the narcissistic pleasure of presenting to another a finished image of ourselves, which they return to us in exactly the

same form: [someone tells] you [they are] a bisexual butch, and you confirm it. But instead, it seems all too likely – especially, perhaps, for bisexuals, whose claims to identity always need that much *more* proof – that no such mirror-image will be returned. Instead, we find ourselves confronted by distortions.[64]

Acceptance of bisexual women into the lesbian community, then, means that the 'lesbian imaginary' becomes peopled with multiple selves (since the bisexual is already irresolute as well as since 'lesbian' becomes overloaded). The form of the identity–desire relation cannot support the complexity of Gonsalves's narrative. One can no longer act as if the self's image is self-identical.

Final remarks

To close I want briefly to return to my earlier comment that a bisexual women's community in Northampton does not seem to be flourishing at present. This may appear strange, given that the inclusion of the term 'bisexual' was argued on the basis of a desire for improved bisexual visibility. As the Gonsalves example and the 'bi seeks . . .' personal ads seem to indicate, however, bisexuality continues to be negotiated in relation to a lesbian community and often under the sign 'lesbian'. In a sense, this development highlights the importance of a bisexual theorizing that does not seek to enforce a separation between the terms 'lesbian' and 'bisexual'. Far from minimizing the importance of bisexuality, theorizing bisexuality in conjunction may be better able to address the production and meanings of bisexuality even where it is not manifest in a conventional 'identity form'.

Such an approach might be able to examine the ways in which bisexuality and lesbianism are conceptualized *only* ever in relationship (though not only to one another). There is, of course, an extensive amount of further work that could usefully emerge from this line of inquiry into the nature of the relationship between women's bisexuality and lesbianism: the ways in which 'race' and racism and class and classism impact the formation and maintenance of the relationship, particularly in a space as predominantly white and middle-class as Northampton; the differences (and similarities) in bisexual women's and lesbians' partial senses of self and community; the impact of temporality in the formation of bisexual women's and lesbian subjectivity.

My fear is that with the growth of the bisexual movement and the increasing emphasis on a discrete bisexuality these beautifully complex histories of contradiction and liaison risk being lost, as bisexuality becomes separated (and separable) from the very contexts in which it has gained a sense of itself.

Notes

Thanks to Bet Power, curator of the Sexual Minorities Archives, Northampton, for allowing me unfettered access to the 'Northampton Collection', and to the Fulbright Commission for making this research possible. Thanks to Ann Kaloski and Phoebe Davidson for astute editorial remarks; to the Bi Academic Intervention works-in-progress group for providing a space to get excited about these ideas (and many others).

1. In *The History of Sexuality: Volume 1: An Introduction*, Michel Foucault suggests that 'terminations of power' (e.g. oppression of women, children, prisoners) do not arise as a result of larger power-inequalities of the same type. In a slightly different sense, 'final form' may be lesbian community or identity, produced *through* meanings of bisexuality (Michel Foucault, *The History of Sexuality: Volume 1: An Introduction*, London: Penguin, 1978).

2. Margaret Mead, 'Bisexuality: What's It All About?', *Redbook* (January 1975); Charlotte Wolff, *Bisexuality – A Study* (London: Quartet, 1977); Fritz Klein, *The Bisexual Option* (New York: Priam Books, 1978). This is not to say that there were no writings on bisexuality between Kinsey and Mead, but none that had a widespread readership or effect. Other writings include: Julius Fast and Hal Wells, *Bisexual Living* (New York: Pocket Books, 1975); Philip Blumstein and Pepper Schwartz, 'Bisexual Women', in J. P. Wiseman (ed.), *The Social Psychology of Sex* (New York: Harper and Row, 1976); Janet Bode, *A View from Another Closet: Exploring Bisexuality in Women* (New York: Hawthorn, 1976).

3. The Kinsey Scale numbers 0 to 6, 0 being exclusively heterosexual, 6 being exclusively homosexual. The 'true bisexual' is understood to be a Kinsey 3, equally attracted to men and to women. While Kinsey's findings shocked America in the late 1940s and early 1950s, the issue of bisexuality was never substantially discussed. See Alfred Kinsey, Wardell Pomeroy *et al.*, *Sexual Behavior in the Human Male* (Philadelphia and London: W. B. Saunders Company, 1948); Alfred Kinsey, Wardell Pomeroy *et al.*, *Sexual Behavior in the Human Female* (Philadelphia and London: W.B. Saunders Company, 1953). See also the UK documentary about Kinsey: *Reputations* (director and producer C. Beavan), BBC2, 4 April 1996.

   It is not clear why there was such a long silence about bisexuality from 1953 until the 1970s. Gayle Rubin and others have written on probable causes of silence and repression of deviant sexual behaviour in the 1950s and 1960s. See Gayle Rubin, 'Thinking Sex: Notes for a Radical Theory of the Politics of Sexuality', in C. Vance (ed.), *Pleasure and Danger: Exploring Female Sexuality* (Boston: Routledge & Kegan Paul, 1984). Rubin's influential piece does not acknowledge bisexuality as a deviant sexuality, however. Work on bisexuality in this period still needs to be done.

4. Virginia Woolf, *Orlando: A Biography* (London: The Hogarth Press, 1928); Radclyffe Hall, *The Well of Loneliness* (London: Jonathan Cape Ltd, 1928); Wilhelm Stekel, *Bisexual Love* (New York: Physicians and Surgeons Book Co., 1934). Virginia Woolf's *Orlando* represented and reconfirmed the medical view of bisexuality as the combining of male and female, masculine and feminine traits in one body. Radclyffe Hall's *The Well of Loneliness* may seem an unlikely choice of early twentieth-century bisexual representation and production, given its prominent role within the canon of lesbian fiction. In the figure of Mary, however, the feminine woman, described by Havelock Ellis as 'the woman to whom the actively inverted woman is most attracted' (Havelock Ellis, *Studies in the Psychology of Sex: Volume 2: Sexual Inversion in Women*, Philadelphia: F. A. Davis Co., 1918), is another understanding of bisexuality. Bisexuality is that human propensity which allows Mary to be attracted to both women and men; it allows for and explains her return to the heterosexual world at the end of the novel. This 'traitorous moment' has haunted twentieth-century femmes ever since, and, more recently, has established a conflicted relationship between femme and bisexual identities. I am aware that *The Well of Loneliness* can also be read as a transsexual autobiographical narrative (in which case our understanding of Mary would shift once again). I examine these meanings of bisexuality as potential, hermaphrodite and androgyne later in this chapter.

5. This bisexual 'explosion' has been particularly noticeable in the USA. The most notable works in this area are: slightly earlier, Fritz Klein and Timothy Wolf (eds), *Two Lives to Lead: Bisexuality in Men and Women* (New York: Harrington Park Press, 1985); Thomas Geller (ed.), *Bisexuality: A Reader and Sourcebook* (Ojai, CA: Times Change Press, 1980); Loraine Hutchins and Lani Ka'ahumanu (eds), *Bi Any Other Name: Bisexual People Speak Out* (Boston: Alyson Publications, 1991); Elizabeth Reba Weise (ed.), *Closer to Home: Bisexuality and Feminism* (Seattle: Seal Press, 1992); Naomi Tucker (ed.), *Bisexual Politics: Theories, Queeries, and Visions* (New York: Harrington Park Press, 1995); Sharon Rose *et al.*, (eds), *Bisexual Horizons: Politics, Histories, Lives* (London: Lawrence & Wishart, 1995). Sue George's *Women and Bisexuality* was the first (non-anthology) book to be published on women's bisexuality for fifteen years, and is still one of the few British books on the subject (Sue George, *Women and Bisexuality,* London: Scarlet Press, 1993).

6. In the UK there are currently twenty-four local bisexual groups; a national bisexual women's network; a national bisexual phoneline; a national HIV and AIDS education and action group, Bisexual Action on Sexual Health (BASH); a national SM bisexual group and newsletter, *Ungagged*; and a national bisexual youth network (Biscuits). The national magazine *Bifrost* folded in 1995, but has been replaced by *Bi Community News*, from which this information is taken (*Bi Community News* (March 1996), 5, pp. 11–12). In the USA there are local bisexual groups in almost every large city; a national bisexual network (BiNet); a national magazine, *Anything That Moves;* and, since the First National Bisexual Conference in the USA in San Francisco in 1990, regular national gatherings. Bisexual space has also been created on the internet, with user-lists and net-sites proliferating. See *Anything That Moves,* issue 10, for details of internet sites and addresses.

7. Robyn Ochs's course on bisexuality was offered again in 1996, under the slightly amended title of 'Identity/Politics: Bisexuality in Context'.

8. Elizabeth Däumer, 'Queer Ethics; or, The Challenge of Bisexuality to Lesbian Ethics', *Hypatia: A Journal of Feminist Philosophy*, Special Issue: Lesbian Philosophy, 7, 4 (fall 1992), pp. 91–105.

9. It is not my intention to draw fast lines between theory, personal narrative and politics. In fact, my work on theorizing bisexuality attempts to integrate a number of processes not always considered 'theoretically pure'. I do think that there is a difference, however, between work that takes *theorizing* bisexuality as its primary concern, that may or may not draw on political or personal moments to speak about bisexuality, to situate bisexuality, or even to imagine bisexuality, and work whose emphasis is on validating a bisexual voice or a particular political practice. I realize that this distinction is tenuous at best.

10. For example, one of the organizers of the 'Lesbian/Gay/Queer: Knowledges and Identities for the 90s' conference at the University of California, San Diego, USA, 20–1 January, 1995, was not interested in including a bisexual speaker at the conference (or the term *bisexual* in the title) because she felt that bisexual theory was not as sophisticated as queer theory (since it re-emphasized identity, rather than behaviours and subjectivities). I found this view profoundly annoying, and yet I could not divorce it from my own view that bisexual theory does need to be more 'engaged' with currently popular theories within feminist and sexuality studies. One difficulty is that, where bisexual writers do not identify the meanings of the term 'bisexuality' that they are using, 'bisexuality' ends up 'unconsciously' carrying a number of different meanings – most commonly androgyny and potential – even where the writer explicitly states otherwise (e.g. Marjorie Garber's readings of Marlene Dietrich and Oscar Wilde in *Vice Versa*: Marjorie Garber, *Vice Versa: Bisexuality and the Eroticism of Everyday Life,* New York: Simon & Schuster, 1995). I discuss these issues in the next section of the chapter.

11. In her article 'Shame in the Cybernetic Fold', Sedgwick identifies this trend within queer theory. Eve Kosofsky Sedgwick, 'Shame in the Cybernetic Fold: Reading Silvan Tomkins', *Critical Inquiry* (winter 1995), pp. 496–522. Partly as a result of inter-ventions within queer theory by bisexuals and, in particular, transsexuals, a new genre

of queer thinking, New Essentialism, which prioritizes the body and personal experience as real – though not unchanging – is growing in popularity in the USA.

12. The usefulness of the term or discipline 'bisexual studies' is disputed by the editors in the Roundtable Discussion at the end of this book.

13. Posts ranged in content from those saying that they would never have sex with a bisexual (20 February 1995 02:15:24 EST), those interrogating the political usefulness of the term, those looking at personal reasons for the discomfort with bisexuals – 'If I do have any problems concerning bisexuality, the source is no more complicated than a broken heart experienced during the formative period of my gay identity' (David Anderson, 21 February 1995 20:00:00 PST) – to those examining the relationship between desire for particular sexes and desire for particular genders – 'identifying as "bisexual" often expresses little of my queer desire for fems (of whatever sex)' (Lynne Degitz, 22 February 1995 17:02:21–0500). Other interesting threads of the debate included the relationship between bisexuality and biraciality, which moved beyond simply stating that both find themselves 'in between' the dominant oppositions of hetero/homo and white/black respectively. Queer Studies list <QSTUDY-L @UBVM.cc.buffalo.edu>, 20 February 1995 to 28 February 1995.

14. One of the first queer volumes that included bisexuality in its title and two articles addressing bisexuality was Joseph Bristow and Angelia R. Wilson (eds), *Activating Theory: Lesbian, Gay, Bisexual Politics*. Other recent anthologies to include articles on bisexuality are S. O. Weisser and J. Fleischner (eds), *Feminist Nightmares: Women at Odds* (New York: NYU Press, 1994); David Bell and Gill Valentine (eds), *Mapping Desire: Geographies of Sexualities* (London: Routledge, 1995); Gordon Brent Ingram (ed.), *Queers in Space: Landscapes of Marginalized Sexualities* (forthcoming, 1997). The new *Journal of Lesbian, Gay, and Bisexual Identity*, ed. W. Blumenfeld, includes articles on bisexuality, and has bisexual researchers on the editorial board. Writers whose work is part of the emerging 'academic bisexual interest' include: (from Australia) Steven Angelides, 'The Economy of (Hetero)sexuality', *Melbourne Historical Journal*, 23 (1995), pp. 39–58; (from the UK) Jo Eadie, 'Activating Bisexuality: Towards a Bi/Sexual Politics', in *Activating Theory*; Clare Hemmings, 'Locating Bisexual Identities: Discourses of Bisexuality and Contemporary Feminist Theory', in *Mapping Desire*; Clare Hemmings, 'From Lesbian Nation to Transgender Liberation: A Bisexual Feminist Perspective', *Journal of Gay, Lesbian and Bisexual Identity*, 1, 1, (January 1996), pp. 37–60; (from the USA) Frann Michel, 'Do Bats Eat Cats? Reading What Bisexuality Does', in Donald Hall and Maria Pramaggiore (eds), *Representing Bisexuality* (forthcoming).

15. Marjorie Garber, *Vice Versa: Bisexuality and the Eroticism of Everyday Life*. The sheer range of Garber's book is staggering. She looks at bisexuality as it has been understood throughout history; its role within sexology, psychoanalysis and psychology; its function in relation to literature, art and culture; and the farthest reaches of its possible meanings (is sexual attraction to a grapefruit bisexual attraction?).

16. Marjorie Garber, *Vested Interests: Cross Dressing and Cultural Anxiety* (New York: Routledge, 1992). For reviews of *Vice Versa* see, for example: in the USA, Frank Kermode, 'Beyond Category', *New York Times Book Review* (9 July 1995), pp. 6–7; Edmund White, 'Gender Uncertainties', *New Yorker* (17 July 1995), pp. 79–81; in the UK, George Melly, 'Sexuality's Double Take', *Guardian* (19 January 1996), p. 17; Syrie Johnson, 'Alice, the Vampire and the Bisexual', *Evening Standard* (22 January 1996), p. 24; Roger Clarke, 'Working Both Sides of the Street', *The Independent Weekend* (20 January 1996), p. 9.

The issue is then raised about where bisexual theorizing is likely to find an academic home. It is interesting that although current bisexual theory often engages directly with lesbian/gay/queer theories, experiences and practices, and, in many ways, sees itself as embedded within that tradition (as well as this chapter, see the chapters by Ann Kaloski and Mariam Fraser in this volume for different perspectives on that tradition), it seems increasingly unlikely that lesbian/gay/queer studies will be a site of acceptance and encouragement of bisexual theory within academia.

17. At the 'Activating Theory: Lesbian, Gay, Bisexual Politics' conference at York University, in 1991, Ann Kaloski and I co-ordinated a workshop on women and bisexuality. One section of the workshop asked the question 'what is bisexual theorizing?', to which no one had even tentative suggestions. At that stage, even the possibility of theorizing bisexuality in any consistent way seemed difficult to imagine.

18. Eve Kosofsky Sedgwick, 'Bi', Queer Studies list <QSTUDY-L@UBVM.cc.buffalo.edu>, 17 August 1994: 15:49:34–0400.

19. Malcolm Bowie, 'Bisexuality', in E. Wright (ed.), *Feminism and Psychoanalysis: A Critical Dictionary* (Oxford: Basil Blackwell, 1992), p. 26.

20. Similarly, in a 1995 *Newsweek* article, bisexuality emerges as individual refusal to accept society's gendering of self, as well as (or, possibly, determining) desire unconstrained by gender of object-choice (John Leland, 'Bisexuality', *Newsweek* (17 July 1995), pp. 44–50).

21. This is reminiscent of a Freudian notion of bisexuality as potential, as the basis of human sexuality from which we (have to) go one way or another. For the development of Freud's position on bisexuality (which is anything but consistent) see Garber's chapter 'Freud and the Golden Fliess' (Marjorie Garber, *Vice Versa*, pp. 169–206).

22. Curiously, in this context, bisexuality becomes stripped of sexuality in itself, while being seen as the 'tie that binds' both the two oppositional poles of heterosexuality and homosexuality. Bisexuality is both *only* sexual, and also *a*sexual. To be a Kinsey 3 is to be equally attracted to men and women, i.e. completely bisexual (see note 3); it is also to be equally unattracted to men and women, i.e. completely asexual. Bisexuality is never about *two*, only about one – asexual, or self-fulfilling – or *three* – continuously and equally attracted to both men and women (Alfred Kinsey *et al.*, *Sexual Behaviour in the Human Male*, pp. 636–59, and *Sexual Behaviour in the Human Female*, pp. 468–76).

23. This view of bisexuality as primarily sexual is evidenced in the case study of lesbian community in Northampton, Massachusetts, which I look at later in this chapter.

24. Bisexual coming-out narratives chart an authentic, chronologically-validated bisexual self. The need to mention one's lasting attractions to people of both sexes also figures prominently in bisexual self-narratives. One of the contributors to the volume *Bisexual Lives* begins her story with a list of her current lovers, with the time that she has been seeing each of them in parentheses – for example, 'Amanda (for two and a half years), Paul (for four and a half years)', and the list goes on (Off Pink Collective, *Bisexual Lives*, London: Off Pink Publishing, 1988, p. 27). The impression that is hard to shake is that here is a *real* bisexual, dedicated to multiple object-choices of both sexes, steadfast in her endlessly mutable, never-satisfied bisexual desire.

25. Sue George, *Women and Bisexuality*, and Amanda Udis-Kessler, 'Challenging the Stereotypes', *Bisexual Horizons*, pp. 45–57, are two of the proponents of bisexuality as historically (and currently) erased and wrongly represented. Udis-Kessler sees negative stereotypes of bisexuals as wholly erroneous, and in no way productive of bisexuality generally. See the Introduction to this volume for a critique of this position. See Marjorie Garber, *Vice Versa*, for an elaboration of the view of bisexuality as repressed by culture.

26. Marjorie Garber, *Vice Versa*, p. 206.

27. Edmund White, 'Gender Uncertainties', p. 81.

28. Elizabeth Däumer, 'Queer Ethics', p. 98.

29. Clare Hemmings, 'Resituating the Bisexual Body: From Identity to Difference', in *Activating Theory*, pp. 129–32.

30. Obviously, lesbians, gay men and heterosexuals also occupy cultural spaces that do not fully reflect their identity. Yet since there are few bisexual spaces, this lack of self-recognition differs in type as well as in degree. I would suggest that although such spaces are now being formed, they are not, as yet, culturally widespread enough to be a primary factor in bisexual self-identification. Lesbian and gay spaces, while not providing a perfect match for all those naming themselves as lesbian or gay, do, however, provide spaces within which they can *negotiate* their particular named identity. Identity is commonly negotiated both within similarly named spaces, and in

relation to differently named or non-named spaces. Heterosexual spaces, are, of course, rarely named as such, yet this is because spaces that are not otherwise named are assumed to be heterosexual by default. The negotiation of a heterosexual identity is still conducted in territory that recognizes the subject *as* heterosexual. The experience of being heterosexual in non-named spaces, or being lesbian or gay in named spaces that do not accurately reflect one's whole identity, but do recognize the subject *as* heterosexual, lesbian or gay, is very different from the experience of being bisexual in lesbian, gay or straight space. The negotiation of the specifics of a bisexual identity within space that does not recognize that identity in whatever form, other than as differently named (i.e. lesbian, gay or heterosexual), is inseparable from the constitution of a bisexual identity. This may be one reason why, whereas lesbians and gay men are commonly happier to relinquish claims on straight culture once they have 'come out', bisexuals are more likely to insist that lesbian and gay culture is still legitimately 'theirs' even if they no longer identify with those names.

31. Michel Foucault, 'Lecture One: Jan. 1976' and 'Two Lectures', in C. Gordon (ed.), *Power/Knowledge: Selected Interviews and Other Writings 1972-1977* (Brighton: Harvester, 1980), pp. 85ff.

32. Jana Sawicki, *Disciplining Foucault: Feminism, Power, and the Body* (New York: Routledge, 1991), p. 26.

33. It is useful to compare bisexual 'mis-reading' to, for example, lesbian femme misreading as straight. Yet when femmes themselves speak of this misreading, it is with the knowledge and culture that they are misread unless with a woman lover who confirms in terms of representation what she *already* knows herself to be. When bisexuals are 'mis-read', it is not with the knowledge that a different environment would provide the 'right' reading. The 'mis-reading' is a particular bisexual experience *of self*, negotiated in different ways and with different meanings and effects from the negotiations of a lesbian femme. See Mariam Fraser's and Ann Kaloski's chapters in this volume for further discussion of the relationship between lesbian and bisexual subjectivities and identities. I touch on these issues of misreading, and the negotiation of bisexual subjectivity under the sign lesbian, in the second part of this chapter.

34. I have conducted research on archival material that is perfect as the basis for evaluating the emergence of a bisexual identity in the context of lesbian spaces, politics and theory. The Northampton Sexual Minorities Archives in Massachusetts, USA, is a grassroots resource run from the curator's house. It includes 'The Northampton Collection' of personal papers, cassettes, slides, newspaper clippings, etc., which documents lesbian events, political discussions, celebrations and personal relationships, etc. in the Northampton area from 1968 to the present. This archival source has never been worked on before, though there is a small amount of work on the Northampton debates themselves: Stacey Young's article on these debates in Northampton draws on published letters and articles in *Gay Community News* (Stacey Young, 'Bisexuality and the Limits of Identity Politics', in *Bisexual Politics*); and Marjorie Garber also briefly mentions these debates in her chapter 'Bi-Sexual Politics' (Marjorie Garber, *Vice Versa*, pp. 80–2).

35. Northampton came to the eyes of the ever-curious US public with a feature article in the *National Enquirer* in April 1992 (Anon., 'Strange Town Where Men Aren't Wanted', *National Enquirer* (21 April 1992), p. 8). The sensationalist article dubbed Northampton 'Lesbianville, USA', and gave the (false) impression that a third of Northampton's population is lesbian. More conservative estimates are that between a tenth and a fifth of the population is lesbian or gay (whether these statistics include bisexuals is not stated). The *National Enquirer* article gave rise to a number of other articles on the town's lesbian community, for example in the *Los Angeles Times* (19 December 1992) and the *Associated Press*, and was covered on CNN national news channel, and *20/20*, a sensationalist news-talk show, in September 1992. All these reports portrayed Northampton as *completely* safe and non-homophobic.

36. An article in *Lesbian Connection* in 1977 on Northampton's lesbian community discusses the creation of an 'attack and defense patrol' in August 1975, in response to several weeks of harassment, 'culminating in an attack by several men with a shovel

and a machete, at a neighborhood bar where lesbians hung out' (Anon., 'Analysis of a Lesbian Community – Part One', *Lesbian Connnection* (July 1977), p. 7; New Alexandria Lesbian Library (NALL), 'The Valley Women's Lesbian Movement: A Herstorical Chronology 1968–1984'). In 1982 and 1983, threats on individual lesbians, the New Alexandria Lesbian Archives (later the Sexual Minorities Archives) and lesbian-owned businesses in Northampton (particularly Womonfyre Books) were the targets of homophobic harassment in the form of death threats left on answer-phones and in letters (NALL, 'The Valley Women's Lesbian Movement').

A video made by Heramedia in 1986 on violence against lesbians includes a section on the violence in Northampton in 1983. Violence against lesbians is explained as to do with men's feelings of exclusion – 'lesbians by definition exclude men and this is seen as a threat to male prerogative and masculinity' (Heramedia, 'Just Because of Who We Are: Violence Against Lesbians', typescript of taped interview for twenty-minute film of same name (New York, 1986), n.p.).

37. Jonathon Freedland, 'This Town Is Big Enough for the Both of Us', *Guardian* (6 November 1995), p. 7.

38. Anon., 'Domestic Partner Law Defeated: Hamp Says No by 87 Votes', *Union News* (8 November 1995), n.p. I am not suggesting here that 'equal rights' would be guaranteed if the Ordinance had passed the referendum. The issue of Domestic Partnership is highly contentious, not least because it assumes that lesbians and gay men want to be 'just like' heterosexuals. Nevertheless, it is clearly seen as a threat to 'heterosexual morality' by those contesting it. For the pros and cons of fighting for Domestic Partnership or marriage rights, see Warren Blumenfeld, 'Same-Sex Marriage: Introducing the Discussion' and 'Point(s)/Counterpoint(s)', *Journal of Gay, Lesbian, and Bisexual Identity*, 1, 1 (January 1996), pp. 77–98.

39. Chris Muther, 'Despite Bi Controversy, 2000 Celebrate Northampton Pride', *Gay Community News* (13–19 May 1990), p. 3. It is not clear what the precise causes of the folding of the Valley Bisexual Network were. Many of the key members of the Valley Bisexual Network began writing for the newssheet *Queer Nation Speaks* (UMass, Amherst) in 1992. This is not to suggest that Queer Nation simply *displaced* the Valley Bisexual Network, however.

40. Jodi Lew, 'Pain and Politics: the Next Pride March', *Valley Women's Voice* (March, 1990), n.p.; Sarah Dreher and Lis Brook, 'Letters to the Editor', *Gay Community News* (11–17 March 1990), pp. 3–4.

41. Robyn Ochs, 'Self-Identifying as Bisexual: a Political Statement', *Gay Community News* (8–14 April 1990), p. 4.

42. Fred Contrada, 'Gay Pride March Slated Saturday', *Union News* (2 May 1990), n.p.

43. This emphasis on the correlation between bisexuality and 'the sexual' is not new. Textually, this is commonly denoted by assigning a lower-case 'b' for 'bisexual' and an upper-case 'L' for 'Lesbian'. In the Northampton Pride March debates, the editor of the lesbian listings magazine *The Calendar* consistently distinguishes between 'Lesbians' and 'bisexuals' (*The Calendar: A Monthly Listing of Events by, for, and about Lesbians in the Connecticut River Valley* (February 1990), p. 1). Those in favour of the inclusion of the term *bisexual* frequently capitalize both 'Lesbian' and 'Bisexual', in order to highlight the political nature of bisexuality – see, for example, Bet Power, 'Who Gets to "Belong" in the Lesbian Community Anyway?', *Gay Community News* (8–14 April 1990), pp. 4–5. I am not sure when this distinction is first made, but it appears in the C.L.I.T. papers of 1976 – 'many of the women of the Black Left are Lesbians or bi-sexual' (Collective Lesbian International Terrors (C.L.I.T.), 'C.L.I.T. Collection No. 2, C.L.I.T. Statement No. 3', *Dyke: A Quarterly* (Spring 1976), p. 47).

The hyphen in 'bi-sexual' also reinscribes bisexuality as *orientation*, psychological characteristic or propensity, rather than identity.

44. This is similar to the mirror stage that Lacan describes in *Ecrits* as the moment of self-recognition, which is co-extensive with the moment of seeing oneself as 'other' (*over there*) and as part of a particular environment (also seen in the reflection). Sexual identity politics' visibility narratives could be seen as a social representation of a truly psychoanalytic moment – only in Lacan, that no identity *per se* exists pre-mirror stage

is made explicit (Jacques Lacan, *Ecrits* (Paris: Editions d'Seuil, 1966); reprinted London: Routledge, 1989, pp. 1–7).

45. The debates were conducted in a series of newspaper articles in local, regional and national newspapers as well as in formal public forums in Northampton. Here I discuss extracts from newspaper debates, in particular by prominent members of the lesbian community (on both sides).

46. Sarah Dreher and Lis Brook, 'Letters to the Editors', p. 2.

47. *Ibid.*

48. At first glance these constructions may appear similar to those articulated by Monique Wittig in her essay 'One Is Not Born a Woman'. Wittig, while seeing 'lesbian' as outside the binary/class dependency of Man/Woman, does not, however, see these constructions as natural or inevitable. On the contrary Wittig asserts that, once the sex class revolution is won, there will be no need for the term *lesbianism* (Monique Wittig, 'One Is Not Born a Woman', *The Straight Mind and Other Essays* (London: Harvester Wheatsheaf, 1992)).

49. Bet Power, 'Who Gets to "Belong" in the Lesbian Community Anyway?', p. 5.

50. *Ibid.*

51. Elisabeth Brook, 'Lesbians Don't Fuck Men', *Sojourner*, 14, 11 (July 1989), p. 6.

52. Questions about the relationship of men to the lesbian movement more generally have, of course, always been an issue. The increasingly close association of the women's movement and lesbianism during the 1970s meant that the sexual aspect of lesbians' relationship to men was also extended into political significance, the sexual form of feminist resistance articulated as no contact (as well as no sex) with men – 'the initial and continuing power of the Women's Movement flows from our actual separation from men to form a movement of women dissatisfied with men' (C.L.I.T., 'C.L.I.T. Collection No. 2', p. 41).

53. Elisabeth Brook, 'Lesbians Don't Fuck Men', p. 6.

54. *Ibid.*

55. Greta Christina, 'Drawing the Line: Bisexual Women in the Lesbian Community', *On Our Backs: Entertainment for the Adventurous Lesbian* (May–June, 1990), p. 14.

56. *Ibid.*, pp. 14–15.

57. Elisabeth Brook, 'Lesbians Don't Fuck Men', p. 6.

58. *Ibid.*

59. Colleen Urban, 'Lesbians Are Not Bisexuals', *Sojourner*, 15, 3 (November 1989), p. 4.

60. Jacques Lacan, *Ecrits*, p. 1.

61. Elisabeth Brook, cited in J. Kelliher, 'Gay Pride March Set for May 4: Event's Title Still Excludes "Bisexual"', *Daily Hampshire Gazette* (12 April 1991), p. 3.

62. Sharon Gonsalves, 'On Bisexuals in the Lesbian Community', *Sojourner*, 14, 9 (May 1989), p. 7. All further references to this article are in the text.

63. Anon., in Elizabeth Armstrong, 'Traitors to the Cause? Understanding the Lesbian/Gay "Bisexuality Debates"', in *Bisexual Politics*, pp. 199–200.

64. Jo Eadie, 'Bisexuality and Narcissism: Some Thoughts Sparked off by the 4th BAI Dayschool', article for distribution to the Bi Academic Intervention Network, 1996.

2

Lose Your Face[1]

Mariam Fraser

I have my identity and I have my sex: I am not new yet.[2]

In *The History of Sexuality* Foucault argues that although sexuality, in contemporary western societies, neither resides within nor is inherently expressive of the truth of the self, we nevertheless *perceive* it to be so: 'A double petition,' Foucault writes, 'in that we are compelled to know how things are with it, while it is suspected of knowing how things are with us.'[3] What of the truth of bisexuality? Some researchers imply that it is a 'riddle'[4] (which presumably requires solving). This position suggests an ignorance of bisexuality, or even ignorances. But as Eve Sedgwick contends: 'far from being pieces of the originary dark, [ignorances] are produced by and correspond to particular knowledges and circulate as part of particular regimes of truth.'[5] To suggest that bisexuality is a riddle then, is not to place it beyond knowledges of sexuality, nor is solving the riddle of bisexuality beyond the fecund propagation of truths. Indeed, the notion of bisexuality as *the* riddle might be no more than another exploitation of *the* secret which must be spoken of *ad infinitum*.[6]

Nevertheless, given the riddled status of bisexuality, it is tempting to invoke a conspiracy of oppression *par excellence*, tempting to try to liberate bisexuality from veils of misrepresentation, misrecognition or 'misinformation'[7] and to 'expose' its hidden truth. In much of the recent literature on bisexuality[8] for example, the constituted (bisexual) self, and its invisibility, are assumed: 'invisibility is, for the present, how we [bisexuals] experience oppression.'[9] This central presupposition – that the bisexual self, although invisible, objectively 'exists' – forces the question as to how such oppression has come about. A narrative subsequently emerges, wherein bisexuality's apparently singular and unique history[10] is perceived to offer a radical and emancipatory potential which other identities, including queer, do not: 'Bisexuality alone calls these assumptions ["the dichotomization between politics and desire"] into question'[11]; the 'bisexual community would pose a significant and unique challenge to the dual gender system and the limitations inherent in compulsory heteromonosexuality';[12] the 'queer community was established on a set of norms of what constituted queer. . . . If we only replicate the system that has oppressed us, then are we as progressive as we would like to think we are?'[13] In other words, if the self-identified bisexual, or bisexuality, stands in an isolated position with respect to lesbian, gay and queer theory and politics, it is precisely this isolation which has enabled it to maintain an autonomy from the tarnishing processes, authorities and legitimizations which enable 'other' identities to be adopted.

To argue that the bisexual self stands as evidence of the truth of bisexuality, or that bisexuality is evidence for the truth of a bisexual self, is to take much for granted. Most importantly, it assumes that bisexuality is anchored to a self; that (like other sexualities) it resides within and is expressive of the truth of the self who possesses it – or who is possessed by it. It may be the case however, that the self does not always bear the great weight of sexuality, and that (bi)sexuality does not always author the 'self', or at least aspects of it, in the way that lesbianism and heterosexuality are frequently perceived to do (whether this is desirable or not). For Foucault, the self (folded force) is itself an aggregate of the very techniques which we employ to describe it.[14] Hence sexuality does not work in isolation from other techniques of the self. Would a sexual identity which does not cohere in material corporeality, for example, be understood as a technique of the self? And what of a sexuality that does not 'belong' to a self? Might bisexuality be an identity without selfhood?

This chapter is based on an analysis of two academic papers written by Claudia Card and Marilyn Frye, both taken from a special issue of *Hypatia* (1985) on the contemporary relevance of *The Second Sex* to western feminism. Published in a major feminist academic journal in the middle of the 1980s, and united by a shared commitment to explore and develop a feminist and lesbian identity politics, they may be seen as indicative of a particular kind of politics and theorizing born of the women's and gay liberation movements of the 1970s. My intention here is to explore the presuppositions which create a ground for the politics put forward in these papers and to consider the implications of these presuppositions for the 'bisexual'[15] woman that Card identifies. I will argue that Card's and Frye's specific figurations of choice and responsibility (and pleasure) as techniques of the self disallow bisexuality, in this context, from also being perceived as a technique of the self. Nevertheless, Card's assumption that the 'bisexual' woman resembles authentic lesbianism[16] produces bisexuality, if not as a sexual identity in the conventional sense, then at least as a presence (named in this way, it cannot be perceived as an absence). This paradox carries the implications of Card's and Frye's work beyond their own analyses and into the cultural politics of 'looking like what you are.'[17] Looking like what she is not, the 'bisexual' woman destabilizes an assumption, an assumption on which much visibility politics rests, that the relation between representation and identity is mimetic. Bisexuality itself appears to be significantly 'different' – as difference is understood by Gilles Deleuze[18] – to lesbianism and heterosexuality.

'A kind of failure of loyalty or lack of commitment'

Card's principal objection to the analysis of 'The Lesbian' in *The Second Sex* is that de Beauvoir perceives homosexuality to be a choice without acknowledging that 'heterosexuality is likewise a choice'.[19] For Card, unless both are seen to be choices, they cannot be evaluated on an equal basis; evaluated as either '"a mode of flight" from one's situation [inauthentic] or "a way of assuming it" [authentic]'.[20] Exploring in more detail de Beauvoir's notion of sexuality as an 'attitude', and especially its relation to choice, Card writes: 'attitudes are often modifiable through insight and understanding . . . like habits, [they] can outlive the judgments upon which they were originally based'.[21] By comparing attitudes to habits Card is able to argue that while we may not be aware of having chosen our attitudes we nevertheless generally consider them to be open to change: 'If attitudes are not themselves directly the objects of choice, choices are among their causes, including such choices as the choice to acquire certain attitudes.'[22] Thus it is that attitudes are 'modifiable'.

That attitudes are not necessarily chosen but nevertheless open to change is central to Card's analysis of sexuality. Referring to Aristotle she argues: 'not everything that is voluntary is chosen, and not everything that is not voluntary is *in*voluntary'.[23] Hence something which is not chosen might nevertheless be voluntary. An attitude – and sexuality, if it is an attitude – falls into this category. And given that attitudes may be voluntary, Card argues that we could (indeed, we should expect to) be held responsible for them.

> We expect people to take responsibility for their attitudes. If sexual orientation is an attitude, then the idea of taking responsibility for one's sexuality belongs to that general expectation. Taking such responsibility requires developing habits of noticing things about oneself, identifying one's attitudes and determining whether they are well-founded or not.[24]

Not only is 'having' attitudes a technique of the self then, but so is taking responsibility for them: Card invites us to develop a 'habit' of 'noticing things' about our attitudes (as opposed to maintaining our attitudes out of habit). She also suggests that we evaluate them: 'Even if attitudes are not chosen, they can still be evaluated as either authentic or inauthentic. They can be honest or dishonest, responsible or not responsible.'[25] In weighing up the (in)authenticity and (dis)honesty of its attitudes, the self casts the light of its objectifying gaze on to its self. However, this self-surveillance is figured by Card as part of a process whereby an individual may achieve a greater sense of self (-awareness).

Card's analysis of attitudes indicates that the crucial factor, for her, is that the ability to take responsibility for one's attitude or sexuality is co-extensive with a responsibility to do so. Frye makes the implications of such responsibility clear, in relation to women's liberation:

> It seems right for all of us to think together . . . to devise collective strategies of resistance and revolution . . . it seems right to require or demand of each other changes of values and characters. . . . In particular, it has seemed that we must require of each other the most fundamental change, namely, a shift of our primary loyalty from its attachment to the masters and their institutions to an attachment to our sisters and our liberation.[26]

What is significant here is that the shift of loyalty from masters to sisters requires, for Frye, not just that individual women be involved with each other, but also that they be responsible for each other. Based on the assumption that the ability to assume responsibility is co-extensive with an obligation to do so, loyalty to others is itself figured as an obligation. Indeed, Frye makes this assumption explicit: 'Loyalty and identity are so closely connected as to be almost just two aspects of the one phenomenon.'[27]

So what are the implications of Card's and Frye's understanding of the role of choice and responsibility, as they contribute to the production of the self, for the 'bisexual' woman that Card identifies? Card describes this woman in some detail:

> 'Disappointed in a man', [de Beauvoir] tells us, a woman 'may seek in woman a lover to replace the man who has betrayed her. Collette [*sic*] indicated in her *Vagabonde* this consoling role that forbidden pleasures may frequently play in woman's existence; some women spend . . . their whole lives in being thus consoled'. Others use women lovers for regeneration until they are able to deal with men again.[28]

Because Card understands de Beauvoir's notion of (in)authenticity to be focused solely on the individual, she speculates that de Beauvoir would not consider this woman to be acting inauthentically because she does take responsibility for herself. Card dryly concurs: 'It seems . . . likely that the woman in these cases, who would probably say she is "bisexual", has her situation very well in hand, from the point of view of taking charge of her own life.'[29] For Card however, the 'bisexual' woman's sexuality *is* inauthentic, because she takes account only of her own pleasure. Drawing on Aristotle, Card argues that the 'bisexual' woman is engaged in a friendship of utility and pleasure rather than a 'true friendship'.[30] In the latter the object of love is the friend, in the former it is utility and/or pleasure. The bisexual woman, according to Card, is less concerned for the woman with whom she is involved and more with what she may gain out of the 'friendship' for herself (for her own use or pleasure). In her introduction Card notes that a 'probable danger for the lesbian is her temptation to exploit other women's conditioning to service and nurturance'.[31] Caring only for her own pleasure, and without loyalty to others, the 'bisexual' woman is found guilty of exploiting such 'conditioning'. Card writes in her footnotes: 'See, e.g. Ulmshneider, "Bisexuality" for discussion of this combination of exploitation and failure to take responsibility.'[32] Hence the 'bisexual' woman is doubly implicated: not only her choice of pleasure, but her failure to take responsibility when she could have done and where she is obliged to, renders her behaviour inauthentic.

If the 'bisexual' woman is loyal to no one but herself and if, as Frye argues, loyalty to others is a constitutive feature of authentic identity, then bisexuality cannot be an authentic identity. This is confirmed by Card, who describes the woman's behaviour as 'a good *example* of inauthenticity in lesbian behavior'.[33] Hence although the woman 'would probably say she was "bisexual"',[34] for Card the very concept of 'bisexuality' is a misnomer; as an example of something else, bisexuality cannot author the self in the way that lesbianism and heterosexuality are usually perceived to do. 'Lesbian' is the subject here, such that even inauthentic lesbianism may be considered to be a technique of self.[35] Bisexuality, by contrast, is merely an example of inauthenticity in lesbian behaviour. This suggests that although there are, presumably, other kinds of lesbian behaviour which are inauthentic, inauthenticity constitutes the whole of bisexuality. In other words, given that bisexuality is not defined in any other way throughout the course of Card's article, its definition as inauthenticity disqualifies it, in this context, from being perceived as a technique of the self: bisexuality is nothing but inauthenticity.[36]

Nikolas Rose argues that 'autonomy, freedom, choice, authenticity'[37] are contemporary technologies of the self which presume an active agent willing to exercise responsibility. This, he suggests, forms 'a grid of regulatory ideals'[38] which divides selves into those who choose to exercise responsibility and 'the marginalized who through wilfulness, incapacity or ignorance cannot or will not exercise such responsibility'.[39] This accords with the common perception of bisexuality as 'a kind of failure of loyalty or lack of commitment'.[40] But Rose presupposes a self who is able to refuse responsibility, while Card's formulation of bisexuality as wholly inauthentic implies that it is not anchored to a 'bisexual' self who could make such a decision. In order to illustrate how the 'bisexual' woman is erased, it is worth exploring further the presuppositions which inform Card's and Frye's conceptions of identity.

Representation and identity

Towards the end of her paper, Frye marks a difference between 'being' and 'acting' lesbian, and relates this difference, which also distinguishes authentic lesbians from inauthentic ones, to the notion of 'communication and community'. These comments are central to both her and Card's understanding of identity. Frye writes:

being lesbian or being heterosexual are not simply matters of sexual preference or bodily behaviors. They are complex matters of attachment, orientation in the world, vision, habits or communication and community. . . . In my own case, being lesbian is an attitude evolved over perhaps fifteen years. . . . It would have been 'inauthentic' to act the lesbian in certain ways too early in that process. It now would be inauthentic *not* to, in certain ways and certain situations.[41]

By drawing a distinction between acting and being, Frye suggests that they are profoundly different expressions of identity: the former is inauthentic, the latter authentic. However, by arguing that '[i]t would have been "inauthentic" to act the lesbian in certain ways too early' in the process of actualizing her lesbian identity and that '[i]t now would be inauthentic *not* to', Frye also implies that there is after all only a shadowy difference between acting and being lesbian. That 'being' lesbian remains a question of 'acting' like one recalls Joan Riviere's analysis of womanliness as a masquerade.[42] Stephen Heath writes of Riviere's womanliness: 'The masquerade says that the woman exists at the same time that, as masquerade, it says she does not.'[43] The same might be said of Frye's lesbian identity, on the basis of her own analysis she appears never to be able to 'be' a lesbian, except in so far as 'being' is about acting.[44] Peggy Phelan makes a similar point, using slightly different terms, about white women and gender identity: 'White women like myself have been encouraged to mistake performance for ontology - to believe that the role is real, and thus sufficient to constitute an identity, a sense of purpose, a reason for being.'[45] Although the parallels between masquerade or performance and ontology are strikingly similar to Frye's analysis of acting and being, it is unlikely that this is what Frye has in mind when she writes of 'acting'. Instead, it appears that Frye is inviting us to believe in the act as a sign of the 'truth' of a lesbian identity. This wish to 'close the gap' between performance or acting and ontology or being suggests, as Carole-Anne Tyler puts it, a 'desire to be self-present' both to oneself and to others. Tyler writes:

As signifiers of our selves with which we are deeply identified, we wish our name and image to transparently reflect our being, like an iconic sign, and to be existentially or naturally bound to it, like an index. Such signs are supposed to be 'motivated' rather than 'arbitrary' or conventional and artificial, and therefore less susceptible to the disarticulations of signifier and signified, sign and referent, which make communication confusing.[46]

Frye's analysis rests on the implicit assumption that the signifiers of the self ('name and image', the act) and being are indeed coincidental or 'naturally bound' to each other. Ideally, for Frye, acting like a lesbian *should* be a guarantee of being a lesbian (this is authentic behaviour). She herself attempts to ensure that there is no gap between the performance of the (lesbian) identity (the act) and the ontological status of 'being' lesbian by acting the lesbian only when she believes she can claim that identity as her own (indeed, she is compelled to act in this way – as she says, 'it would now be inauthentic *not* to'). In short, Frye is urging us to believe that we may, in good faith, recognize and identify (and perhaps identify with) what it is that we see. If this were guaranteed, 'communication', as Tyler notes, would not be confusing. In terms of a philosophy of representation, while 'being' lesbian (if this were possible) would be defined by self-identity or self-presence,[47] 'acting' the lesbian – although a likeness or copy – would 'participate' in the original. Thus even though one could never actually 'be' a lesbian, acting like one would express 'a special kind of internal resemblance to the original'.[48] Perhaps one, as Tyler says, which is 'motivated' rather than arbitrary.

Card's and Frye's conception of identity belies an implicit assumption that the 'relationship between representation and identity is linear and smoothly mimetic. What one sees is who one is.'[49] Believing that the field of the visible may be mastered, that what one sees is not only who one is but also what one knows (such that the visible constitutes the subject not only ontologically but epistemologically), this conception of identity 'reflects the ideology of the visible, an ideology which erases the power of the unmarked, unspoken, and unseen'.[50] Indeed, the inauthenticity of the 'bisexual' woman appears in large part to rest on her ability to 'pass' as an authentic lesbian and, in so doing, to disrupt the mimetic relation between representation and identity (inauthentic behaviour is produced out of a discrepancy between acting and being). Outlining Aristotle's notion of a 'family resemblance', Card argues that the term 'resemblance' may be applied to anything which is called by the same name but which does not 'possess any one characteristic in common'.[51] This, she argues, is true in the case of the woman who calls herself 'bisexual': her 'attitudes are "lesbian" in so far as they resemble genuine lesbian attitudes, which also normally include receptivity to regeneration [*sic*] and nurturance from women'.[52]

It is precisely the 'bisexual' woman's resemblance to 'genuine lesbian attitudes', her 'theft'[53] of the signs of an authentic lesbian identity, that enables her to be misrecognized as an authentic lesbian and to exploit, as Card puts it, 'other women's conditioning to service and nurturance'. While she and Frye might both be acting, Frye's act is authentic while that of the 'bisexual' woman is not. In this context then, the 'problem is not the mask but its assumption or not, its fit or misfit, with the latter pointing to it as mask.'[54] Because the woman who calls herself 'bisexual' fails to pass, the 'misfit' – the discrepancy between acting and being, between what we may see and what we may know – is revealed. And in this misfit the 'bisexual' woman illustrates that acting and being are not after all the same or 'naturally' bound. Thus, however much she desires it, and the 'bisexual' woman bears witness to this, Frye will not be able to 'close the gap between performance and utterance, performative and constative, subject and T-shirt, the one who is "outing" and the one who is out'.[55]

The issue of passing then, or resemblance (as its implications are understood by Card), raises a series of problems for theories of identity based on a belief that representation and identity are mimetic. It also reveals the extent to which these theories assume not only that the visible signifiers of identity, the representation, will correspond to the identity itself, but also (and this second presupposition in fact creates a ground for the first) that an identity will be produced as visible at all. Lisa Walker, in her article 'How to Recognize a Lesbian: The Cultural Politics of Looking Like What You Are',[56] demonstrates how the privileging of visible signifiers of difference in the work of Donna Haraway, Sue-Ellen Case and Judith Butler results in the elision of identities which are not constructed as visible. Her analysis is concerned with 'women of color who can "pass" for white and femme lesbians who can pass for straight'.[57] Walker argues that Case, for example, constructs a paradigm in which the 'visibility' of ethnicity is implicitly perceived to be closer to 'authenticity'[58] than the 'invisibility' of whiteness. Thus the white butch and femme lesbian couple whom Case describes are brought closer to 'social reality' through a comparison with Native Americans:

> Katie King describes this transference of meaning from one sign to another as the 'magical' quality of signs invested with political value: 'Signs have a sort of magic attached to them, and magic operates by contiguity, or nearness, in other words, it works by rubbing off on you'. In Case's argument, . . . the association of the butch and femme couple with the Native American brings the former even closer to 'social reality', so that the 'ghosting of the lesbian subject' [the invisibility of lesbian women in feminist theory] is corrected by 'coloring' her in.[59]

Walker objects to the notion that an 'authentic' identity can be achieved only when signs of this identity are clearly visible. While agreeing that the celebration of visible difference is an effective strategy for reclaiming signifiers of difference which have been negatively portrayed,[60] she also suggests that this may in its turn replicate the same 'dominant ideologies'[61] which have employed visibility 'to create social categories on the basis of exclusion'.[62] Walker adds, 'In this situation, members of a given population who do not bear that signifier of difference or who bear visible signs of another identity are rendered invisible and are marginalized within an already marginalized community.'[63]

However, as Phelan's discussion of Jennie Livingston's film *Paris Is Burning* makes explicit, neither visibility nor invisibility can be held up as the inherently desirable political strategy. Phelan points out that while being passed against one's consent may be problematic, it is also the case that some might wish to pass. The male models[64] who walked the stage of Harlem clubs in the late 1980s, for example, employed the accoutrements of femininity in order 'to be passed over, not vulnerable to the hostile gaze of heterosexual culture'.[65] In this instance, the security conferred by invisibility, its power, is actively chosen. Beverley Skeggs's analysis of passing in the context of white working-class women also suggests that the problem with passing may be that 'someone may catch you out'.[66] Skeggs argues that white working-class women's attempts to pass as middle class 'does not involve ironic mimicry . . . because it wants to be taken seriously; because it speaks from a position of powerlessness and insecurity'.[67] This is because passing, Skeggs argues, usually presupposes the existence of an authoritative 'norm' to which the 'passer' attempts to conform: 'Passing . . . assumes a fit between the reality of one group and the naturalising of its definition.'[68] Thus, for example: 'The middle class do not need to pass.'[69] Similarly, Card's and Frye's definition of a lesbian is naturalized – it includes the ability to make choices and to assume responsibility for, and be loyal to, others. Failing to pass, the 'bisexual' woman is exposed as an inauthentic lesbian. She is 'caught out'.

What all these analyses share, whatever their position on the desirability (or not) of passing, is an emphasis on the role of the other in the construction of the self. Phelan argues that the trope of visibility in the production of identities ties the subject to others since we cannot see ourselves and are therefore dependent upon a detour through the eyes of the other to recognize and confirm our identities. The 'problem' with the gaze, Phelan argues, is that it 'promise[s] to show all, even while it fails to show the subject who looks, *and* thus fails to show what the looker most wants to see'.[70] Theories of identity based on representation then, are frequently premised upon the fear of loss or failure. And, given this fear of the failure of 'self-seeing', it remains that while we might wish to be 'self-present' to ourselves and to others, the other might not always 'provide a reassuring image of the self'.[71] The black and/or femme lesbian is passed against her consent in Walker's analysis, while Card refuses to accept the name 'bisexual' which she suggests the woman in her example 'would probably say she is'.[72]

However, the 'bisexual' woman's 'resemblance' to authentic lesbianism has implications for more than the 'bisexual' woman alone. She is herself an other to or through which the authentic lesbian might look to see her identity reflected. As noted above, by passing through the lesbian community the 'bisexual' woman introduces the possibility that that community, and the authenticity of lesbian identities, are not after all 'ideal', that not everyone in the 'community' shares the identity and therefore will not necessarily reflect the authentic lesbian back to herself in the way that she would like. Tyler writes: 'The community of signifying clones whose identities are clear, communications transparent, and desires identical is . . . a fantasy based on the repression of differences within both the self and the community.'[73] The 'communication' on which the community is founded cannot be guaranteed since, as the relation (of both similarity/her resemblance and difference/her inauthenticity) between the 'bisexual' woman and the authentic lesbian in Card's analysis indicates, there is a 'two-way traffic in signs whose inevitable doubleness can secure no identity – or identity politics – on a permanent basis'.[74]

This inevitable 'doubleness' introduces the issue of difference not only between self and other but also within the self. Tyler argues that:

> The subject is . . . an effect of impersonation or 'mimicry' which results from and expresses an alienating identification with something outside it. . . . The subject is only retroactively the cause of what it brings into being, an imitation of a reflection or copy of which it 'will have been' the original (so that there can be a copy at all).[75]

In other words, as Frye's own analysis of her lesbian identity inadvertently reveals, 'being' lesbian is a question of acting or imitating an image of what a lesbian is supposed to be like. Phelan writes: 'We imagine what people might see when they look at us, and then try to perform (and conform to) those images.'[76] Thus the subject is an effect of the imitation of the image, an image whose source lies outside the self and, according to Phelan, in the other. From this perspective, Frye 'is' a lesbian only to the extent that others recognize her performance of (a lesbian) identity as authentic. It is the success (figured here as recognition) of the performance itself, the copy or imitation, which *subsequently* enables Frye to claim a lesbian identity as 'her own'. Representation and identity then, because of this detour through the image which is confirmed (or not) by the other, cannot be identical: 'Our representations appear to belong to us as sovereign subjects although they come to us from the Other. This is so especially for "our" representations, the signifiers which represent us, with which we are deeply identified, and which in fact constitute us in the first place.'[77] If it is the case that identity is produced retroactively, through the imitation which is only subsequently claimed as an 'original' identity, then the imitation cannot be the same as the original identity. As Paul Patton points out: 'a perfect imitation is no longer an imitation at all but another instance of the same thing. In other words, the detour through the eyes of the other ensures that imitation or copying depends upon the maintenance of a difference between the copy and the thing imitated.'[78] The imitation or copy and the original are necessarily different for the individual to come into being, because otherwise there would be nothing with which to tell them apart.

Tyler argues that such differences must be erased or repressed if the 'desire to be self-present'[79] both to oneself and to others is to be fulfilled: to this end the subject narcissistically perceives 'similarity where there is only difference'.[80] This may be illustrated in the way that Card recuperates the 'bisexual' woman into a model of identity based not on difference but on sameness.

Sameness

As noted above, Card's argument rests on the presupposition that all identities may, and should, be evaluated according to the same criteria. This is manifest in her claim that heterosexuality must be seen as a choice in order that heterosexuality and lesbianism (which, she argues, is usually perceived to be a choice) may be evaluated on an equal basis.[81] And just as heterosexuality and lesbianism are compared as though they were the same, so are the 'bisexual' woman and the authentic lesbian. Significantly, on the basis that the 'bisexual' woman's attitudes 'resemble genuine lesbian attitudes',[82] Card concludes that she is in fact an inauthentic lesbian. In other words, Card redefines the 'bisexual' woman on the basis of resemblance gone awry. Foucault writes:

> The meeting point of the axes is the point of perfect resemblance, and from this arises the scale of differences as so many lesser resemblances, marked identities: differences arise when representation can only partially present what was previously present, when the test of recognition is stymied. For a thing to be different, it must first no longer be the same; and it is on this negative basis, above the shadowy part that delimits the same, that contrary predicates are then articulated.[83]

Assuming that in Card's analysis the authentic lesbian is, ideally, 'the point of perfect resemblance' where the gap between representation and identity, copy and original, is (perceived to be as) closed (as possible), the inauthentic lesbian signifies a 'lesser resemblance' or imitation. And in so far as the inauthentic lesbian is different from the authentic lesbian only because she is not the same as her, the nature of the difference between the two is constructed as 'a difference *from* or *within* something. . . . Difference is transformed into that which must be specified within a concept, without overstepping its bounds.'[84] In short, it is the resemblance between the authentic and inauthentic lesbian that enables Card to assume that they are in essential respects the same and therefore that their difference is no more than a 'difference within resemblance, so to speak'.[85] The difference between the two then, according to Card, is secondary. Sameness remains primary.[86]

By evaluating the 'bisexual' woman on the same basis as the authentic lesbian, Card achieves 'sameness of outcome'.[87] According to Card, it is not the 'bisexual' woman who passes as, or resembles, an authentic lesbian but rather an inauthentic lesbian who passes as an authentic one. And because, by definition, the inauthentic lesbian has failed to pass (it is her having been 'caught out', as Skeggs puts it, that reveals her inauthenticity), she may be contained within the arena of visible representation, among 'marked identities'. The potential difference between the 'bisexual' woman and the authentic lesbian is tamed and, constructed as an inauthentic lesbian, the woman becomes 'facialized' as Deleuze and Guattari would have it.

For Deleuze and Guattari abstract machines of faciality ensure 'the almightiness of the signifier as well as the autonomy of the subject'.[88] The face delimits anything other than 'appropriate significations' and any subjectivity that does not 'conform in advance to a dominant reality'.[89] It does this in two ways. First, it constitutes the dichotomies out of which concrete faces are produced (recognized and identified): 'it is a man *or* a woman, a rich person or a poor one, an adult or a child, a leader or a subject, "an x *or* a y".[90] And, as Card's account suggests, such dichotomies might also include and produce the concrete faces of an authentic and an inauthentic lesbian. Second, given a concrete face, the machine judges 'whether it passes or not, whether it goes or not. . . . This time, the binary relation is of the "yes–no" type. . . . At every moment, the machine rejects faces that do not conform, or seem suspicious.'[91]

In relation to racism, Deleuze and Guattari suggest that there is no 'outside' of the face; instead, there are only degrees of deviance established in relation to the 'White-Man' face.[92] In other words, they illustrate how the face – 'a deviance detector'[93] – recuperates deviance into a model of identity based on sameness: 'There are only people who should be like us and whose crime it is not to be. ... Racism never detects the particles of the other; it propagates waves of sameness until those who resist identification have been wiped out.'[94] Card's redefinition of the 'bisexual' woman as an inauthentic lesbian has a similar effect. Because she is defined through a degree (or even degrees) of deviance (a lesser version of the identity produced by the face), she remains contained within the face. Even deviance, according to Deleuze and Guattari, is facialized: 'At any rate, you've been recognized, the abstract machine has you inscribed in its overall grid.'[95] It is a wave of sameness that erases the 'bisexual' woman and washes up in her place an inauthentic lesbian that is *able* to be recognized and identified: failing to pass, she is facialized.

Given that in Card's account the notion of bisexuality is almost entirely wiped off the face, it cannot be the case that, were the 'bisexual' woman not 'misrecognized' as an inauthentic lesbian, bisexuality would be revealed as an authentic sexual identity. Where Card is concerned, there is no 'bisexual' woman to misrecognize or even to be invisible; there is only an inauthentic lesbian. This suggests not only that the 'problem' of bisexuality cannot be solved by expanding the field of the visible (in order that it might be recognized as an authentic identity) but also that the resemblance between bisexuality and lesbianism does not pertain to an essential similarity. Instead, bisexuality appears to be of an entirely different order altogether.

Difference

Drawing on Foucault, I suggested at the beginning of this chapter that contemporary western concepts of the self are often the product of the discourses which seek to explain them. The analysis of the ways in which both (in)authenticity is ascribed to the self of the lesbian and 'bisexuality' is erased as a technique of the self illustrates how this is so. In order to explain 'who' the lesbian is, Card draws on a number of techniques of the self (self-evaluation, loyalty and choice are just a few). Her own erasure of bisexuality, because it does not conform to these techniques, serves to assure Card that the self is indeed produced in this way. That the self she constructs is bound by the very presuppositions which preceded it suggests, from a Deleuzian perspective, that:

History, subjectivity, and the meaning of Being are products in consciousness; to take any particular form of these as the starting point for interpretation and understanding fails to attain the underlying level of the processes by which such forms of consciousness are produced.[96]

For Deleuze, what we may consciously 'know' is always static and therefore prevents forces from acting. Hence: 'we only deal in inverted and flattened representations. Life is replaced by an image.'[97] Because the notion of authentic and inauthentic lesbianism, and the self in which they cohere, are always already representations, produced through conscious knowledge, they inevitably seal flows of force within them. Is bisexuality the same?

If it were the case that the difference between bisexuality and (in)authentic lesbianism was negatively predicated, then bisexuality would signify a degree of deviation from what remained an essential similarity – perhaps that they are all identities which may be possessed (or seen to be possessed). In this instance, bisexuality would 'belong' to the self in the way that lesbianism and heterosexuality are usually perceived to do. However, because bisexuality is defined as wholly inauthentic (where inauthenticity does not refer to a technique of the self), it is neither anchored to the self nor does it, relatedly, express the 'inner' truth of the soul of the 'bisexual' woman. In this respect, the 'problem' of bisexuality is very different to the 'problem' of the femme identity that Walker, for example, describes. She writes:

> while a butch woman of color might not be recognized as a lesbian because she is not white, she might be perceived as a lesbian because her sexual style is considered 'blatant'. A femme woman of color, on the other hand, will probably not be recognized as lesbian, first because she is not white and then because she is not butch.[98]

Although the femme woman of colour is not recognized as lesbian (on both counts), she remains a lesbian nevertheless (if she did not, Walker herself would not be able to identify her). In other words, Walker assumes that even those identities which are not 'marked', or visible, may in some way cohere in the self. Where Card's construction of bisexuality is concerned, however, even presence, or visibility, does not guarantee that it is an identity in the conventional sense (as Walker's analysis of visibility and identity suggests that it might be). This is because bisexuality seems to signify the deception itself, the moments during which the inauthentic lesbian passes as an authentic one (perhaps bisexuality is passing itself). Indeed, it is only when discussing the nature of this deception, this inauthenticity, that Card employs the term 'bisexual'. Having established 'inauthenticity', the term no longer appears to be necessary to her; as noted above, the 'bisexual' woman is redefined as an inauthentic lesbian. Bisexuality is thus neither produced as a technique of the self (such that it might subsequently be 'misrecognized' or 'invisibilized'), nor is it productive of, or embedded within, material corporeality. Further, because passing itself cannot be seen (although that which passes, as well as that which fails to pass, may be), bisexuality cannot be said to be entirely visible but neither is it simply invisible. In both these respects, bisexuality exceeds the faciality of the authentic and the inauthentic lesbians as well as the femme woman of colour that Walker describes to illustrate the problematic relation between representation and identity.

This is the 'difference' between bisexuality and lesbianism, a difference which may be illustrated with reference to simulacra. Patton writes:

> the difference between a simulacrum and what it simulates, by contrast [to a copy and its imitation of the original], is of another order altogether. The simulacrum is not in essential respects the same as what it simulates, but different. Although it reproduces the appearance of the original, is does so as an effect. Here, the apparent identity of the two is the secondary, derived relation, while it is their difference that is primary.[99]

A simulacrum is not a copy of a copy, since this would maintain an essential similarity: 'The simulacrum would then be a second-order copy, the difference between copy and original redoubled.'[100] Equally, bisexuality cannot be seen as an imitation of an inauthentic lesbian since this would presuppose that it participated, albeit in a lesser way, of the original (self-present) identity. Nevertheless, this conclusion is not necessarily to suggest that bisexuality (as it is constituted here), because it is not possessed by the self which it might have expressed, is not a body at all. Instead, it may be understood as a different kind of body, a body without the organs which would stratify and regulate it.[101]

For Deleuze a body is understood 'as pure flows of energy, capable of multiple variations';[102] it is defined not by what it 'is' but by what it can 'do', by the affects of which it is capable.[103] Where molar entities – such as the binaries of men and women – are concerned, the flow of forces are limited and ordered by the three strata of organism, significance[104] and subjectification: their capacity both to affect and be affected is circumscribed (as noted above, the self itself is folded and stabilized force). The Body without Organs (BwO) is 'what remains when you take everything away':[105] 'no longer an organism that functions but a BwO that is constructed. No longer are there any acts to explain, dreams or phantasies to interpret, childhood memories to recall, words to make signify. . . . There is no longer a Self [*Moi*] that feels, acts and recalls.'[106] The BwO is a field for the production of the immanence of desire.[107] It is never possessed, 'never yours or mine',[108] but rather traverses surfaces (such as the molar identities of lesbianism and heterosexuality), enabling flows of energy to seep out from and within them. Passing through the lesbian community, the BwO of bisexuality is a deterritorializing force which intervenes in the processes of recognition and identification. The effect is to destratify the mimetic relation between representation and identity and to destabilize the molar lines[109] of possession, faciality, visibility and sameness which order identities. The BwO of bisexuality cannot therefore be understood to be different from lesbianism and heterosexuality simply because it is not the same as them (this is the difference between 'x' and 'y'). It is not a copy of a copy, but a simulacrum; if it resembles lesbianism, then this resemblance is produced as an effect of a more fundamental difference.

For example: it is precisely resemblance that ensures that bisexuality is recognized just enough to be in a position to deterritorialize, and thus to release energies contained by, the molar entities that Card and Frye produce. Deleuze and Guattari write of the BwO:

> You have to keep enough of the organism for it to reform each dawn; and you have to keep small supplies of signifiance and subjectification, if only . . . to enable you to respond to the dominant reality. Mimic the strata. You don't reach the BwO . . . by wildly destratifying . . . the worst that can happen is if you throw the strata into demented or suicidal collapse, which brings them back down on us heavier than ever.[110]

The BwO of bisexuality is not an imitation of molar entities (which would suggest that it was basically the same as molar entities). Rather, its effect is to mimic the stratifications which produce them and, in doing so, it *comes* to resemble them. Bisexuality appears, for example, to be an identity that may be possessed (by the 'bisexual' woman) but then, *because* it is not, it destabilizes the presupposition that the relation between representation and identity is a smooth one. What is significant, then, is that the BwO of bisexuality is a field of production rather than a site of expression. As Philip Goodchild notes, in Deleuze's thought 'the unconscious processes [such as the BwO] that produce meaning will be of a different nature from the meanings produced – the unconscious is a place of production, not expression . . . meaning is purely a surface effect'.[111] As a simulacrum, the BwO of bisexuality refers to 'gestures which develop before organised bodies [and] . . . masks before faces'.[112] Hence the resemblance between bisexuality and lesbianism, rather than pertaining to a basic sameness, is produced as an effect of a primary and unrecuperable difference, a simulation:

> Simulation is the production of an effect rather than the reproduction of an appearance. The effect in question may be an effect of resemblance, or may be produced by means of an effect of resemblance, but these have no particular privilege in the world of simulacra.[113]

If bisexuality *were* wholly destratified, then it would not be present in Card's text at all, it would not be a BwO. Conversely, if bisexuality were not a BwO, it would not be a force of deterritorialization, as it is. The production of bisexuality in these texts illustrates the capacity of the BwO to intervene in arenas which appear to be highly stratified and ordered. In this respect, the BwO of bisexuality traces a molecular path away from some of the presuppositions on which a number of theories of identity based on representation rest:

> The body without organs is not the proof of an original nothingness, nor is it what remains of a lost totality. Above all, it is not a projection;

it has nothing whatsoever to do with the body itself, or with an image of the body. It is the body without an image.[114]

Nevertheless, there is an ambivalence in the conclusions that I have drawn about bisexuality. A critique which focuses almost entirely on negativity finds, finally, a positive (if unrepresentable) role for bisexuality. And I have argued this even though, as Michael Hardt notes, Judith Butler and others criticize Deleuze precisely because the 'power' of the negative is erased. Describing the terms of such critiques, Hardt writes, 'Philosophies of affirmation remain impotent because they have deprived themselves of the power of negation, they have lost the "magic" of the labor of the negative.'[115] The BwO of bisexuality illustrates however, that affirmation is not opposed to critique. Indeed, Deleuze refers to a 'total critique', 'an unrestrained attack on the established values and the ruling powers they support'.[116] Hardt adds, and the BwO of bisexuality demonstrates this point, that '[t]his is not to say that all that is present is negated, but simply that what is negated is attacked with unrestrained force'.[117]

I chose an extract from Kathy Acker's *In Memoriam to Identity* to frame this article because Acker longs for something 'new'. If a space is created in which forces may act freely, then nothing is preserved and nothing remains the 'same'. This suggests that we need to do more than 'complicate', as Walker puts it, 'our ideas about what counts as radical self-presentation for minority identities'.[118] Perhaps we need to do differently.[119] This reading of bisexuality is offered to this end: not so much as a solution to the 'contemporary emergency' but in the hope of a 'quantum leap'.[120]

Notes

I would like to thank Celia Lury, Phil Goodchild and Nick Millett for their helpful comments on earlier versions of this paper. Thanks also to the readers, Clare Hemmings and Ann Kaloski, for their encouragement and constructive criticism.

1. I have taken this title from Gilles Deleuze and Claire Parnet, *Dialogues*, trans. Hugh Tomlinson and Barbara Habberjam (London: Athlone, 1987), p. 47.
2. Kathy Acker, quoted in Rosi Braidotti, *Nomadic Subjects* (New York: Columbia University Press, 1994), p. 39.
3. Michel Foucault, *The History of Sexuality, Volume 1: An Introduction* (Harmondsworth: Penguin, 1990), p. 78.
4. Martin S. Weinberg, Colin J. Williams and Douglas W. Pryor, *Dual Attraction: Understanding Bisexuality* (New York: Oxford University Press, 1994), p. 4.
5. Eve Sedgwick, *Tendencies* (London: Routledge, 1994), p. 25.
6. Michel Foucault, *The History of Sexuality, Volume 1: An Introduction*, p. 35.
7. Brenda Marie Blasingame, 'The Roots of Biphobia: Racism and Internalized Heterosexism', in Elizabeth Reba Weise (ed.), *Closer to Home: Bisexuality and Feminism* (Seattle: Seal Press, 1992), p. 49.
8. See Loraine Hutchins and Lani Ka'ahumanu, *Bi Any Other Name: Bisexual People Speak Out* (Boston: Alyson, 1991), or Elizabeth Reba Weise (ed.), *Closer to Home*.
9. Karin Baker, 'Bisexual Feminist Politics: Because Bisexuality Is Not Enough', in Elizabeth Reba Weise (ed.), *Closer to Home*, p. 266.
10. *Ibid.*, p. 265.
11. Elizabeth Reba Weise, 'Introduction', in Elizabeth Reba Weise (ed.), *Closer to Home*, p. xi.

12. Karin Baker, 'Bisexual Feminist Politics', p. 266.
13. Brenda Marie Blasingame, 'The Roots of Biphobia', p. 49.
14. Michel Foucault, 'Technologies of the Self', in Luther H. Martin, Huck Gutman and Patrick H. Hutton (eds), *Technologies of the Self: A Seminar with Michel Foucault* (London: Tavistock, 1988). I am employing the term 'techniques of the self' in two different capacities. The first is closely allied to Foucault's own understanding of the term, where 'techniques' refers to the specific practices which are deployed by individuals upon their selves in order to transform themselves (towards a desired state such as authenticity). While sexuality is not usually understood to be a technique of the self *per se*, it frequently plays a key part in narratives which are employed as a technique through which the individual is rendered (and renders itself) intelligible. (See, for example, Marilyn Frye's account of her 'acquisition' of a lesbian sexual identity, below.)
15. Claudia Card, 'Lesbian Attitudes and *The Second Sex*', *Hypatia/Women's Studies International Forum*, 8, 3 (1985), pp. 209–14 (p. 213).
16. *Ibid.*, p. 213.
17. I am taking this phrase from Lisa Walker's 'How to Recognize a Lesbian: The Culture Politics of Looking Like What You Are', *Signs: Journal of Women in Culture and Society*, 18, 4 (1993), pp. 866–91 (p. 866).
18. I will return to this below.
19. Claudia Card, 'Lesbian attitudes and *The Second Sex*', p. 209.
20. *Ibid.*, p. 209.
21. *Ibid.*, p. 212.
22. *Ibid.*, p. 212.
23. *Ibid.*, p. 212. Emphasis in the original.
24. *Ibid.*, p. 212.
25. *Ibid.*, p. 212.
26. Marilyn Frye, 'History and Responsibility', *Hypatia/Women's Studies International Forum*, 8, 3 (1985), pp. 215–17 (p. 216).
27. *Ibid.*, p. 216.
28. Claudia Card, 'Lesbian Attitudes and *The Second Sex*', p. 213.
29. *Ibid.*, p. 213.
30. *Ibid.*, p. 213.
31. *Ibid.*, p. 209.
32. *Ibid.*, p. 213, note.
33. *Ibid.*, p. 213. My emphasis.
34. *Ibid.*, p. 213.
35. Card writes: 'it is not just that the *woman* is being inauthentic: her *lesbianism* is inauthentic' (*ibid.*, p. 213). Emphasis in the original. Notably, the woman remains in possession of 'her lesbianism' even though it is inauthentic.
36. This is not to suggest, however, that inauthenticity could never be a technique of the self. I am grateful to Celia Lury for pointing out that one could, for example, be 'a *master* of insincerity'.
37. Nikolas Rose, 'Authority and the Genealogy of Subjectivity', in Paul Heelas, Scott Lash and Paul Morris (eds), *Detraditionalization: Critical Reflections on Authority and Identity* (Oxford: Blackwell, 1996), p. 320.
38. *Ibid.*, p. 320.
39. *Ibid.*, pp. 320–21.
40. Judith Butler, *Bodies That Matter: On the Discursive Limits of 'Sex'* (New York: Routledge, 1993), p. 112.
41. Marilyn Frye, 'History and Responsibility', p. 217. Emphasis in the original.
42. Joan Riviere, 'Womanliness as Masquerade', in Victor Burgin, James Donald and Cora Kaplan (eds), *Formations of Fantasy* (London: Methuen, 1986).
43. Stephen Heath, 'Joan Riviere and the Masquerade', in Victor Burgin, James Donald and Cora Kaplan (eds), *Formations of Fantasy*, p. 54.
44. The brevity of the extracts cited here may imply that Frye *is* able to 'be' a lesbian without 'acting' like one 'early' on (she argues that during this period '[i]t would have

been "inauthentic" to act the lesbian'). However, Frye writes that '[i]n my case, being lesbian is an attitude evolved over perhaps fifteen years – from my earliest awareness of aptitude for passionate connection with women to a way of being which actualizes that possibility' (Marilyn Frye, 'History and Responsibility', p. 217). This suggests that 'earlier' Frye is not so much 'being' a lesbian as being in the process of 'actualizing' a lesbian identity (which, until actualized, cannot be claimed as an authentic identity).

45. Peggy Phelan, *Unmarked: The Politics of Performance* (London: Routledge, 1993), p. 105.

46. Carole-Anne Tyler, 'Passing: Narcissism, Identity, and Difference', *Differences: A Journal of Feminist Cultural Studies*, 6, 2+3 (1994), pp. 212–48 (p. 216).

47. As in Plato's Forms which are 'nothing other than what they are'. Paul Patton, 'Anti-Platonism and Art', in Constain V. Boundas and Dorothy Olkowski (eds), *Gilles Deleuze and the Theater of Philosophy* (New York: Routledge, 1994), p. 147.

48. *Ibid.*, p. 147.

49. Peggy Phelan, *Unmarked*, p. 7.

50. *Ibid.*, p. 7.

51. Claudia Card, 'Lesbian Attitudes and *The Second Sex*', p. 213.

52. *Ibid.*, p. 213.

53. Carole-Anne Tyler, 'Passing: Narcissism, Identity, and Difference', p. 241.

54. Stephen Heath, 'Joan Riviere and the Masquerade', p. 50.

55. Carole-Anne Tyler, 'Passing: Narcissism, Identity, and Difference', p. 221.

56. Lisa Walker, 'How to Recognize a Lesbian', pp. 866–91.

57. *Ibid.*, p. 869.

58. *Ibid.*, p. 877.

59. *Ibid.*, p. 877.

60. The accent on visibility politics since the 1960s bears witness to this. The late 1960s and 1970s lesbian and gay liberation movement's slogan 'Out and Proud', for example, with its emphasis on coming out of the (private) closet into the 'open' for everyone to 'see', is an example here. More recently, the catchword 'VisiBIlity', which was printed on T-shirts and badges at the 1993 National Bisexual Conference in Britain, captured this logic in a word. See Rosemary Hennessey, 'Queer Visibility in Commodity Culture', in Linda Nicholson and Stephen Seidman (eds), *Social Postmodernism: Beyond Identity Politics* (Cambridge: Cambridge University Press, 1995), for a critique of the queer emphasis on visibility and the 'theatricalization' of the political.

61. Lisa Walker, 'How to Recognize a Lesbian', p. 888.

62. *Ibid.*

63. *Ibid.*

64. 'Male models' in this context refers to 'Latino and African-American gay men, transvestites, and transsexuals' (Peggy Phelan, *Unmarked*, p. 93).

65. *Ibid.*, p. 104.

66. Beverley Skeggs, *Becoming Respectable: An Ethnography of White Working Class Women* (London: Sage, forthcoming).

67. *Ibid.*

68. *Ibid.*, p. 19.

69. *Ibid.* It is arguable that most dominant identities, as Skeggs points out with respect to middle-classness, are 'invisibilized'. Richard Dyer shows how the power of whiteness is secured not through its representation as superiority but rather as an 'invisible' norm. Richard Dyer, 'White', *Screen*, 29, 4 (1988), pp. 44–64. Phelan too notes that passing as heterosexual (by choice or not) is easy because heterosexuality is usually assumed (Peggy Phelan, *Unmarked*, p. 96).

70. *Ibid.*, p. 104. Emphasis in the original. In so far as Phelan appears to be unwilling to admit that there may be other ways in which the subject might 'see' itself, her evaluation of the gaze is framed in terms of an apparently inevitable 'loss' and 'failure'. The very negativity of this evaluation suggests that Phelan continues to privilege the role of the visible in the production of identity even as she attempts to move away from it. In this respect Phelan shares what Martin Jay, in relation to Foucault, has described as a profound mistrust of the visible: 'the ocularcentrism of those who praised the

"nobility of sight" [is] not so much rejected as reversed in value. Vision [is] still the privileged sense, but what that privilege produce[s] in the modern world [is] damned as almost entirely pernicious.' Martin Jay, *Downcast Eyes: The Denigration of Vision in Twentieth-Century French Thought* (Berkeley: University of California Press, 1994), p. 384.

71. Carole-Anne Tyler, 'Passing: Narcissism, Identity, and Difference', p. 225.
72. Claudia Card, 'Lesbian Attitudes and *The Second Sex*', p. 213.
73. Carole-Anne Tyler, 'Passing: Narcissism, Identity, and Difference', p. 233.
74. *Ibid.*, p. 227.
75. *Ibid.*, pp. 218–19.
76. Peggy Phelan, *Unmarked*, p. 36.
77. Carole-Anne Tyler, 'Passing: Narcissism, Identity, and Difference', p. 218.
78. Paul Patton, 'Anti-Platonism and Art', p. 149.
79. Carole-Anne Tyler, 'Passing: Narcissism, Identity, and Difference', p. 216.
80. *Ibid.*, p. 219.
81. Claudia Card, 'Lesbian Attitudes and *The Second Sex*', p. 209.
82. *Ibid.*, p. 213.
83. Michel Foucault, 'Theatrum Philosophicum', trans. Donald F. Bouchard and Sherry Simon, in Donald F. Bouchard (ed.), *Michel Foucault: Language, Counter-Memory, Practice: Selected Essays and Interviews* (Oxford: Blackwell, 1988), pp. 183–4.
84. *Ibid.*, pp. 181–2. Emphasis in the original.
85. Paul Patton, 'Anti-Platonism and Art', p. 153.
86. As Rosalyn Diprose has put it (in relation to gender): 'The constitution of identity and difference is such that there is no sexual difference to speak of: only sameness or a lack.' Rosalyn Diprose, *Ethics, Embodiment and Sexual Difference* (London: Routledge, 1994), p. 36.
87. Rosalyn Diprose, 'Nietzsche and the Pathos of Distance', in Paul Patton (ed.), *Nietzsche, Feminism and Political Theory* (London: Routledge, 1993), p. 13.
88. Gilles Deleuze and Felix Guattari, *A Thousand Plateaus: Capitalism and Schizophrenia*, trans. Brian Massumi (Minneapolis: University of Minnesota, 1988), p. 181.
89. *Ibid.*, p. 168.
90. *Ibid.*, p. 177. Emphasis in the original.
91. *Ibid.*, p. 177.
92. *Ibid.*, p. 178.
93. *Ibid.*, pp. 177–8.
94. *Ibid.*, p. 178.
95. *Ibid.*, p. 177.
96. Philip Goodchild, *Deleuze and Guattari: An Introduction to the Politics of Desire* (London: Sage, 1996), p. 15.
97. *Ibid.*, p. 28.
98. Lisa Walker, 'How to Recognize a Lesbian', p. 886.
99. Paul Patton, 'Anti-Platonism and Art', p. 154.
100. *Ibid.*, p. 153.
101. It may seem odd to be concluding with a Body without Organs of bisexuality given Deleuze and Guattari's views on bisexuality. They write: 'Bisexuality is no better a concept than the separateness of the sexes. It is as deplorable to miniaturize, internalize the binary machine as it is to exacerbate it; it does not extricate us from it' (Gilles Deleuze and Felix Guattari, *A Thousand Plateaus*, p. 276). In the introduction to *Inside/Out* Diana Fuss, writing about another binary opposition, heterosexuality and homosexuality, makes a similar point. Here, Fuss suggests that sexualities other than hetero- and homosexuality – such as 'bisexuality, transvestism, transsexualism . . .' – rather than being 'left out' of the homosexual/heterosexual equation, might themselves be assimilated into the inside/outside opposition, so securing its logic ever more tightly (Diana Fuss, 'Inside/Out', in Diana Fuss (ed.), *Inside/Out: Lesbian Theories, Gay Theories* (New York: Routledge, 1991), p. 2). Although she does not expand at any length, presumably Fuss is referring to the feature that bisexuality, transvestism and transsexualism are sometimes perceived to have in common: that they 'are' the

opposition, they 'hold' it within themselves and, as a consequence of this definition, reinforce (rather than deconstruct) that opposition. Both Deleuze and Guattari and Fuss base their analyses on particular definitions of bisexuality. Deleuze and Guattari appear to confine bisexuality to androgyny and then suggest that it holds within it the two molar entities of male and female. Fuss presupposes the existence of a bisexual 'self' which is able to hold the hetero/homosexual opposition within itself. This view seems to be particularly common. Elizabeth Däumer, for example, notes that contemporary perspectives on bisexuality tend to perceive it as that which, 'rather than broadening the spectrum of available sexual identifications, holds in place a binary framework of two basic and diametrically opposed sexual orientations.' Elizabeth Däumer, 'Queer Ethics; or, the Challenge of Bisexuality to Lesbian Ethics', *Hypatia*, 7, 4 (1992), pp. 91–105 (p. 96). Although bisexuality may surely take these forms, the conclusions that I am drawing here are based on Card's construction of bisexuality.

102. Rosi Braidotti, *Nomadic Subjects: Embodiment and Sexual Difference in Contemporary Feminist Theory* (New York: Columbia University Press, 1994), p. 165.
103. Gilles Deleuze, 'Ethology: Spinoza and Us', trans. Robert Hurley, in Jonathon Crary and Sanford Kwinter (eds), *Incorporations* (New York: Zone, 1992).
104. Signifiance (rather than signification) refers not to 'acts' of signification, but to the general tendency of *thought* towards producing significations.
105. Gilles Deleuze and Felix Guattari, *A Thousand Plateaus*, p. 151.
106. *Ibid.,* p. 162.
107. Desire is understood here to be 'a process of production without reference to any exterior agency, whether it be a lack that hollows it out or a pleasure that fills it in' (*ibid.*, p. 154). Whenever a BwO is made into an organism, a signification or a subject – whenever desire is betrayed – it is uprooted from its immanence: 'The BwO howls: "They've made me an organism!" "They've wrongfully folded me!" "They've stolen my body!"' (*ibid.*, p. 159).
108. *Ibid.,* p. 164.
109. Molar lines stratify and subjectify forces, and congeal them into entities, while molecular lines destabilize, deterritorialize, or destratify these entities.
110. *Ibid.,* p. 160–1.
111. Philip Goodchild, *Deleuze and Guattari*, p. 15.
112. Gilles Deleuze, *Difference and Repetition,* trans. Paul Patton (London: Athlone, 1994), p. 10.
113. Paul Patton, 'Anti-Platonism and Art', p. 155.
114. Gilles Deleuze and Felix Guattari, *Anti-Oedipus: Capitalism and Schizophrenia* (Minneapolis: University of Minnesota, 1994), p. 8.
115. Michael Hardt, *Gilles Deleuze: An Apprenticeship in Philosophy* (London: University College London Press, 1993), p. 115.
116. *Ibid.,* p. 116.
117. *Ibid.,* p. 116.
118. Lisa Walker, 'How to Recognize a Lesbian', p.888.
119. As Deleuze puts it: 'The theory of thought is like painting: it needs that revolution which took art from representation to abstraction. This is the aim of a theory of thought without image' (Gilles Deleuze, quoted in Paul Patton, 'Anti-Platonism and Art', p. 141).
120. Adrienne Rich, 'Motherhood: The Contemporary Emergency and the Quantum Leap', in *On Lies, Secrets and Silence* (London: Virago, 1980).

3

'Her Libido Had Flowed in Two Currents': Representations of Bisexuality in Psychoanalytic Case Studies

Phoebe Davidson

The tendency for some adults to be sexually attracted to both men and women has been seldom addressed and theorized in psychoanalytical works. Why is adult bisexuality so rarely addressed by analysts?

I have chosen the following two case studies to illustrate how theories of bisexuality have been applied and how these historical accounts may still influence analytical theorizing of bisexuality. Freud's 'The Psychogenesis of a Case of Homosexuality in a Woman', first published in 1921,[1] is significant because Freud acknowledges a bisexuality universal to all, although he does not explicitly see bisexuality as an adult sexual category.[2] My contention is that, although Freud had well-formed theories of bisexuality, he was not able to apply them adequately. Thus bisexual elements in this case are distorted and obscured by Freud's over-identification with the girl's father and denial of the heterosexual elements within her sexuality. My second case study is Melanie Klein's 'The Psychogenesis of Tics', first published in 1925.[3] In this study a tentative structure resembling Freud's theories of bisexuality is maintained, but any contradictions posed by that bisexuality are dealt with by splitting homosexual attitudes from heterosexual attitudes and pathologizing the homosexual part. Both these case studies illustrate how the dominant attitudes to gender and sexuality of the time influence clinical practice.

For a contemporary reading of bisexuality I have chosen the work of Marie Maguire,[4] a psychoanalytical psychotherapist influenced by both Freudian and Object Relations schools.[5] Maguire writes about gender issues in psychotherapy from a feminist perspective.[6] I have chosen some case studies from her book to show how bisexuality can be considered without being pathologized, albeit not unproblematically.

Case study 1: Freud's 'A Case of Homosexuality in a Woman'

'A beautiful and clever girl of eighteen, belonging to a family of good standing'[7] is brought by her parents to Freud for analysis. She pursues a 'society lady' of whom her parents disapprove; this woman lives with a woman friend with whom she has intimate relations and carries on a number of promiscuous affairs with men. The parents' concern is that the girl has not shown any interest in young men and that the present relationship is a continuation of attachments to women.

Freud's difficulty with this case is that the girl is coming to treatment because of her parents' wishes and not because she is ill. The task in hand was, therefore, 'converting one variety of the genital organisation of sexuality into the other'.[8] Freud then hypothesizes about *male* homosexuals, rather than the *female* homosexual at hand. He continues:

> It is only where the homosexual fixation has not yet become strong enough, or where there are considerable rudiments and vestiges of a heterosexual choice of object, i.e. in a still oscillating or in a definitely bisexual organisation, that one may make a more favourable prognosis for psychoanalytic therapy.[9]

Thus a bisexuality has been acknowledged in theory, but has this been adequately addressed within this case?

Freud notes that the girl has passed through the feminine Oedipus complex[10] and has substituted a slightly older brother for her father. When she was between the ages of thirteen and fourteen she displayed a strong, but passing, affection for a small boy. Freud infers from this that she had a strong desire to be a mother and have a child. However this affection was transitory and after this she becomes indifferent to the boy and begins to take an interest in mature women. This brings on a severe chastisement from her father.

This change in types of object-choice comes about because of her mother's new pregnancy and the birth of a third brother. Freud says, 'Before it happened, her libido was concentrated on a maternal attitude, while afterwards she became a homosexual attracted to mature women, and remained so ever since.'[11] Freud hypothesizes about why this change happened and its cause. Why did the girl start to desire mothers? The mother saw her as an inconvenient competitor and so the girl has no cause for affection for her mother herself. Freud's explanation is that just as she is reviving her Oedipus complex at puberty she suffers her greatest disappointment. She consciously wants to have a male child because what she unconsciously desires is her father's child and an image of him. But it was not herself who bore the child but her rival, her mother. Enraged, resentful and embittered, she turns away from men. Freud states, 'After this first great reverse she forswore her womanhood and sought another goal for her libido.'[12] He continues, 'After her disappointment, therefore, this girl had entirely repudiated her wish for a child, her love of men, and the feminine role in general.'[13]

Thus Freud attempts to explain how this woman came to love other women by claiming that she repudiated men. Joanna Ryan and Noreen O'Connor[14] argue that the concept of repudiation in explaining homosexuality is central both in 'Psychogenesis . . .' and elsewhere in Freud's writing. Just as masculinity in men can be seen as being based on repudiation of what is understood as female, homosexuality has been interpreted as a rejection of desire for the opposite sex. In 'Psychogenesis' the term 'repudiation' is used to mean expulsion, exile or banishment – thus this woman came to love other women through the act of repudiating men. Thus repudiation of men and the love of women are made virtually constitutive of each other in Freud's thinking.

Ryan and O'Connor counter Freud's theory of repudiation thus:

> The possibility of a woman choosing another woman as a love-object without repudiating men, or femininity, or motherhood, is foreclosed upon, and we are left with female homosexuality as inevitably a negative and reactive choice.[15]

The main focus of their argument is that repudiation denies any positive desire for a woman and does not allow any exploration of that desire. They ask whether a choice between two alternatives always amounts to repudiation or a rejection of the one not chosen. Thus, 'if a woman chooses a woman as a love-object, it means or is explained by having repudiated men. This may well be true in some instances, but it is not necessarily generally so.'[16] I think that what is being tentatively opened up here is the acknowledgement that heterosexuality and homosexuality are not two opposing characteristics – that individuals may experience desire for both sexes.

Ryan and O'Connor go on to suggest that Freud was blind to the part that was repudiated within the case study, the girl's heterosexuality. However, I would argue that Freud was not blind to the negative image, the supposedly repudiated heterosexuality. Freud acknowledges the heterosexual elements in the girl's sexuality thus:

> The girl's inversion, however, received its final reinforcement when she found in her 'lady' an object which promised to satisfy not only her homosexual trends, but also that part of her heterosexual libido which was still attached to her brother.[17]

Freud believes that the girl had transferred her sweeping repudiation of men on to him. He notes the following:

> Once when I expounded to her a specially important part of the theory, one touching her nearly, she replied in an inimitable tone, 'How very interesting', as though she were a *grande dame* being taken over a museum and glancing through her lorgnon at objects to which she was completely indifferent.[18]

It is not clear from his case study whether Freud was completely indifferent to his analytical interpretation being dismissed in such a way. However, Freud claims that as soon as he recognized what he assumed was the girl's attitude to her father he broke off the analysis and advised her parents to send her to a female doctor. Freud's over-identification with father–daughter dynamics in this case becomes clear, as he was unable to challenge the girl's revenge against her father because he had, in fact, become her father through countertransference.

Yet there was also an important positive[19] transference from the patient to the analyst. Her dream content reveals, according to Freud, an anticipation of the cure for inversion and a longing for a man's love and children. In her waking life the girl tells Freud she wishes to marry only to escape her father and believes she can have sexual relationships with men and women at the same time.

Freud does not believe her dreams. His belief is they are expressed as an attempt to win his favour so she could disappoint him later on, just as her father had disappointed her. He says he is warned by *some slight impression*, and tells the patient that he does not believe her and that she intends to deceive him just as she habitually deceives her father.

But why? Why is so it impossible to see heterosexual and homosexual desire co-existing? The content of the dreams is written off like some disobedient daughter but what about the attachment for the small boy[20] and, as Maguire suggests, the heterosexual desire which co-existed with her rage towards her father?[21] Freud explains this thus:

> In addition, these presages of later homosexuality had always occupied her *conscious* life, while the attitude arising from the Oedipus complex had remained *unconscious* and had appeared only in such signs as her tender behaviour to the little boy.[22]

Thus the heterosexual meanings within the dreams are ignored in the case study and a separation between her heterosexuality and her homosexuality is maintained. To strengthen this split her heterosexuality has been assigned an unconscious meaning. Thus her sexuality has been split between her conscious and her unconscious, and is continued thus:

> From her very early years, therefore, her libido had flowed in two currents, the one on the surface being one that we may unhesitatingly designate as homosexual. This latter was probably a direct and unchanged continuation of an infantile fixation on her mother. Possibly the analysis described here actually revealed nothing more than the process by which, on an appropriate occasion, the deeper heterosexual current of libido, too, was deflected into the manifest homosexual one.[23]

First, although Freud says that the current on the surface was homosexual and later goes on to say categorically that this is a case of congenital homosexuality, there is no proof that the girl's libido was primarily homosexual in her early years and she had, according to Freud, passed through a normal Oedipus. Thus the heterosexual has been ignored for the sake of the homosexual, and the bisexual elements within this case study, although elegantly explored and theorized, have not been acknowledged.

Second, in regard to the 'two currents', Freud posits that one of the facts revealed by psychoanalytic investigation is that 'a very considerable measure of latent or unconscious homosexuality can be detected in all normal people'.[24] So the homosexual and heterosexual elements have been split and one made latent or unconscious. However the girl in this case study was perfectly conscious of some heterosexuality – for example in her belief that she could have relationships with men and women. It is interesting to speculate how far this split has been taken in general theories of latency. It would be pertinent to ask whether the general misinterpretation of heterosexuality and homosexuality as diametrically opposed categories (i.e. 'flowing in two currents') which must be kept and understood separately has been theorized into the psychoanalytic canon.

One of the problems in this case study was Freud's over-identification with and over-reliance on the father–daughter relationship, particularly in relation to the dream material, which helped to obscure the bisexual elements. Would Melanie Klein's case studies, which represent a shift from Freud's patriarchal viewpoint to the centrality of mother and child, view bisexuality in a clearer way? I intend to discuss the following case study at length and then compare how Freud and Klein theorize bisexuality.

Case study 2: Klein's 'The Psychogenesis of Tics'

Melanie Klein's writings[25] state that the sexual development of children is bound by the emotions ensuing from their object relations, that is, relations to (usually) people. Klein conceptualizes positions which not only are developmental stages but are descriptions of mental structures found in adults as well as children. Symbolization in Klein is a key factor, as Noreen O'Connor states: 'She stresses the importance of a balance between anxiety which initiates symbol formation and phantasy and a capacity for anxiety tolerance on the part of the ego.'[26] The internal world of the child is peopled by either part objects (e.g. the mother's breast, father's penis) or whole objects (e.g. the mother *per se*). These objects may either reflect external reality or be based on phylogenetic or inherited memory.

The primitive ego cannot understand why an object can be both good and bad. Thus the paranoid-schizoid position is dominated by defences against anxieties and persecution; the main mechanisms are splitting, projection and introjection. Thus splitting may occur in the self (introjection) and the object related to (projection) may be split into ideal (a good object) and destructive (a bad object) parts. This helps the primitive ego to organize its own internal chaos and assuage intolerable anxiety. Thus a bad feeling or a disturbance at the mother's breast may be felt as a bad object and spat out.

The depressive situation comes about when the child recognizes its former part object as a whole object (e.g. mother rather than breast). The feelings associated with this position are guilt and loss. The child fears that it may have destroyed its mother through destructive rage. The child then feels a need to repair the relationship and restore the mother. Successful negotiation of this position is marked by the ability to integrate good feelings (e.g. the child's projected love and gratifying experience) and bad feelings (e.g. the child's rage and frustrating experience with mother). Integration of feelings of hate, envy and jealousy towards the parents as a couple are developed at this position.

Reading Klein is difficult. Her case studies are unlike Freud's 'scientific observation'[27] in that she usually provides only interpreted material and gives little reason for why she has arrived at such an analysis. The style of her writing has been seen as reflecting a texture of the primary process thinking, the way that children construct the world.[28]

I have chosen the following case study because it is one of the very few examples where Klein examines heterosexuality and homosexuality together. Klein uses this case study to emphasize the psychopathology of tics, which are central to her analysis of Felix's repressed sexuality. However I have chosen to concentrate on Felix's actual homosexual and heterosexual relationships to see if this casts any light on theorizing bisexuality.

Felix comes for treatment with Melanie Klein between the ages of thirteen and sixteen. Klein observes that he illustrates a neurotic character; he holds himself separate from his family and school friends, has a marked lack of emotions and a tic.

At the age of three Felix has a surgical operation on his penis. At this time his father also warns him about masturbation. This caused anxieties which, Klein believes, strengthens his castration complex and turns him away from a heterosexual to a homosexual attitude. At school he displays an aversion to games until, when Felix is eleven, the return of his father from the war. His father's threats of punishment at this fear of sport[29] meant that Felix overcompensates for his original fear of games and sport holds his interest to the exclusion of other matters. He stops masturbating at this time.

The only fragments of masturbatory phantasty[30] he can recall at the start of his analysis with Klein are as follows:

> He is playing with some little girls; he caresses their breasts and they play football together. In this game he is continually disturbed by a hut which can be seen behind the little girls.[31]

In analysis the hut represents a lavatory which stands for his mother and has the significance of degrading her. For Klein, the game of football shows an acting out of intercourse phantasies. Games represent a form of release of sexual tension, one which was permitted by his father. Thus this appears to be a heterosexual phantasy. During analysis it becomes clear that the over-interest in games is an overcompensation for anxiety. His interest in games relents and he becomes more interested in school work. He starts to masturbate again.

Klein relates the movements within Felix's tic to his phantasy of wishing to take his mother's place in relation to his father in sexual intercourse. This conceals an active homosexual phantasy of taking the place of his father in intercourse with a boy. This phantasy (and the one concealing it) is, to Klein, narcissistic. For Klein, narcissism is not merely a withdrawal from relationship to an investment in one's ego alone as Freud sees it, but an intense relation to mainly internal objects. Thus, according to Klein, he has chosen himself as his love object. But behind these phantasies she finds details of Felix's original identification with his father in heterosexual intercourse with his mother.

Felix's first homosexual relationships are aroused by reading a book about the love of a man (who Klein believed was a symbol of his father) for a boy (who Klein believed was a symbol of Felix). He develops a romantic crush on a fellow student, A, who is much admired not only by his schoolmates but also by a master. It is the relationship of the fellow student to the master that determines Felix's feelings for the boy. Klein's analysis reveals that A represents an idealization of Felix himself (i.e. narcissism). A's relationship with the master represents Felix's desire both to be loved as a son by his father and to take his mother's place in relation to his father. Thus, Klein concludes: 'His love for A was principally based on identification and corresponded to a narcissistic object relation.'[32] The relationship is not acknowledged and Felix transfers his affections to another boy, B. B represents, according to Klein, Felix's father and is meant to replace him. Klein stops this relationship, because, she says, of the complications, but she does not explain further. What I believe is significant about the case is that the homosexuality has been interpreted as narcissistic.[33]

Felix's first heterosexual object-choice is, according to Klein, influenced by his homosexual attitudes, and she ignores the earlier heterosexual phantasy. This choice is an actress, who according to Klein possesses male attributes. Thus for Klein she becomes a mother with a penis.[34] Felix's second relationship is with a woman older than him. She represents to Felix his mother both denigrated and superior. Klein imposes a temporary break in this relationship in order to release anxieties, stating:

> It could now be seen that the turning away from the originally loved but forbidden mother had participated in the strengthening of the homosexual attitude and the phantasies about the dreaded castrating mother.[35]

Representations of bisexuality in Freud and Klein

So how is bisexuality, then, represented within Freud and Klein? Both had difficulties with bisexuality, the concept of heterosexuality and homosexuality co-existing in one person.

They also had difficulty with the temporality of bisexuality; significant *heterosexual* attitudes at the beginning of both of these case studies are ignored. I would argue that temporality, the concept of different relationships/fantasies with people of different sexes over time, becomes difficult to comprehend if theories of sexuality are based on a linear strategy. It is precisely the way that both Freud and Klein use Oedipus[36] as a standard route to a resolved adult sexuality, usually heterosexuality, which causes a conceptual problem. Sexuality is perceived as a maturation process: a bisexuality could be perceived at the beginning, in infancy, but it certainly has no place at the end of this process, in adulthood.

Furthermore both Freud and Klein split the heterosexuality from any homosexuality in these case studies to make the bisexuality absent. Freud tended to convert his case material to ignore any difficulty and make heterosexuality absent when it clearly was not. Thus the girl's heterosexual elements are ignored and the homosexual elements are taken as the whole of her sexuality. In regard to Klein, the boy's homosexual elements are pathologized and his heterosexuality encouraged. Marie Maguire states: 'Through her abandonment of Freud's theory of bisexuality Klein reinforced the equation of homosexuality with pathology.'[37] But Klein conceptualizes the same layered constructions of a homosexuality with a heterosexuality beneath, to explore sexuality, as did Freud. I would argue that she doesn't abandon Freud's theories of bisexuality, because she uses his theoretical constructions to examine and understand both manifest and latent sexuality, whether heterosexual or homosexual, together in one individual. But instead of acknowledging the homosexuality, as shown in her case study, she has pathologized it. Pathologizing homosexuality thus within a bisexual framework causes problems because the heterosexuality becomes normalized and bisexuality is negated.

Rachel Cunningham challenges Klein's denial of homosexuality thus:

> It seems then that in the Kleinian view, at least as it is asserted now, our reproductive urge to keep the human race going is phylogenetically inscribed. Thus, if a child develops into an adolescent who is sexually and emotionally attracted to his/her own sex, a betrayal of truth, of the prescribed order to things, is meant to have occurred, a perversion of what is meant to be.[38]

This pathologization of homosexuality is seen in that Klein saw fit to tell Felix to stop one homosexual relationship, *without* an explanation why, and to put a temporary stop to one heterosexual relationship, *with* an explanation from Klein as to why. Furthermore Felix's homosexual relations are deemed narcissistic whereas his heterosexual ones are not. But it is striking that Felix's object relations at the start of the analysis could well be narcissistic in total, a flight from relationships, i.e. his aloofness from his family and schoolmates, whether his relationships were homosexual or heterosexual. To use Klein's terminology, she has split a perceived oscillation between heterosexuality and homosexuality, a possible bisexuality, in Felix's case into heterosexual good behaviour and homosexual bad behaviour, thus helping to contain and regulate her own anxieties about sexuality not fitting into convenient categories.

Case study 3: Marie Maguire's clients

There is a growing tendency for homosexuality today to be more culturally accepted rather than stigmatized. Does this then mean that this growing acceptance has been reflected in psychoanalytical theorizing, and what are the implications for bisexuality when homosexuality is less likely to be pathologized and the heterosexuality less likely to be privileged? I have chosen some case studies of clients exhibiting bisexual features from Marie Maguire. What is important in her case studies is how bisexuality has been more accepted, rather than obscured and pathologized.

Maguire's patient Ms L has in the past had sexual relationships with both sexes. At present she loves women and desires them slightly but is also having affairs with men.

She has a dream about an enormous penis which was originally attached to a man. Ms L then starts to play with it and to put it in her mouth. She is disturbed by someone and she puts the penis in a drawer. Afterwards she pulls it out again but it has shrunk. When she tried to play with it again it doesn't work. She tries to eat it but it tastes foul.

Maguire interprets her attempt to devour the penis as an attempt to strengthen her identification with her father and to separate from her mother. In discussion about the dream the client indignantly responds to Maguire's suggestion that she wants a penis by saying that she only wants to try having a penis to experiment with, to play with, but not to have permanently. The penis symbolized a quality she wanted, which she believed men had, a ruthless determination to put her needs first in professional and sexual life.

Maguire draws on Freud to hypothesize that when a girl becomes heterosexual her desire to have a penis attached to her body, or to ingest it, becomes a desire to enjoy it sexually.[39] Freud believes in regard to female sexuality that the first conception of sexual intercourse is an oral one. Sucking on the penis is similar to sucking on the mother's breast. Maguire says that her patient had not decided whether she wanted a male or female sexual partner; unconsciously she felt torn between her mother and father. Maguire comments:

> Her image of a combined nipple-penis provided a temporary solution to this bisexual conflict. She told me that in the dream she had put the penis into her mouth as a baby does when it explores the world around it, sucking on it as she once sucked on the nipple. 'The penis was like a tough, springy plastic toy', she said, 'a kind of eroticised nipple'.[40]

This unconscious split between father and mother was reflected by Mrs K, who was in treatment for bulimia with Marie Maguire. She 'constantly oscillated emotionally' between men and women in regards to sexual object-choice. Maguire sees this oscillation as representative of her internal mother and father. Mrs K has split the parental couple and wishes to have exclusive possession of each. She cannot bear the idea of either her mother or her analyst being part of a sexual couple. '"It makes me feel ill", she said.'[41] Maguire believes that she needed to accept her parents as a couple so that she could let go of her obsession with them and build her own independent adult emotional life.

I would like to dwell on this question of the parental couple because I think that it is significant in any pathologization of bisexuality. Hanna Segal believes that the successful negotiation of Oedipal conflict, i.e. psychological maturity, is the ability to feel hate, jealousy and envy of the parents as a couple; phantasies of running away with either parent are a defence against such feelings. She says, 'Any deviation from sexuality of that kind [i.e. a resolved heterosexuality] is an internal attack on the parents as a couple, and in that sense is not really a complete healthy development.'[42]

Cunningham counters this by stating that, if an individual is able both to bear and to appreciate the idea of a heterosexual couple together rather than wanting to split it, then there is potential for maturity and emotional depth. She adds, significantly, that the ability to tolerate the togetherness of the parental couple is none too easy a task for many people.

Is it pertinent to ask, therefore, whether bisexuality is seen in psychoanalytical theory as a representation of an unconscious desire to keep parents apart? Many bisexual people have had long-term, loving, intimate relationships with both men and women. Furthermore, as Cunningham points out, if the ability to tolerate the parental couple is difficult for a lot of people, this does not explain why any neurotic tension in bisexuality should be pathologized over and above, say, difficulties in heterosexual relationships.

Furthermore Maguire, commenting on gendered power differences, notes that the integration of the parental couple has not happened within psychoanalytical theory. She emphasizes the importance of seeing how maternal and paternal power interact within the psyche. She suggests that theorizing so on the part of the psychoanalytical establishment would have to involve a recognition that any notion of sexual equality in our current society is, in fact, illusory.

There are, however, problems with how bisexuality is seen in Maguire's case histories. Maguire acknowledges that Freud has influenced her understanding of bisexuality. She emphasizes the 'precariousness of all sexual orientation and the subtle oscillations there are in all of us between heterosexual and homosexual desire'.[43] Freud does talk about oscillations, which could describe a bisexuality, thus: 'In all of us, throughout life, the libido normally oscillates between male and female objects.'[44] But he is contradictory because in the passage mentioned above he uses the phrase 'in a still oscillating or a definitely bisexual organisation', indicating a difference between oscillations and bisexuality. But in Maguire's text there has been a slippage of meaning to where the salient features of bisexuality are oscillations rather than seen as possible pluralities of desire co-existing simultaneously. Thus she states: 'Yet at the same time Freud's concept of bisexuality enabled him to explore the intricate oscillations of homosexual and heterosexual desire which influence the choice of love object.'[45] This can be seen in Maguire's case study where she describes Mrs K who constantly oscillated emotionally between men and women. In this case this may well be a defence against intimacy, but Maguire describes Mrs K's sexuality thus: 'For instance, she insisted that although she wanted a permanent love relationship with one person, psychically she would always be bisexual.'[46] But Maguire has difficulties with the realities of her sexuality. By using the term *oscillations* Maguire is describing a sexuality which can be split, e.g. moving backwards and forwards from a heterosexual to homosexual object-choice and vice versa and thus bisexuality is not seen as pluralities of desire towards men and women existing simultaneously. Furthermore, according to Maguire's logic, once Mrs K has made a choice she will no longer be bisexual.

This split in bisexuality by using the term *oscillations* can be further seen in Maguire's comment about Ms L, who had not made up her mind whether she wanted a male or female sexual partner more. Thus, it can be read that an anticipation of a choice has been made for Ms L rather than an acceptance of the plurality of her desire. Maguire does remain open about the sex of preferred partner – she refers to some patients feeling the need to choose a partner of one sex with whom to make a permanent relationship. She continues that patients who 'are in conflict with sexual orientation' usually make it clear that they need an atmosphere of absolute analytical neutrality. Maguire notes the difficulty, particularly in the case of Sharon below, of not steering a course for clients to make a heterosexual object-choice.

Moreover Maguire does have an important point in insisting that identification and sexual orientation are separated theoretically as far as possible. She believes that by doing so she may make it clear whether homosexuals, like heterosexuals, suffer because they have identified with parental figures towards whom they feel profound ambivalence, rather than because of their sexual orientation *per se*. She uses a case study of a lesbian, Sharon, who exhibited many similarities to the girl in Freud's case study above. Like Freud's beautiful and clever girl of eighteen, Sharon appeared to have made an Oedipal shift from mother to father but had chosen to become lesbian rather than heterosexual. Sharon had changed significantly in brief psychotherapy by using the transference with her analyst to strengthen positive identifications with maternal figures and to loosen the power of negative paternal internalizations without altering her sexual orientation. Thus a neurotic tension had been resolved without altering her sexuality and an acknowledgement has been made, unlike Freud's repudiation above, that homosexuality does not mean a rejection of desire for the opposite sex.

This is reflected in Cunningham's belief that it is possible for homosexuals to be relatively un-neurotic. She believes that a child who has loved a parent of the same sex and remains linked to that parent has the potential to form loving and lasting homosexual relationships. Thus would it not be possible that a love of both parents would allow for a plurality of sexual desire and sexual, intimate relationships for both sexes to exist? This could allow for a recognition of bisexuality as un-neurotic.

Furthermore sexuality is not everything,[47] as Cunningham notes: 'The road to psychological maturity is a hazardous one for most individuals and much of the terrain to be covered lies *outside* the field of sexual identification and object choice.'[48] However, these difficulties are compounded for those who are not heterosexual. Thus it is relevant to ask whether analysts have dealt with both their own homosexual feelings and their own internalized cultural homophobia. Can they recognize the cultural pressure towards homosexuality which may exacerbate feelings of depression, paranoia and low self-esteem in individuals?[49]

The first problem, however, is that homosexuality has not been properly integrated into the psychoanalytic movement, still less the homosexual content of bisexuality. Various schools, most notably the Institute of Psychoanalysis, where 90 per cent of all consultant psychotherapists in London and 50 per cent in the country as a whole have trained,[50] operate a bar on homosexuals as training candidates. Cunningham notes that feelings about homosexuality remain raw and unprocessed in many analysts. Homosexuality is 'not a repressed entity or complex, but a disavowed one, projected or split off into the external world ["Them"] where it can only be seen as threatening, pernicious.'[51] Using Object Relations theory she berates the lack of health/emotional maturity on this matter in the psychoanalytic movement thus: 'as a vital area of the human psyche is spat out as unpalatable and is persistently denied access except as a bad object to be theorised about from a defensive distance'.[52]

Cunningham notes that it is likely from the continuous hostility towards homosexuality that a psychic bisexuality has been rarely achieved by psychoanalysts. She continues,

> Yet surely psychic bisexuality is crucial for broad human understanding and clinical empathy. Perhaps many analysts have not had their bisexuality adequately understood and received in their own analyses and are therefore unable to view this issue without anxiety.[53]

There are, however, several problems with this suggestion. Because of the way that bisexuality is often split, as shown by the case studies above, there would be a tendency to see only the heterosexuality or only the homosexuality. What are the implications for clients exhibiting bisexual elements? First, a person's bisexuality stands in danger of being split and only the heterosexual or the homosexual side being adequately addressed. For bisexual clients this splitting would be painful, as a portion of one's avowed identity is split off and disowned, and would be disorientating for clients sexually attracted to both men and women.

There are further problems with the pathologization of homosexuality within the psychoanalytic field which affect an acceptance of bisexuality. Most notably in Klein's preceding constructions homosexuality has been pathologized and heterosexuality has been encouraged and thus bisexuality would have to be either homosexual or heterosexual. Yet if bisexuality were to be accepted, the element of homosexuality would have to be accepted, and, if bisexuality were to be pathologized, what would happen to the heterosexuality? This awkward contradiction is one reason why analysts do not find it easy to address bisexuality. A true acknowledgement of bisexuality would necessitate a re-evaluation of the hierarchy in the split between homosexuality and heterosexuality. This would prevent bisexuality being merely considered a combination of oppositional, 'oscillating', traits.

Furthermore the temporality of bisexuality, the seeming movement in sexual relations between one sex and another, is not clearly theorized. Both Freud and Klein ignored significant heterosexual elements at the beginning of the case studies shown above. This tendency can further be seen in Maguire's client Ms L indignantly refuting the suggestion that she wanted a penis *permanently* when actually she wanted a penis to see what it felt like as a *temporary* measure.[54]

Maguire acknowledges the tendency for psychoanalytical writers to present views as timeless and universal. She notes that, while feminist literature stresses the importance of historical and cultural factors on the formation of gendered identity, this is rarely reflected in psychoanalytical writing. Significantly, notions of normal/abnormal development expressly in the case of homosexuality are presented in psychoanalytical discourse as universal truths irrespective of evidence that norms are culturally weighted. In referring to the conflicts within anorexic or bulimic women Maguire does refer to a 'socially required oedipal choice', thus recognizing the social pressures on making a choice of partner, presumably heterosexual.

Maguire does acknowledge and explore bisexuality in her case studies. She further notes that 'Many actively heterosexual women have a strong component of bisexuality, and the mother's sensual pleasure in the daughter need not be harmful unless she is unduly seductive'.[55] She cites Weller and Wrye's hypothesis that mother–daughter relations can be erotic in their own right and that sexual wishes and fantasies may be directed towards an oedipal mother who is separated from the self and who is a source of pleasure as well as identification.[56] However, because she relies on the inheritance of Freud she has difficulty in accepting the realities of bisexuality. Thus her use of the term *oscillations* allows for a possible split to occur in a bisexuality into heterosexual and homosexual elements. Furthermore her focus on the object-choice of the relationship determining sexuality rather than a choice in deciding relationships, as seen in the case of Mrs K above, has allowed bisexuality to be seen as either heterosexual or homosexual when in relationship.

Lastly, even if analysts were able to see a bisexuality, that is no guarantee that bisexuality will not still be seen as an immature phenomenon rather than an adult sexual category. Cunningham suggests that psychic bisexuality is necessary for clinical empathy – but if empathy is seen as a hallmark of emotional maturity there is a contradiction with bisexuality which is often seen as a hallmark of emotional immaturity.

However, the main problem with considering adult bisexuality in an analytical framework is an over-emphasis on sexuality as a maturation process with a presumed end result of heterosexual marriage. Oedipus could be resolved in a number of ways but, as Bowie infers, Freud's descriptions of the standard route by which this complex can be resolved have a 'marked normative and normalizing air'. From an original bisexuality 'male children are expected to become masculine, female children feminine and all children, in due course, heterosexual adults'.[57] Thus bisexuality is seen as an immature state, a point of departure rather than a destination point of a resolved, conscious and integrated adult sexuality. This is why adult bisexuality is so rarely addressed in psychoanalytical literature.

Notes

1. Sigmund Freud, *Case Histories II* (London: Penguin, 1991).
2. In Sigmund Freud's 'Three Essays on Sexuality', in *On Sexuality* (London: Penguin, 1991), sexuality is viewed as a maturation process with an implicit aim of heterosexual marriage.
3. Melanie Klein, *Love, Guilt and Reparation* (London: Virago, 1988).
4. Marie Maguire, *Men, Women, Passion and Power* (London: Routledge, 1995).
5. The term *Object Relations* pertains to and is developed from Klein in the work of W. R. D. Fairburn, *Psychoanalytic Studies of the Personality* (London: Routledge, 1994); Harry Guntrip, *Schizoid Phenomena, Object Relations and the Self* (London: Karnac, 1992); D. W. Winnicott, *Maturational Process and the Facilitating Environment* (London: Karnac, 1990); D. W. Winnicott, *Playing and Reality* (London: Tavistock, 1971) and other works by the same author.
6. Maguire recounts that her involvement with the Battersea Action and Counselling Centre and the Women's Therapy Centre was formative (*Men, Women*, p. 4).
7. Freud, *Case Histories II*, p. 371.
8. *Ibid.*, p. 375.
9. *Ibid.*, p. 376.
10. The term *Oedipus* refers to emotions, usually unconscious, involving the desire of a child to possess sexually the parent of the opposite sex and to identify with the parent of the same sex. *Feminine Oedipus* refers to the desire of a female child to possess sexually her father and to identify with her mother.
11. Freud, *Case Histories II*, p. 381.
12. *Ibid.*, p. 383.
13. *Ibid.*, p. 384.
14. Joanna Ryan and Noreen O'Connor, *Wild Desires and Mistaken Identities: Lesbianism and Psychoanalysis* (London: Virago, 1993).
15. *Ibid.*, p. 42.
16. *Ibid.*, p. 43.
17. Freud, *Case Histories II*, p. 386
18. *Ibid.*, p. 390.
19. The feelings and identifications experienced by the patient towards the analyst are known as *transferences* and reflect earlier powerful feelings usually towards parents. *Positive and negative transferences* refer to positive and negative feelings and identifications. Freud's reference here is to a positive transference which he believes is a revival of the girl's passionate love for her father. Counter-transference is the feelings and identifications on the analyst's part towards the patient.
20. Freud conflates maternal instinct and sexual instinct in this passage, as elsewhere within the text.
21. Maguire, *Men, Women*, p. 202.
22. Freud, *Case Histories II*, p. 396 (italics in original).
23. *Ibid.*, p. 396.

24. *Ibid.*, p. 399.
25. Melanie Klein, *Envy and Gratitude* (London: Virago, 1988).
26. Noreen O'Connor 'Is Melanie Klein the One Who Knows Who You Really Are?', *Women: A Cultural Review*, 1, 2 (1990), p. 182.
27. For further reading on Freud's case histories being not as scientific as he claims, refer to Charles Bernheimer and Clare Kahane, *In Dora's Case: Freud-Hysteria-Feminism* (London: Virago, 1985).
28. Jay Greenberg and Stephen A. Mitchell, *Object Relations in Psychoanalytic Theory* (London: Harvard University Press, 1983), p. 120.
29. This threat of punishment coincided with a traumatic physical examination of his nose.
30. Freud uses the term 'fantasies', Klein uses the term 'phantasies'.
31. Klein, *Envy and Gratitude*, p. 108.
32. *Ibid.*, p. 112.
33. It is fairly standard to find a link between narcissism and homosexuality in psychoanalytical texts. Freud is explicit in describing homosexuality as narcissistic object-choice: Freud 'On Narcissism: An Introduction' (1914), in Penguin Freud Library, vol. 11 (London: Penguin, 1984). This link can be shown in the following passage from Hanna Segal, a contemporary exponent of Klein in an interview with Jacqueline Rose in *Women: A Cultural Review*, 1, 2 (1990). She says: 'I would not call it [homosexuality] normality because it is a developmental arrest' (p. 211). She continues: 'But my clinical judgement is that homosexuality is of necessity a narcissistic condition, as the name itself betrays' (p. 212). She concludes by stating that narcissism in homosexuality is inbuilt.
34. Klein, *Envy and Gratitude*, p. 115.
35. The figure of the mother with a penis appears in Kleinian theory as a primitive amalgam of mother containing not only milk and a breast, but also containing attributes of the father, i.e. his penis: Hanna Segal, *Introduction to the Work of Melanie Klein* (London: Karnac, 1988), pp. 103–16. However it is notable that this woman's 'masculine' attributes have been made part male by being given a penis, thus dispensing with any awkward contradictions arising out of Felix's desire for a woman with masculine characteristics.
36. See Sigmund Freud in 'Some Psychological Consequences of the Anatomical Distinction between the Sexes', in *On Sexuality* (London: Penguin, 1991) and Melanie Klein in 'Our Adult World and Its Roots in Infancy', in *Envy and Gratitude*.
37. Maguire, *Men, Women*, p. 205.
38. Rachel Cunningham, 'When Is a Pervert Not a Pervert?', *British Journal of Psychotherapy*, 8 (1991), p. 56.
39. From correspondence from Freud to Jones quoted by Peter Gay in *Freud: A Life for Our Times* (London: Macmillan, 1988), p. 501.
40. Maguire, *Men, Women*, p. 76.
41. *Ibid.*, p. 184.
42. Segal, *Introduction*, p. 207.
43. Maguire, *Men, Women*, p. 198.
44. Freud, *Case Histories II*, p. 384.
45. Maguire, *Men, Women*, p. 202.
46. *Ibid.*, p. 185.
47. Although both Freud and Klein (certainly at the time her case study was used) liberally attribute sexuality to everything.
48. Cunningham, 'When Is a Pervert Not a Pervert?', p. 50.
49. Maguire, *Men, Women*, p. 208.
50. Andrew Samuels, 'Therapists with a Problem', *Capital Gay* (5 May 1995).
51. Cunningham, 'When Is a Pervert Not a Pervert?', p. 50.
52. *Ibid.*, p. 51.
53. *Ibid.*
54. Maguire, *Men, Women*, p. 75.
55. *Ibid.*, p. 189.
56. *Ibid.*, p. 206.
57. Malcolm Bowie, *Feminism and Psychoanalysis: A Critical Dictionary* (1992), ed. Elizabeth Wright (Oxford: Blackwell, 1995), p. 28.

4

The Sexual Reproduction of 'Race': Bisexuality, History and Racialization

Merl Storr

Why write about bisexuality?

In the summer of 1995, I attended a conference at the University of Middlesex called 'New Sexual Agendas'. I was disappointed. I didn't find many new sexual agendas; but I did find a lot of old ones. At one plenary session, the respected feminist scholar Mary McIntosh gave a paper which had a lot to say about the new sexual identities emerging within lesbian and gay communities in the 1990s. In this paper she set out her view that such identities would prove to be transient, and she singled out bisexuality for special attention, arguing that, despite its current vogue, ultimately it would always be subsumed by existing (and enduring) straight and gay institutions or identities.

During questions at the end, a member of the audience expressed astonishment at McIntosh's statements about bisexuality and pointed out that her entire paper was predicated on a binary division between straight and gay. McIntosh replied that bisexuality simply cannot be a viable sexual identity because 'the bisexual' is not a cultural figure in the way that 'the homosexual' is, and she cited Foucault to back her claim that 'the homosexual' 'entered the stage' of sexual discourse[1] at a specific historical point in a way that 'the bisexual' did not. The questioner responded by pointing out that McIntosh was herself actually *foreclosing* bisexuality as a possibility through her rigidly binary, straight-versus-gay approach to sexuality. McIntosh replied again: yes, she *did* see the world in terms of that straight/gay split, and she made no apology for that: it was a sociological observation, that was how she thought the world was, love it or loathe it – and, she added, she happened to love it. As the exchange between McIntosh and her questioner continued, I heard cries of 'Let's have another question!' from the audience; apparently bisexuality was even less deserving a topic of discussion for the audience than it was for McIntosh herself.

This might just be an everyday tale of bi academic folk; certainly those of us who heard Elizabeth Wilson speak at the 'Activating Theory' conference in 1992 will be reminded of a similar dismissal of bisexuality in her paper, and a similar exchange with questioners afterwards.[2] But it is interesting because it encapsulates some of the common assumptions of lesbian, gay and queer scholarship about the history of homosexuality and, correlatively, the non-history of bisexuality. It is now widely accepted by lesbian, gay and queer scholars that sexuality has a history and that 'the homosexual', in the sense of a particular 'type' of individual, is a phenomenon that did not emerge until comparatively recently in 'western' societies.[3] A common view of that history is that sexuality is regulated by a binary opposition between heterosexuality and homosexuality which was either inaugurated or consolidated by the sexologists who wrote during the late nineteenth and early twentieth centuries, including Magnus Hirschfeld, Richard von Krafft-Ebing and Havelock Ellis, among others – although there is some disagreement over the correct dating of the emergence of homosexuality as such,[4] and hence over whether sexologists actually created the hetero/homo opposition or merely reformulated an already extant opposition in new ways. The existence of this binary tends to be asserted by scholars such as McIntosh as a matter of sociological observation and as 'how the world is', although some are less prepared to admit to loving it than she, often presenting it as oppressive in its grip on contemporary sexuality. Eve Sedgwick, for example, writes:

> Many of the major nodes of thought and knowledge in twentieth-century Western culture as a whole are structured – indeed, fractured – by a chronic, now endemic crisis of homo/heterosexual definition, indicatively male, dating from the end of the nineteenth century. . . . an understanding of virtually any aspect of modern Western culture must be, not merely incomplete, but damaged in its central substance to the degree that it does not incorporate a critical analysis of modern homo/heterosexual definintion. . . . from the turn of the century . . . every given person, just as he or she was necessarily assignable to a male or a female gender, was now considered necessarily assignable as well to a homo- or a hetero-sexuality, a binarized identity that was full of implications, however confusing, for even the ostensibly least sexual aspects of personal existence. It was this new development that left no space in the culture exempt from the potent incoherences of homo/heterosexual definition.[5]

In the context of this binary organization that 'leaves no space in the culture exempt', *bi*sexuality appears as a category subsumed by that binary – a co-existence of, or oscillation between, the binary's poles – and hence not really a category at all. Thus the way that the history of sexuality, and the legacy of that history for contemporary culture, are understood tends to foreclose bisexuality both as a historical – indeed, historiographical – concern and as a contemporary issue. My argument in this chapter is that this foreclosure of the history of bisexuality must be resisted – not just because bisexuality is an important topic in its own right, although that certainly is the case, but also because critical enquiry into bisexuality has particular importance for understanding the constitutive role of 'race' in the history of 'western' sexuality. Returning to the last *fin de siècle*, I shall focus on two major sexologists: Havelock Ellis, 'the most influential of the late Victorian pioneers of sexual frankness'[6] whose works include the key and, in its day, highly controversial study *Sexual Inversion*; and Richard von Krafft-Ebing, more conservative author of the 'canonical'[7] legal-medical textbook *Psychopathia Sexualis*, which was first published in German in 1886 and ran to twelve editions, the last of which appeared in 1903 and will be the focus of my discussion in what follows.

If it is truly the case that the history of sexuality is regulated by, and perhaps even produced by, a binary opposition between heterosexuality and homosexuality in the way that McIntosh and others suggest, then, in response to Emma Donoghue's recent question, 'Who Hid Bisexual History?',[8] one might find oneself wearily replying that perhaps there never was any bisexual history to hide after all. But it is important, and even necessary, to note that the pervasive assumption that the hetero/homosexual binary is *the* defining feature of the history of 'western' sexuality is precisely that – an assumption.[9] To be sure, hetero/homo definitions and identities are central to the ways in which sexuality is structured in the contemporary 'west', and it would be impossible to attain any accurate understanding of contemporary 'western' sexuality without taking the dominance of that binary typology into account. But it is a serious error to assume that that binary typology was *the* dominant typology from the moment of its inception (whenever that may actually have been), or to imply that, at some given historical moment, 'the homosexual' 'entered the stage' with the hetero/homo binary already set and scripted. As Sedgwick herself notes in a passage which follows that cited above, late nineteenth-century sexological discourse offered a 'rich stew'[10] of sexual definitions which greatly exceeded the terms of hetero- or homosexuality, including erotic practices and relations which both marked and transgressed divisions between human and animal, animate and inanimate (whether dead or non-living), and interpersonal and intrapersonal (masturbation was a recurrent focus of attention). Far from being regulated by the dourness of a single binary opposition, the texts of Hirschfeld, Krafft-Ebing and Ellis (and indeed Freud, who was in so many ways their son and heir[11]) are a veritable cornucopia of polymorphous perversities and perversions, marvellously rich and strange in the face of their own attempts to submit their unruly subjects to the rigours of scientific taxonomy. If the hetero/homosexual binary is truly now *the* dominant organizing principle of sexuality, the question of how it emerged into its dominant position from the richness of the nineteenth century is one with which historians of sexuality have yet to get to grips.[12] Moreover, the articulation of bisexuality as a practice and/or an identity at various points in the twentieth century,[13] as well as of other sexual practices and identities for which the gender (or even the existence) of sexual partner(s) is not the organizing principle, arguably throws doubt on the absolute nature

– 'no space in the culture exempt' – of the hetero/homo binary as characterized by writers such as Sedgwick. The undoubted force of the hetero/homo binary in the late twentieth century notwithstanding, it is by no means necessarily the case that all sexual subjects in the 'west' have experienced themselves straightforwardly or solely within its terms, and to assume otherwise risks reducing sexual history and culture to the very structure that many scholars of sexuality seek to oppose. The proliferation of 'queer' identities and practices in the current *fin de siècle* – not just homosexual (or indeed heterosexual) queer but bisexual, transgender, rubber, leather, SM, piercing, fetishist, polyamorous, butch, femme and other formations[14] – should alert us to the possibility that the homo/hetero binary is not the only force at work in the production and regulation of sexual subjects. The fact that some or even most[15] sexual articulations can now be (and usually are) subsumed under the terms of that binary is, of course, a product of the complex play of power and resistance, both historically and in the present. But as, precisely, an outcome of social, cultural and historical forces, that fact is *contingent*: it is no more necessary, in itself, than the potential subsumption of sexual practices under other organizing principles – vanilla versus SM, say, or polyamorous versus monogamous, or even principles which are not binary at all, such as the focusing of pleasure in particular body parts, or in particular physical environments (cottages, backrooms, sex parties, suburban semis), or in particular modes or states of dress. The production of sexuality, always discursive and localized, is always also multiplicitous and complex, and its reduction to a single binary opposition is a phenomenon that historians and theorists of sexuality should be concerned to interrogate, not simply to reproduce.

Thus, for the queer reader of the present *fin de siècle*, the sexological texts of the previous *fin de siècle* appear to offer tantalizing narratives of our polymorphous antecedents; not just homosexuals and bisexuals, but SM practitioners, fetishists, transgendered subjects and many others can find images of their forebears there – speaking to us, as it were, at and from the very moment of their production and regulation by the discourses of science and law. Of course, the search for sexological ancestors must proceed with caution. First, there must be caution against conflating polymorphism with freedom and hence imagining sexuality before the dominance of the hetero/homo binary as a pre-lapsarian flowering of eroticism, when in fact, as a reading of the texts themselves makes plain, the forces of discursive power are very much in play: the very classification of these figures is as much an act of routinizing and regulating desire as is their apparent elision by the hetero/homo binary. Second, there must be caution against the projection of contemporary sexual maps on to the landscapes of the past, expressed at its crassest in the search for sexual identities as if they were historical constants, as if the Urnings and Uranodionings of the late nineteenth century simply 'were' homosexuals and bisexuals in the sense in which we understand those terms today; indeed, the term 'bi-sexual' itself then meant something different than it does for us now, as I shall discuss shortly. Despite the many similarities, it is important to bear in mind that many late nineteenth-and early twentieth-century sexual paradigms were indeed different from our own: the distinction between the consensual and the non-consensual is entirely absent from Krafft-Ebing, for example, while the distinction between the congenital and the acquired seems to have been unanimously regarded among sexologists as of paramount importance, for both scientific and legal reasons. Seen in this light, 'Who Hid Bisexual History?' appears just to have been the wrong question after all: the point is not to 'find' a 'hidden' bisexual history, but rather to interrogate the sexual past with caution and respect, acknowledging our positionalities as contemporary queer viewers without simply reducing what we see to distorted reflections of ourselves.

Historians have already begun to work on uncovering the history of sexuality as marked by the racial positionings of sexual subjects – in particular, the feminist literature on the history of eugenics and of 'maternalist imperialism' in Europe and North America is now very extensive.[16] In contrast with advances made in this regard, it is arguable that inadequate attention has thus far been paid to the ways in which 'race' operates discursively in the production of sexuality *as such*, particularly in the sexological canon which played, and arguably continues to play, a crucial role in the formation of sexuality as we know it today.[17] This neglect of 'race' in the sexual discourses of the past reflects and is reflected by the state of certain contemporary sexual-dissident theories, notably queer theory, which, despite the reiteration of 'difference' as a key concern, nevertheless fails to encompass racial dynamics at the heart of sexuality. Judith Butler, for example, offers a dazzling theoretical analysis of sexuality and the body articulated around the concepts of iteration, citation and performativity which explicitly suggests that racism, homophobia and misogyny should be seen not as 'parallel or analogical relations' but as 'vectors of power [which] require and deploy each other';[18] and yet her recent turn to an explicit analysis of 'race' – discussions of Nella Larsen's *Passing* and of Jennie Livingston's documentary film *Paris Is Burning*[19] – is curiously stilted. Butler's theoretical position is articulated around a notion she calls 'heterosexual matrix',

> that grid of cultural intelligibility through which bodies, genders, and desires are naturalized. . . . a hegemonic discursive/epistemic model of gender intelligibility that assumes that for bodies to cohere and make sense there must be a stable sex expressed through a stable gender (masculine expresses male, feminine expresses female) that is oppositionally and hierarchically defined through the compulsory practice of heterosexuality.[20]

This notion of 'heterosexual matrix' is for Butler extraordinarily fruitful for the analysis of gender, sexuality and the production of sexed and gendered bodies. But it fails to note any racial dimension to that production, any racial logic at the heart of the matrix, particularly in the constitution of heterosexuality as procreation – surely not an incidental feature of the discourse of heterosexuality as 'natural', and a crucially *racialized* feature in ways that I hope to make clear.

The notion of 'race' is a slippery one, in the writings of the sexologists and elsewhere. As Lucy Bland notes of early twentieth-century British usages of the term, '"Race" might mean the "human race", the "Anglo-Saxon race", "the British race", etc., depending on the context. The ambiguity of meaning allowed a slippage between the different usages.'[21] In fact the movements of slippage are complex, with an array of terms unstably distinguished from each other. For example, Krafft-Ebing uses the terms 'species' and 'race', but the latter has an unstable relationship with the former. Thus he claims that 'desires arise in the consciousness of the individual, which have for their purpose the perpetuation of the *species* (sexual instinct). . . . The duration of the physiological processes in the sexual organs, as well as the the strength of the sexual desire manifested, vary, both in individuals and in *races*'[22] – where 'race' operates as a subdivision of 'species', the purpose of sexual instinct being the perpetuation of the latter; but later in the same text he writes of 'the sexual instinct which is indispensable for the preservation of the *race*',[23] with the implication that 'race' refers to the single human 'race' or 'species' rather than to its supposed subdivisions. Havelock Ellis, by contrast, uses 'species' relatively rarely, and is more likely to use 'race' interchangeably in both senses: 'that propagation of the race which, as a matter of fact, we find dominant throughout the whole of life';[24] 'we seem to find a special proclivity to homosexuality . . . among certain races and in certain regions'.[25]

As I hope these quotations make clear, 'race', with all its instability, is the organizing principle of sexuality for these sexologists, procreation and the propagation of 'the race' (whatever that might mean at any given point) being the meaning and purpose of sexuality as such. Indeed, the very distinction between the normal and the 'perverse' arises from the racial imperative of sex as procreation; according to Krafft-Ebing, 'With opportunity for the natural satisfaction of the sexual instinct, every expression of it that does not correspond with the purpose of nature – i.e., propagation – must be regarded as perverse'.[26] In this the sexologists of the *fin de siècle* are exemplars of nineteenth-century racialism; as Robert Young suggests, 'Race became the fundamental determinant of human culture and history: indeed, it is arguable that race became *the* common principle of academic knowledge in the nineteenth century'.[27] It is arguable that all of the sexologists' most important claims arise from this common principle. Ellis's insistence, for example, that all homosexuality, even that which appears to be 'acquired', must ultimately be based on congenital conditions arises from the racial imperative to procreation:

> the argument for acquired or suggested inversion logically involves the assertion that normal sexuality is also acquired or suggested. . . .

This theory is wholly unworkable. . . . We should . . . have to admit that the most fundamental human instinct is so constituted as to be equally well adapted for sterility as for that propagation of the race which, as a matter of fact, we find dominant throughout the whole of life.[28]

Thus the vicissitudes of sexuality, perverse or otherwise, as articulated by sexology simply cannot be understood in isolation from 'race': 'race' is precisely what sexuality is all about.

This is particularly true of bisexuality, the formulation of which in *fin-de-siècle* sexology can be fully understood only in the context of racialization, and the investigation of which thus highlights the constitutive role of 'race' in sexology's understanding of both 'normal' and 'inverted' sexuality. While there are a number of figures in sexological texts which might have an appeal to contemporary bisexual readers as ancestors – notably the 'psychosexual hermaphrodite' attracted to members of both sexes, and the 'acquired invert' who, in Krafft-Ebing in particular, appears as a malleable figure who can be persuaded from heterosexuality to homosexuality and, with encouragement from suitable professionals, might be coaxed back again – it is on the term bi-sexual'[29] itself that I wish to focus here. 'Bi-sexual', in both Ellis and Krafft-Ebing, stands in a particular relation to both 'race' and the 'heterosexual matrix', and reveals the mutually constitutive congruence of the two. 'Bi-sexual' in these texts indicates a coincidence of male and female characteristics, and it is primarily a physical phenomenon although it has a number of important psychosexual effects. It is a term which has vital explanatory value for the understanding of the perverse. Ellis, for example, writes:

We can probably grasp the nature of abnormality better if we reflect on the development of the sexes and on the latent organic bi-sexuality in each sex. At an early stage of development the sexes are indistinguishable, and throughout life the traces of this early community of sex remain. . . . Putting the matter in a purely speculative shape, it may be said that at conception the organism is provided with about 50 per cent. of male germs and about 50 per cent. of female germs, and that as development proceeds either the male or the female germs assume the upper hand, killing out those of the other sex, until in the maturely developed individual only a few aborted germs of the opposite sex are left. In the homosexual person, however, and in the psychosexual hermaphrodite, we may imagine that the process has not proceeded normally . . . ; the result being that we have a person who is organically twisted into a shape that is more fitted for the exercise of the inverted than of the normal sexual impulse, or else equally fitted for both.[30]

Bisexuality as a physical phenomenon is not the same as hermaphroditism the latter is an anomaly of sexual *development*, but the former is the originary state *from* which later developments are made. Krafft-Ebing gives a similar account of bisexuality as an originary state. In a move which echoes the recurrent nineteenth-century claim that 'ontogeny recapitulates phylogeny', Krafft-Ebing explicitly locates bisexuality as the origin not just of the development of the individual but also of the development of the 'species' or 'race': 'The primary stage [of evolution] undoubtedly was bi-sexuality such as still exists in the lowest classes of animal life and also during the first months of foetal existence in man';[32] interference in the evolution of sexual types, in the form of hereditary degeneration or physical intervention, may result in 'intermediary sexual gradations between the pure type of man and woman.'[33] Krafft-Ebing shares the conviction, common at that period,[34] that a strongly marked differentiation between the sexes is a product of advanced evolution and civilization, and that in 'civilised races' the sexes are more different from each other than is the case among 'less developed races': 'The higher the anthropological development of the race, the stronger these contrasts between man and woman, and vice versa.'[35] (Ellis, on the other hand, taking the unorthodox view that women are more highly evolved than men, claims that 'modern civilisation is becoming . . . feminine'[36] and that as men evolve they will become more like women.) Interestingly, Krafft-Ebing uses 'mono-sexuality', a term which some bisexual theorists in the 1990s have reactivated to describe those whose orientation is towards one sex only, to describe the state of sexual–racial development which has evolved beyond the duality of bisexuality to a single-sexed harmony in which the sex predominating in the primary sexual characteristics corresponds with that predominating in the secondary: 'The type of the present stage of evolution is mono-sexuality, that is to say, a congruous development of the secondary bodily and psychical sexual characteristics belonging to the respective sexual glands.'[37]

Clearly, then, 'bi-sexuality', which both Ellis and Krafft-Ebing see evidenced in such secondary characteristics as male nipples, facial hair in women and the clitoris as a bisexual analogue of the penis, is an important feature of the 'heterosexual matrix' as it appears in *fin-de-siècle* sexology, arguably even its very heart: two sexes evolved from one originary bisexual state into a 'mono-sexual' congruence between primary and secondary characteristics, analogous to the twentieth-century congruence between 'sex' and 'gender' identified by Butler. Moreover, the notion of 'bi-sexuality' is what allows sexology to preserve a heterosexual logic even in cases of sexual inversion, characterized as 'A mono-sexual psychic apparatus of generation, in a monosexual body which belongs to the opposite sex . . . a feminine psycho-sexual centre in a masculine brain, and *vice versa*',[38] or as 'a distinctly general, though not universal, tendency for [male] sexual inverts to approach the feminine type. . . . In inverted women a certain subtle masculinity or boyishness is equally prevalent . . . Even in inversion the imperative need for a certain sexual opposition . . . still rules in full force'[39] – this need for opposition sometimes leading, Ellis argues, to inter-racial sexual relationships among inverts, especially among women in American prisons. Moreover, the logic of bisexuality is a racial logic, both in the sense that it is a mark of evolution and its supersession by sexual dimorphism is, for Krafft-Ebing at least, a characteristic of racial superiority, and in the related sense that the two-sexed sexuality present in and developed from bisexuality is entirely organized around that principle of the propagation of 'the race' which so thoroughly dominates the whole of human and animal life that neither procreative nor non-procreative sexuality is intelligible outside it.

European discourses of 'race' at the *fin de siècle* were distinctively imperialist in character. According to Robert Young, 'In the imperial phase, from the 1880s onwards, the cultural ideology of race became so dominant that racial superiority, and its attendant virtue of civilization, took over from economic gain or Christian missionary work as the presiding, justifying idea of the empire'.[40] In fact all of the 'justifying ideas' of empire mentioned by Young – economics, Christianity and racial superiority – had their corollaries in sexology; these are perhaps seen especially clearly in Krafft-Ebing. Krafft-Ebing's recurrent focus on masturbation, for example, as a primary factor in the development of perverse sexuality, is part of a tradition of seeing energy, particularly sexual energy and/or semen[41] itself, in economic terms, as something which may be 'saved' or 'spent' but which, if spent, should be spent wisely and not simply squandered. As Stephen Heath points out, the Victorian sexual imaginary mirrors the middle-class concerns of the day with commerce and economy, where *thrift* is the overriding principle for the regulation of both body and purse ('spending' is the term in common Victorian use as a colloquialism for orgasm): '*Thrift* is the supreme Victorian middle-class virtue: moderation, wise frugality, good housekeeping, the proper use of money and energy, ordered and regular expenditure; *unthrift* is thus waste, excess, ruinous expenditure, everything that is most immoral, a profound social disturbance'.[42] Krafft-Ebing's repeated warnings against masturbation, which 'despoils the unfolding bud of perfume and beauty'[43] and can lead young people into perversity if left unchecked, thus forms part of a more general sexual analogue of that 'Protestant ethic' of thrift, frugality and asceticism which Weber was to identify as a key component of the 'western' 'spirit of capitalism' just as the final edition of *Psychopathia Sexualis* was appearing in print.[44] More explicitly, Krafft-Ebing invokes the moral and spiritual superiority of Christianity over the beliefs of other 'races' in his discussion of sexual development through history, with particular reference to Islam – significantly at a time when Germany had considerable economic and military interests in (among other places) Turkey:

> Christianity raised the union of the sexes to a sublime position. . . .
> Thence emanates the fact that the love of man, if considered from the
> standpoint of advanced civilisation, can only be of a monogamic nature

and must rest upon a stable basis. . . . From the moment when woman was recognised the peer of man, when monogamy became a law and was consolidated by legal, religious and moral conditions, the Christian nations attained a mental and material superiority over the polygamic races, and especially over Islam.[45]

It is the imperialist concern with 'race' and 'civilisation', however, which is most strongly marked in Krafft-Ebing, and which is most inextricably entwined in the notion of bisexuality. One passage in particular, giving a detailed account of Krafft-Ebing's view of bisexuality and of its sexual and racial dynamics, is worth quoting at length:

> The author of this book has made an attempt to utilize facts of heredity for an explanation [of congenital homosexuality]. . . .
>
> All attempts at explanation made hitherto on the ground of natural philosophy or psychology, or those of a merely speculative character are insufficient.
>
> Later researches, however, proceeding on embryological (onto- and phylogenetic) and anthropological lines seem to promise good results. . . .
>
> . . .[T]hey are based (1) on the fact that bisexual organization is still found in the lower animal kingdom, and (2) on the supposition that mono-sexuality gradually developed from bisexuality. . . .
>
> *Chevalier* . . . proceeds from the original bisexual life in the animal kingdom, and the original bisexual predisposition of the human foetus.
>
> According to him the difference in the gender, with marked physical and psychical sexual character, is only the result of endless processes of evolution. The psycho-physical sexual difference runs parallel with the high level of the evolving process. The individual being must also itself pass through these grades of evolution; it is originally bisexual, but in the struggle between the male and female elements either one or the other is conquered, and a monosexual being is evolved which corresponds with the type of the present stage of evolution. But traces of the conquered sexuality remain. Under certain circumstances these latent sexual characteristics . . . may provoke manifestations of inverted sexuality. . . .
>
> If the structure of this opinion is continued, the following anthropological and historical facts may be evolved [*sic*]:
>
> . . . This destruction of antipathic sexuality is at the present not yet completed. In the same manner in which the appendix in the intestinal tube points to former stages of organization, so may also be found in the sexual apparatus – in the male as well as in the female – residua, which point to the original onto- and phylogenetic bisexuality. . . .
>
> Besides, a long line of clinical and anthropological facts favor this assumption . . .

. . . Manifestations of inverted sexuality are evidently found only in persons with *organic taint*. In normal constitutions the law of mono-sexual development, homologous with the sexual glands, remains intact. . . .

The facts quoted seem to support an attempt of an historical and anthropological explanation of sexual inversion.

It is a disturbance of the law of the development of the cerebral centre, homologous to the sexual glands (homosexuality), and eventually also of the law of the mono-sexual formation of the individual (psychical 'hermaphroditism'). In the former case it is the centre of bi-sexual predisposition, antagonistic to the gender represented by the sexual gland, which in a paradoxical manner conquers that originally intended to be superior; yet the law of mono-sexual development obtains.

In the other case victory lies with neither centre; yet an indication of the tendency of mono-sexual development remains in so far that one is predominant, as a rule the opposite. . . .

In the first case it must be assumed that the centre which by right should have conquered was too weak. . . .

In the second case both centres were too weak to obtain victory and superiority.[46]

A number of features appear in this passage which point towards the inherently racial nature of bisexuality for Krafft-Ebing. First, Krafft-Ebing is insistent that the explanation for sexual phenomena is to be sought in the fields of anthropology – the study of 'race', with the characteristic ambiguity between 'human race' and particular 'races' – and embryology, thus reiterating the congruence of ontogeny with phylogeny and, at the same time, locating such phenomena firmly on racial ground. Second, an ambiguity appears in the meaning of 'antipathic sexuality', a phrase widely used throughout the text as though it were simply interchangeable with 'inversion' and 'homosexuality' but which here is taken to refer to a physical, rather than psychosexual, phenomenon in the appendix-like persistence of male physiological features in all female bodies and vice versa, and which occurs in a passage (immediately following that quoted) in an apparently different sense again, as a subdivision of inversion rather than as a synonym for it: 'The antipathic sexual instinct is only the strongest mark left by a whole series of exhibitions of the partial development of psychical and physical inverted sexual characters.'[47] These slippages in meaning may perhaps be read as symptomatic of a discursive move which attempts both to universalize and to minoritize, to render certain phenomena both general and particular so that the power-effects of the discursive attention upon the latter are circulated and diffused throughout the former. The same is arguably true of those slippages, often noted but not explained by historians, in the meanings of the term 'race': the slippages are not merely incidental to the power-effects of racial and sexual discourses, but are integral to those very effects, a crucial part of the production and regulation of sexual–racial subjects. Sexual abnormality, racial inferiority haunt the bodies even of those to whom the particularity of those conditions does not actually apply; no subject is exempt from sexual or racial interrogation.

Third, the dynamic of bisexuality itself is articulated here in the language of conquest and racial struggle. A conflict between opposing forces properly ends in the conquest of one side by another, but traces of the defeated force remain and may, under certain conditions, rise up to overthrow the rule of the conqueror. The imperialist logic, and the imperialist anxiety, are evident here, and homosexuality is clearly imagined as a rising up of an inferior force against its rightful ruler: precisely, a *racially* inferior force, since it is on the basis of the demands of 'race' and procreation that Krafft-Ebing's entire theory of 'bi-sexuality' and 'mono-sexuality' is built, with bisexuality itself presented as 'primitive'. Moreover, in the case of men – a case which Krafft-Ebing in common with other writers then and since takes as paradigmatic – it is the *female* element which should be the conquered, the male which should conquer; and this resonates with the imperialist feminization of conquered peoples throughout the nineteenth and early twentieth centuries to which scholars of imperialism have recently drawn much attention, particularly in contexts of European colonial rule over peoples imagined as 'Oriental', with connotations of exoticism, decadence and excess[48] – recall Krafft-Ebing's comments on the inferiority of Islam to Christianity, specifically in relation to its sexual and marital practices. The point is that this imperial dynamic is not simply an accidental feature of Krafft-Ebing's conception of bisexuality. The development of mono-sexuality through conflict between opposing forces of male and female elements is the whole point of Krafft-Ebing's theory here. Taken together, it is the racial logic of dimorphic evolution and heterosexual procreation, and the imperial logic of conquest and overthrow, which constitute his conception of 'bi-sexuality' as such. 'Race' is the very stuff of bisexuality; in the sexual sphere, no sense can be made of the one without the other.

Unravelling the racial logics of sexuality is important and ongoing work, and clearly it raises questions about how today's sexual dissidents are to articulate their own identities *as* dissident while also paying attention to the racialized roots of those identities. The problematics of sexual–racial ethics is an area too large and complex to discuss adequately here. However, there are some questions pertaining to certain *current* understandings of the term 'bisexual' that I would like briefly to mention. The first of these lies in the consequences of sexologists' positioning of bisexuality as an originary state from which other kinds of sexuality emerge. For both Ellis and Krafft-Ebing, bisexuality is an original physical state – both phylogenetically, as a primitive state of 'species', and ontogenetically, as a predisposition of the foetus – from which the mono-sexuality of two distinct and coherent sexes, male and female, ultimately evolves. This same logic can be seen at work in Freud's notion of bisexuality, albeit with a different inflection: for Freud, bisexuality is an originary *psychical* disposition from which the child evolves, passing through the Oedipal crisis and the rigours of repression to develop into either heterosexuality or homosexuality: 'freedom to range equally over male and female objects – as it is found in childhood, in primitive states of society and early periods of history, is the original basis from which . . . both the normal and the inverted types develop'.[49] Freud's famous claim that, thanks to this original bisexuality, 'all human beings are capable of making a homosexual object-choice and have in fact made one in their unconscious'[50] gives credence to – and is arguably one of the major sources, if not *the* major source, of – the popular claim that everyone is 'really' or at least 'potentially' bisexual, a claim which many bisexual activists now disavow[51] but which has had, and continues to have, considerable influence on the available meanings of sexual identities, and by no means only bisexual identities. But, as Freud's references to 'primitive states of society' suggests, it is impossible to divorce the claim that bisexuality is a universal, original state from the cluster of racial meanings – evolution, procreation, conquest, superiority – which constitute it. The claim that 'everyone's bisexual really' rests on a covert racial and imperialist discourse of sexuality.

Second, the notion of monosexuality, which, as mentioned above, has recently been reactivated as a term for those who are exclusively heterosexual or homosexual, has similarly proved to have a racial logic at its heart. Bisexual activists who deploy the term in this new way do not intend to invoke racial or imperialist connotations, but we cannot, like Humpty-Dumpty, simply make words mean anything that we want them to mean. Words do not simply fall out of the sky; words have histories, and words have power. Mono-sexuality, as a term used in contradistinction with bisexuality, is a sexological word whose meaning is constituted by the racial imperative of sex as procreation. Perhaps it is possible to use the term 'monosexual' in ways that genuinely do not invoke that imperative and do not rest upon the term's opposition to a racially constituted notion of 'bisexuality'. But I would argue that bisexual politics needs to reflect seriously on the implications of 'monosexual' and 'bisexual', and that explicit attention must be paid to the racial heritage of both of those terms, before any such use is attempted.

I return, in conclusion, to my opening question: why write about bisexuality? Writing about bisexuality is important, not just in its own right but also because a focus on the concept of 'bi-sexuality' as it appears in sexology in particular demonstrates the constitutive importance of 'race' and racial logic in the history of 'western' sexuality. Most lesbian/gay and queer historians of sexuality to date have given a great deal of attention to the hetero/homo binary, and clearly, given the current dominance of that binary, this is important work. But an exclusive focus on that binary as if its dominance were simply a historical given – even as if it were the only important dynamic at work in sexuality at all – is a distortion of historical complexity; and foreclosure of any critical interrogation of bisexuality through such a focus also forecloses crucial questions about 'race'. It is possible to make sense of the sexological concept of 'bi-sexuality' only by paying close attention to the racial imperatives and slippages at the heart of these texts, imperatives and slippages towards which queer theorists have often gestured under the rubric of 'difference' but the specific formations of which have thus far received too little attention. 'Bi-sexuality' demonstrates the specific ways in which sexual categories are always also racial categories; in which the relationship between 'sex' and 'race' is not additive, but mutually constitutive; in which our contemporary sexual identities – which many sexual dissidents today understand and experience as progressive and liberatory – have historically been constituted as racialized identities. Dislodging the hetero/homo binary from its currently privileged position may force us to recognize that even the 'outlaws' of sexual dissidence are unwitting legislators for the reproduction of 'race'.

Notes

I would like to thank Lucy Bland, Phoebe Davidson and Jo Eadie for their helpful comments on earlier drafts of this piece.

1. This use of the term 'discourse', which I shall be continuing in my own discussion, comes from Foucault, who uses it to refer to the operation of power as knowledge. 'Discourse' is simultaneously material and representational in operation, and both produces and regulates subjects in its web. Unfamiliar readers are referred to introductory texts on Foucault such as Jana Sawicki, *Disciplining Foucault* (London and New York: Routledge, 1991).
2. Wilson's paper was subsequently published: Elizabeth Wilson, 'Is Transgression Transgressive?', in Joseph Bristow and Angelia R. Wilson (eds), *Activating Theory* (London: Lawrence & Wishart, 1993).
3. The literature on this is now vast. As representative texts, see Lillian Faderman, *Odd Girls and Twilight Lovers* (New York: Penguin, 1992); David M. Halperin, 'Is There a History of Sexuality?', in Henry Abelove, Michèle Aina Barale and David M. Halperin (eds), *The Lesbian and Gay Studies Reader* (New York and London: Routledge, 1993); Martha Vicinus, '"They Wonder to Which Sex I Belong"', in Abelove *et al.* (eds), *The Lesbian and Gay Studies Reader*; Jeffrey Weeks, *Coming Out* (London: Quartet Books, 1977). The central text for this body of scholarship is Michel Foucault's celebrated *The History of Sexuality*, trans. Robert Hurley (London: Peregrine Books, 1984).
4. See Mary McIntosh, 'Queer Theory and the War of the Sexes', in Bristow and Wilson (eds), *Activating Theory*, for a useful summary of the various positions in this disagreement.
5. Eve Kosofsky Sedgwick, *Epistemology of the Closet* (Berkeley and Los Angeles: University of California Press, 1990), pp. 1–2.
6. Sheila Rowbotham and Jeffrey Weeks, *Socialism and the New Life* (London: Pluto Press, 1977), p. 141.
7. Carroll Smith-Rosenberg, 'Discourses of Sexuality and Subjectivity', in Martin Bauml Duberman, Martha Vicinus and George Chauncey, Jr (eds), *Hidden from History* (London: Penguin, 1991), p. 269.
8. Emma Donoghue, 'Divided Heart, Divided History', in Sharon Rose, Cris Stevens *et al.* (eds), *Bisexual Horizons* (London: Lawrence & Wishart, 1996), p. 75.
9. This point about the binary reading of history by scholars such as Sedgwick was eloquently made by Lucy Bland and Frank Mort in 'Thinking Sex Historically', paper given at 'New Sexual Agendas' conference, 14 July 1995.
10. Sedgwick, *Epistemology of the Closet*, p. 8.

11. This is perhaps most clearly to be seen in Freud's 'Three Essays on the Theory of Sexuality' (1905), an early and seminal work located very much within the nineteenth-century sexological tradition even as it breaks away from it. See Sigmund Freud, 'Three Essays on the Theory of Sexuality', trans. James Strachey, in *Pelican Freud Library*, Vol. 7 (London: Pelican, 1977).

12. Cf. Sedgwick, *Epistemology of the Closet*, p. 9.

13. For an account of bisexuality from the 1960s onwards, see Sue George, *Women and Bisexuality* (London: Scarlet Press, 1993); see also Faderman, *Odd Girls and Twilight Lovers*, and Marjorie Garber, *Vice Versa* (London: Hamish Hamilton, 1996).

14. Cf. Gayle S. Rubin, 'Thinking Sex', in Abelove *et al.* (eds), *The Lesbian and Gay Sudies Reader*.

15. Certainly not *all* sexual practices can be subsumed under the hetero/homo divide: when one masturbates, is that a heterosexual or a homosexual act? To be sure, 'masturbator' has not thus far operated as a sexual identity in the twentieth century, even within those queer discourses which seek to reclaim otherwise 'outlawed' sexualities, but the fact that it has not done so is a point that should be interrogated rather than simply foreclosed with the alibi of a totalitarian hetero/homo binary regime. See Paula Bennett and Vernon A. Rosario II (eds), *Solitary Pleasures* (New York and London: Routledge, 1995).

16. See, for example, Lucy Bland, *Banishing the Beast* (London: Penguin, 1995); Antoinette Burton, 'The White Woman's Burden', *Women's Studies International Forum*, 13, 4 (1990); Anna Davin, 'Imperialism and Motherhood', *History Workshop Journal*, 5 (1978); Vron Ware, *Beyond the Pale* (London and New York: Verso, 1992).

17. Exceptions to this neglect have included Jonathan Dollimore's *Sexual Dissidence* (Oxford: Oxford University Press, 1991); Diana Fuss, *Identification Papers* (New York and London: Routledge, 1995); Anne McClintock, *Imperial Leather* (London and New York: Routledge, 1995).

18. Judith Butler, *Bodies That Matter* (New York and London: Routledge, 1993), p. 18.

19. *Ibid.*, pp. 121–40 and pp. 167–85.

20. Judith Butler, *Gender Trouble* (New York and London: Routledge, 1991), p. 151, note 6.

21. Bland, *Banishing the Beast*, p. 231.

22. Richard von Krafft-Ebing, *Psychopathia Sexualis, with Especial Reference to the Antipathic Sexual Instinct*, trans. Franklin S. Klaf (London: Staples Press, 1965) (English translation of the 12th edition), p. 16, my italics.

23. *Ibid.*, p. 46, my italics.

24. Havelock Ellis, *Studies in the Psychology of Sex, Volume I: Sexual Inversion* (London: University Press, 1897), p. 130.

25. *Ibid.*, p. 22; second italic original, first and third italics mine.

26. Krafft-Ebing, *Psychopathia Sexualis*, pp. 52–3.

27. Robert J. C. Young, *Colonial Desire* (London and New York: Routledge, 1995), p. 93.

28. Ellis, *Studies*, p. 130.

29. The hyphenation of terms such as 'bi-sexual' and 'mono-sexual' is inconsistent in these texts, especially in the translation of Krafft-Ebing. However, the most common occurrence is of hyphenated 'bi-sexuality', and I shall reflect that convention in the texts quoted.

30. Ellis, *Studies*, pp. 132 -3.

31. See Cynthia Eagle Russett, *Sexual Science* (Cambridge MA and London: Harvard University Press, 1989), p. 50.

32. Krafft-Ebing, *Psychopathia Sexualis*, p. 28.

33. *Ibid.*, p. 30.

34. See Russett, *Sexual Science*, pp. 131–50.

35. Krafft-Ebing, *Psychopathia Sexualis*, p. 30.

36. Havelock Ellis, *Man and Woman* (London: Walter Scott Publishing Co., 1904), p. 448.

37. Krafft-Ebing, *Psychopathia Sexualis*, p. 30.

38. *Ibid.*, p. 427, note 89.

39. Ellis, *Studies*, pp. 119–20.

40. Young, *Colonial Desire*, p. 92.
41. The anxiety is strongly oriented around *male* bodies, with Krafft-Ebing in particular harping on the perils of masturbation for masculinity. Anxieties about female masturbation took a somewhat different form: see e.g. Bram Dijkstra, *Idols of Perversity* (Oxford: Oxford University Press, 1986), esp. pp. 66–81.
42. Stephen Heath, *The Sexual Fix* (London: Macmillan, 1982), p. 18; cf. pp. 20–3 on spermatorrhea. Cf. Lawrence Birken, *Consuming Desire* (Ithaca, NY: Cornell University Press, 1988); Dijkstra, *Idols of Perversity*; Thomas W. Laqueur, 'The Social Evil, the Solitary Vice, and Pouring Tea', in Bennett and Rosario (eds), *Solitary Pleasures*; Russett, *Sexual Science*, on similar descriptions of neurasthenia in economic terms.
43. Krafft-Ebing, *Psychopathia Sexualis*, p. 189.
44. Max Weber, *The Protestant Ethic and the Spirit of Capitalism*, trans. Talcott Parsons (London: Allen & Unwin, 1930). Weber's essays on the 'Protestant ethic' first appeared in German in 1904–5.
45. Krafft-Ebing, *Psychopathia Sexualis*, pp. 2–3.
46. *Ibid.*, pp. 226–9.
47. *Ibid.*, p. 230.
48. See e.g. Joanna de Groot, '"Sex" and "Race"', in Susan Mendus and Jane Rendall (eds), *Sexuality and Subordination* (London: Routledge, 1989); Rana Kabbani, *Europe's Myths of Orient* (Bloomington: Indiana University Press, 1986); Edward Said, *Orientalism* (New York: Vintage, 1978).
49. Freud, 'Three Essays', p. 57, note 1.
50. *Ibid.*, p. 56, note 1.
51. See e.g. George, *Women and Bisexuality*, pp. 181–2.

TWO

Literature,
Criticism,
Literary Theory

5

Returning to the Lesbian Bildungsroman: *A Bisexual Reading (of) Nancy Toder's* Choices

Ann Kaloski

She was hungry for experience. She wanted to try everything at least once. Maybe even twice.[1]

In December 1980 Nancy Toder's new novel, *Choices*, was reviewed in the journal *Off Our Backs*.[2] The book's positive lesbian reception seemed assured; it had, apparently, everything required for a good read, 'plot, action, erotica, and multidimensional characters' (but read on).[3] The reviewer's interpretation of the four main characters is worth quoting at length:

Sandy is a therapist, . . . a quick-witted, tough gay activist. Her lover Michelle is a teacher and writer, a soft, loving stubborn complement to Sandy's occasional brittleness. Jenny at 30+ is the standard myopic, tight-assed straight academic woman who once had a lesbian lover. Many of us have a Jenny or two in our past. Barry, Jenny's husband, is a rare thing in contemporary literature: he is a nice Jewish man who is not a stereotype, who is not a neurotic sex fiend, and who has more than a little generosity in his character.[4]

Spot the misfit! Lesbians and heterosexual men are portrayed with warmth and some subtlety, in contrast to bisexuals who are, it seems, typecast as narrow. Not only is Jenny dismissed as 'standard myopic, tight-assed' (add your own insult), but her place in the collective lesbian history is only symbolic: she is retained as past 'mistake', but not as 'real person'.

So how was I, and other bisexual women, supposed to read this tale of lesbian identity affirmation? Why, one might ask, would we want to, given the portrayal of the bisexual protagonist as a 'hungry' woman who experiments before (re)turning to heterosexuality? Yet I've always liked coming-out fiction, despite a complex relationship to the texts. I first came across *Choices* shortly after the novel was published. My reading then left me feeling displaced and unacceptable, someone who couldn't or wouldn't make a decision to be a lesbian and was thus 'letting the side down'. The text appeared to validate lesbianism and (even) to accommodate heterosexuality, but to position bisexuality as a place of denial and self-delusion. Although reading about same-sex desire was pleasurable and self-affirming to a point, that lesbian point needled me and left me feeling irritated and dissatisfied. I wanted the novel's encouragement to love women but the text wouldn't let (bisexual) me relax into its happy tale of lesbian love. Recently I picked up *Choices* again, and found that the lesbian point no longer hurt, and that the portrayal of bisexuality was relatively sympathetic, given the novel's aim to profess lesbian love.

What was happening here? There are three points about the reading process I wish to emphasize. First, the potency of reading as an active process which produces a narrative from the text. Second, the (re)construction of the reader through cultural changes. And third (and consequently), the efficacy of cultural shifts in rejigging texts.[5] My stance in this chapter is that the reader both forms and is formed by her texts. And while I don't wish to generalize too much from my responses, they do seem to be fairly typical of their respective eras, and to suggest tantalizing possibilities for contemporary re-readings of coming-out fiction.[6] I'm intrigued by the spectre of bisexual women in the lesbian *Bildungsroman*; and in this chapter I explore the integral yet shadowy existence of bisexuality within the genre, a presence which both defines a certain form of lesbian/feminist identity, *and* which also opens up the writing to a bisexual understanding.[7] What kind of a spin could a bisexual reading put on this tale?[8]

Expecting to fly

The lesbian coming-out genre is, almost by definition, lesbian/*feminist* fiction. It developed in the 1970s and early 1980s, mainly in the USA, and both produced and was produced by a particular congruence of feminist and lesbian politics.[9] Despite the popularity of the genre amongst lesbians, coming-out fiction has generated little critical work. A common explanation for this lack rests on the supposed simplicity of coming-out novels. As Elizabeth Wilson suggests in her wittily titled essay 'I'll Climb the Stairway to Heaven: Lesbianism in the Seventies', lesbian writings positioned a utopian form of lesbianism as the ultimate destiny of real women.[10] According to Wilson this impulse led to a sense of 'repetition rather than exploration' in 1970s lesbian novels, with the rehashing of the same old story of a lesbian search for a dream.[11]

I shall be challenging this position on two counts. First, I shall suggest ways in which the repetitiveness of coming-out fiction can be read as a complicated strategy in the creation of a lesbian/feminist identity, operating both transgressively and conservatively, By this I mean to suggest that the repetition works to simultaneously create, enforce and re-enforce lesbian/feminist subjectivity, *and* – by virtue of repetition, always containing within it the potential, indeed probability, of 'mistake', and of change – functions as a site of subversion. Wilson uses the term 'repetition' pejoratively, and while I agree that coming out – again – *can* be boring and static, I think she misplaces the political and personal force of the coming-out refrain; underestimating the tendency of repetition to fail and thus produce vacillation and difference.[12] I read coming-out novels as a body of fiction that self-consciously rehearses a particular form of lesbian/feminist identity, and in doing so I ask how the repetitive performance of coming-out fiction operates, and to what end. Second, I argue that alongside, and in counterpoint with, this repetitive gesture, coming-out fiction offers a more complex and exploratory form of narrative than is usually appreciated by critics. I shall attempt to demonstrate that these supposedly ingenuous stories can accommodate multiple readings. Put more specifically I'm asking, first, how coming-out fiction 'does power', and, second, how that power can be destabilized through a bisexual reading.

Wilson is not the only lesbian critic to present a negative image of coming-out fiction, and it seems that most critics in the 1970s and early 1980s just could not be bothered with the genre.[13] Bonnie Zimmerman is a notable exception. In her 1983 essay 'Exiting from Patriarchy: The Lesbian Novel of Development' she demonstrates once again her ability to let loose an ordinary lesbian awareness into the critical arena.[14] That is, rather than impose a traditional critical framework on to what she terms 'developmental literature', she allows the stories to generate their own critical anatomy, through identifying the role played by the genre in lesbian lives.

Recent criticism has begun to reappraise coming-out fiction, valuing its style as one among many genres of lesbian/feminist writing and venturing, in retrospect, to acknowledge its multifariousness. Gabriele Griffin, for instance, reframes lesbian developmental novels of this period as fiction in which the 'deviant' homosexual woman becomes the 'defiant' lesbian hero, and she unpacks popular texts, demonstrating ways in which lesbians 'claimed cultural space'.[15] Nicki Hastie also highlights the lesbian pleasures of sharing coming-out fiction, and seeks to develop ways of analysing and updating the lesbian *Bildungsroman* by reading lesbian/feminist fiction of the late 1980s and 1990s within a coming-out model.[16] Welcome though this is, the effort at reappraisal has failed as yet to take any account, on the level either of narrative or of readership, of connections forged in and by the genre between lesbianism and bisexuality.

One critic who acknowledges the presence of bisexual women alongside lesbians as participants in lesbian fiction is Paulina Palmer. I shall look in some detail at the manner in which she locates bisexuals and bisexuality in her argument, because her stance seems to indicate either an interesting aberration or a decided shift in lesbian literary criticism. The first sentence of her preface to *Contemporary Lesbian Writing* illustrates her position: 'Gone are the days when a book on the topic of lesbian writing could be expected to appeal only to those readers who identify as lesbian or bisexual.'[17] Palmer clearly recognizes that lesbians and bisexual women share (or perhaps shared) patterns of consumption. None the less she maintains the custom of labelling this fiction lesbian, and bisexuality takes up only a small sub-section of her book.[18]

Despite this imbalance, Palmer's invocation of bisexuality cannot be dismissed as mere tokenism. Although bisexual women are the more silent partners in her text, Palmer's comments about bisexuality tend to come towards the end of a section, suggesting, in their tone, not so much an addition to her argument as a provisional conclusion. She argues that within the theory and the fiction of lesbian/feminism, lesbianism operates as 'the signifier of feminism', and she recognizes that this perspective blocks self-conscious articulations of women's desires for each other which evade the designation 'lesbian'. Palmer's analysis of the politics of lesbian fiction leads her to include bisexuals, and there seems to be a genuine desire on her part to question the relationship of lesbian/feminism to bisexuality. Her text remains profoundly ambivalent, however. Palmer admits that lesbian fiction of the 1970s and early 1980s portrayed bisexual women as either 'weak' or 'manipulative', but she can still write, in 1993: 'The emergence of these stereotypes, simplistic and unjust though they are, is understandable and, in the case of some women, they perhaps contain a grain of truth.'[19]

Ouch! Did lesbians never betray their sisters in the 1970s? Palmer slips between decrying 'stereotypes' and identifying 'some women' as a threat *because* of their bisexuality, and thereby perpetuates the standardized damning of bisexual women. Coming from this undoubted sympathetic lesbian critic this is an indication of how deeply ingrained the prejudices between lesbians and bisexual women can be. Nevertheless, Palmer seeks to expose, if not yet rectify, what she sees as an injustice, and her (relatively) positive stance on bisexuality compares favourably to her position on queer, which she treats with some scepticism and little sympathy.[20] Palmer does not present a libertarian attitude to sexual mores; she is not arguing that all sexual choices, regardless of their implication for feminism, are equally valid. Instead, she attempts to reassess lesbian/feminist thinking, shifting and sifting rather than tearing apart, and in this process finds herself including bisexual women.

Alongside Palmer's acceptance of some valency between bisexual women and lesbians is another productive critical stance: her appreciation of and delight in coming-out fiction. She notes that the genre has received little critical attention because the stories have, on the one hand, been subsumed into 'feminist fiction' by heterosexual literary critics, and, on the other, been lost in the clamour for postmodern disruption by lesbian (and gay) theorists. Lesbian coming-out fiction, it seems, is just not distinct enough, or clever enough to stand alone. Palmer's own mix of lesbian/feminist thinking hints at ways to read coming-out fiction as a bisexual woman, and in the next section of this chapter I begin to fill in the traces of Palmer's impressions, and attempt to show that a sympathetic reading of coming-out fiction need not be an exclusively lesbian act, but can be a form of 'les/bi' criticism: that is, a mode of theorizing which assumes a lesbian/bisexual affinity. Rather than focusing on differences *between* lesbians and bisexual women, this reading attempts to ventilate the differences *among* lesbians and bisexual women.

The needle and the damage done

The coming-out novel on which I have chosen to focus is less well known outside the Anglophone lesbian/feminist community than, say, *Rubyfruit Jungle* or *Oranges are Not the Only Fruit* – texts which have been marketed as 'women's books', albeit with an upfront lesbian theme.[21] The novel I have chosen is, in contrast, a 'lesbian novel'. I begin from the sense of ambivalence provoked by my different readings. It is an ambivalence which, I argue, is explicitly generated by the text, and I hope, therefore, that my speculative reading won't do violence to the text and won't force the novel into shapes that reflect my desires to the exclusion of the desires of the text. Rather, this bisexual reading is attempting to look at the ways in which the textual desires of a lesbian story of self-development can encode bisexuality.

In *Choices* – 'the classic story of lesbian love', if we are to believe the blurb on the book cover – Nancy Toder tells the story of the coming into adulthood of two women, Sandy and Jenny. The novel focuses on how they make and live out decisions about their sexuality. The first part of the novel is set in the girls' college in the USA, and charts in some detail how their attraction for each other becomes actively sexual, and, through shifting focalization, reveals the different responses of Sandy and Jenny to their love. Part II is set several years later, when Sandy and Jenny meet at a psychology conference. Sandy is now in a steady relationship with a woman, Shelly, and Jenny is in a heterosexual marriage with Barry. This section of the novel depicts the way in which Sandy copes with meeting the woman who broke her adolescent heart, and how Jenny responds to encountering her former 'best friend'.

One way to look at the differences *among* lesbians and bisexual women is to read *Choices* for the contrasting narratives of Sandy and Jenny. Sandy's story is, of course, the lesbian tale, whereas Jenny's tale is more ambivalent. I suggest that Jenny's desires, passions and behaviour can be named bisexual and that, despite Toder's stated intention to help lesbians in their 'communal search for definition and courage', the representation of Jenny does facilitate a bisexual reading.[22] It is perhaps the genre's liberal humanist framework which makes this possible. Although Toder's primary intention is to write a novel depicting 'positive' and 'fulfilled' lesbians, she is also quite consciously concerned with decision-making, and, as the writer remarks in the introduction, '*Choices* is the story of several women's struggles to articulate their love for women'.[23] Toder's aim is to produce a wonderfully biased novel, where 'The whole world is seen from a lesbian perspective' but in doing so she does attempt a kind of honesty in depicting the difficulties of living as a 'pure' lesbian.[24] The book's dedication is symptomatic of this liberal persuasion:

> This book is dedicated to all the brave women who have defied so much in their love for women, and to those women who, for whatever reasons, were unable to make that commitment or live by it; in our common pain and rage, let us affirm that our daughters will have more choices.

Here, to turn away from lesbianism – whether as a bisexual or as a 'pretend heterosexual' – is to fail: only lesbians are 'brave'. Toder both asserts the primacy of lesbianism and declares her understanding of the 'realities' of lesbian life, something with which, of course, not all women can cope. Irritating though her attitude is, the attempt at a sympathetic portrayal of 'failed lesbians' does open up the text to a bisexual reading, and Jenny cannot quite be contained by the novel's triumphalism.

The lesbian story frames the text. The novel opens with Sandy at the airport on her way to college, looking – in her mother's relatively affectionate term – like a 'hoodlum' in black clothes: leather jacket and short skirt, backcombed hair, and gum in her mouth (pp. 1–2). But the reader soon realizes that beneath this hard exterior lies a frightened girl when the supposedly streetwise Sandy is airsick. In contrast, this is Jenny's introductory image:

> Jenny had set her hair on big curlers and was filing her nails. . . . She *looked* like a baby doll in her pink sheer baby-doll pyjamas. The product of an assembly line gone berserk – the long dark hair wrapped around fat ugly curlers, fixed in place by a pink hair net. (emphasis in text) (pp. 7–8)

This icon of US femininity clues in the reader: Jenny plays the game.[25] She has already learnt to hide her curiosity, and broken her parent's strict rules about behaviour and appearance only in secret. But Jenny isn't just a good-time girl. Within this lesbian text a bisexual reading picks up other codes: 'She was hungry for experience. She wanted to try everything at least once. Maybe even twice' (p. 7). What will happen to Jenny's free-floating desires?

Everybody knows this is nowhere

What happens is that Jenny and Sandy fall in love. But while it is clear that their attraction is mutual, it is Jenny who first broaches the subject: '"Sandy . . . I don't know exactly how to say this . . . I have these feelings . . ."' (p. 29). It is Jenny who first says the life-changing words: 'I want to kiss you'; Jenny who is 'the first to explore further'; Jenny who first reaches over to unbutton her girlfriend's blouse; Jenny who first becomes less shy, noticing how 'scared and timid Sandy was' (pp. 32–3). Yet, whereas by the end of the novel Sandy is portrayed as decisive and 'mature' (though still, of course, with a sense of fun!), Jenny's exit is ambivalent, and produces intriguing readings. Shelly's lesbian interpretation is that Jenny has chosen a life which is 'Comfortable. Secure. Safe' at the expense of 'passion' (p. 258). Sandy is less sure. She recognizes, with some respect at last, that Jenny is different from her, and that choosing lesbianism wouldn't be 'as right for her as it was for me' (p.258). This phrase does, I think, give space for beginning to perceive varying ways of loving women. Lesbianism isn't depicted as 'right' or 'wrong' for Jenny, but rather as not '*as* right for her'.

Could there be a different ground for Jenny? To/in a bisexual reading, bisexuality is an obvious different ground, but bisexuality is not named in the concluding throes of the text. The novel clearly faces difficulties in trying to assert a particular form of lesbian/feminism, and in also attempting to 'be fair' to women and the decisions they make about their sexuality. Toder seeks to end the novel in a relatively sympathetic way to women who desire other women, and yet cannot 'attain' lesbianism, but her liberalism is challenged by the location of bisexuality throughout *Choices* as traitorous or irresponsible. In Jenny, Toder indicates the possibility of same-sex desire in women outside of a lesbian identity, but the narrative is caught in its own framework: women need a sexual identity label, but a bisexual identity, Toder implies, is not possible. Jenny can therefore only be positioned in the text as 'not-lesbian' or as 'not-heterosexual'. Textually, she is 'no place'.

Jenny's displacement from a coherent universe is further complicated through her narrative. Ever sympathetic, Toder takes the reader into Jenny's thoughts after she has returned from a walk by the ocean with Sandy. The meeting was dramatic (and later in this chapter I'll revisit this encounter), and motivated Sandy into kissing her former girlfriend. Afterwards, Jenny is confused, knowing that all has changed for her. She cannot forget the adult passion of the beach kiss, but at the same time 'one of the few things she was sure of' was that she didn't want to lose Barry (p. 254). This isn't presented as materialistic (after all, Jenny has a well-paid job), nor, at this point, as cowardly (Jenny loves and desires her husband). Her strong and renewed ardour for Barry *could* be attributed to displaced lust, but the narrative is more complex than this. Certainly, Jenny has been aroused by Sandy, but she is also affected by the passion of arguing with Barry, and the strength of his desire for her. Jenny knows that she has to be brave, a door is open and she has to see what's on 'the other side', but it is not clear to Jenny, nor to the reader, what Jenny's 'other side' consists of. She looks obsessively at her reflection in mirrors, water, windows but cannot see another 'self'. She has no idea what she might be. It is hard to read this 'other' Jenny as lesbian, given that she knows lesbians, and has been avidly reading about lesbians and recognizing much of herself in the descriptions. Jenny knows she desires women, and wants *something*, but this something includes Barry. Jenny defies any settled romantic ending to her story. She neither returns completely to her husband, as in the plot of many sensationalist heterosexual novels which use lesbian encounters as a titillating motif, nor does she enter 'lesbian nation'.[26] Her husband realizes: 'Things are going to change now', but there is no blueprint for that change (p. 255). Barry asks: 'Where are you, Jenny?' and 'What happens now, Jen?', and to both of these questions Jenny replies 'I don't know' (p. 254–5). In the liberal environment of a lesbian reading of *Choices*, this realm of not-knowing is a sad place for Jenny. Her 'choices' lie outside of the text, but only just outside. While the narrative lines of Sandy's story do, at least, give a semblance of completeness, Jenny's tale is left frayed and fraught, with the nature of her identity unknown.

This 'dual-narrative' reading goes some way toward interpreting *Choices* as a novel about different forms of same-sex desire among women despite the novel's difficulties in locating bisexuality. In an interview given shortly after the publication of *Choices* Toder asserts:

> Another thing is that it [*Choices*] validates our anger. A woman in Boston told me that one valuable thing for her was the feeling that we have the right to be angry at our ex-lovers, women who went straight. The book has an intrinsic sense of lesbian rage being positive and valuable and appropriate.[27]

Despite this unambiguous view of her book as authenticating lesbian anger towards women who 'turn', I am arguing that the text does not sustain such an unequivocal mien. The book, both by intention and by process, is written for and about 'women'.[28] Toder attempts to present aspects of two women's lives in an honest way, and in doing so *almost* writes the option of a bisexual identity into the narrative. But the bisexual story fits only in so far as Jenny is either lesbian or not-lesbian. Once the text raises the possibility of Jenny 'find[ing] a new balance' and acknowledging the reality of sexual desire for women and men, Jenny's vibrant articulateness deserts her: 'what was there to say? She said nothing' (p. 255).

The lesbian narrative locates Jenny as unable to see an image of her self, as unable to voice a description of her self, and as not knowing where she belongs. At the same time a kind of lesbian innocence and purity is prioritized by Toder, personified in Sandy. She is depicted as an 'innocent' who 'couldn't *possibly* imagine' something so perverse as bisexuality. She is 'tough', but with a clarity of understanding which cuts through suggestions of sexual depravity, and lesbianism is depicted as a wholesome way of life. ('Honey, I'm home' announces Shelly, returning from work (p. 108).) A great deal of textual energy is spent in demonstrating Sandy's purity. In college, for instance, when Jenny wants to keep their sexual relationship a secret, and date boys, this reasoning doesn't 'make any sense' to Sandy (p. 43). Her feelings for Jenny are blindingly naive: 'They can't hurt us, not if our love is strong, not if we stick together' (p. 44). Leaving aside (for the moment) the portrayal of Jenny as cowardly and manipulative for wanting Sandy <u>and</u> boys, Sandy's 'innocence' – here and in adulthood – involves a large degree of ignorance: 'For an intelligent woman you certainly have some blind spots, Sandy' (p. 166).

Change your mind

Through tracking the stories of Jenny and Sandy I have implied that the attempt at a lesbian coherence works only with the complicity of a lesbian audience who read coming-out stories to validate 'real lesbians' and 'justifiable anger' (at bisexual women). But what of a bisexual reading? I have, crucially, argued that such a reading is not necessarily opposed to lesbian interpretations, but partakes of many lesbian reading pleasures. Yet a bisexual reading, unlike a lesbian reading, can *never* be a complete reading, and it/she will experience the ambivalences produced by the (lesbian) attempt at a wholesome text.[29] Reading the two narratives in this way doesn't do justice to bisexual irritation with and attraction to the text, which inspired my reading in the first place. I'd therefore like to try another route, and move back into the novel in an attempt to expose *how* the textual manoeuvres of coming-out fiction (don't) cope with the bisexual sub-text. How is the ambivalence of the narrative produced and maintained?

One of the most damning and intriguing indictments of bisexuality in *Choices* occurs soon after Sandy has bumped into Jenny at the psychology conference. Sandy is very disturbed by their brief meeting and, as Toder puts it, 'conflicting feelings alternated inside her. Like an electric current, AC–DC' (p. 132). This image prods Sandy into remembering the first time she came across 'AC–DC' as a synonym for bisexuality:

> The woman had great difficulty explaining it. 'You know, AC–DC,' she kept repeating. Finally she said, 'Swings both ways.' 'Oh, you mean bisexual,' Sandy said, 'Yeah,' the woman said, 'AC–DC.'
> A shiver ran through Sandy's body. (p.132)

As I read and reread *Choices* I kept returning to that shiver. It seemed somehow pivotal, both incisive *and* wavering: a vacillating image which might help shed some light on the seductive ambivalence of the text.

In the passage from *Choices* quoted above, the reader is party to Sandy's thoughts and feelings, and the narrative persuasion is towards identification with Sandy. A bisexual reading is therefore led to turn against herself or itself, identifying with Sandy's incomprehension and disgust. This is, in some ways, similar to the reading process described by Judith Fetterley in *The Resisting Reader*, where she focuses on male-authored fiction from the USA which positions women as the constricting space from which 'one' escapes into manhood.[30] Fetterley argues that, because of the narrative structure of this (US) American literature, for a woman to enjoy the experience of reading 'she is required to identify against herself'.[31] Although I think it would be ridiculous to shift wholesale male–female thinking on to a lesbian–bisexual paradigm, Fetterley's model provides serviceable currency for attempting to understand my ambivalence in reading *Choices*.

Lesbians (as lesbians) clearly lack political and social power in most cultures. However, as I have already suggested, the sign 'lesbian' can operate as a mark of female power, and the fact that many bisexual women experience lesbian as a zone of exclusion and authority needs to be acknowledged. One of the reasons some bisexuals feel they have no home place is because they have been excluded from lesbian territory: often literally as when bisexuals are banned from lesbian (and gay) centres, and also narratively, as in lesbian fiction when the lesbian 'gets the girl', leaving the bisexual woman isolated in her 'indecision'. Where does that 'authority' come from? Or, to return to one of my starting questions, how does lesbian fiction 'do power'? I am arguing that coming-out stories construct a certain form of lesbian/feminism which attempts to deny the validity of bisexuality as a possible 'choice', whilst simultaneously kindling a narrative which produces and even encourages a bisexual reading.

If I continue the comparison with Fetterley's male–female model, Sandy's lesbian shiver can be read as a 'masculine' gesture of unburdening rather than a more 'feminine' gesture of assimilation. The (US) American men Fetterley depict long to free themselves from their wives and girlfriends and from their feminizing effects. Similarly, Sandy is portrayed as wanting to eliminate her ex-girlfriend, and shake away any hint of collaboration with bisexuality. The passage from *Choices* continues thus:

> The evening breeze had suddenly turned cold. She stopped walking, took a deep breath, and looked out over the ocean. The deep breath didn't help her chill, and the constant lapping of the waves tonight had an irritating effect, rather than calming her as it usually did. (p. 32)

Sandy's body begins to let her down once she is infiltrated with the thought of bisexuality. The threat – of bisexuality – is enough to make her breath control ineffectual and her lesbian mastery fails. Bisexuality is positioned as the (feminine?) force which disrupts the (masculine?) lesbian norm. Sandy can no longer walk forward, and she must focus her energy towards disciplining her breath. The hindering of lesbian development by bisexuality is a fairly common lesbian complaint.[32] Yet although Sandy's progress falters, bisexual irritation arouses her, and she cannot be still. Sandy vacillates, like an AC/DC current. Lesbian/bisexual boundaries are destabilized, and she becomes – metaphorically – bisexual. Is this a point where the (bisexual) sub-text exposes the ambivalence of the (lesbian) coming-out novel?

Sugar mountain

In order to answer this, and to continue my destabilizing of the narrative wholesomeness, I shall reroute my argument via the connections between fiction and sexual identity. The creating and the identifying of lesbian myths has been important in cultivating a sense of lesbian selfhood:

> When lesbians meet – as friends, lovers, or community – we create bonds and trust among ourselves by telling our coming-out stories.

> Coming out is the rite of passage through which the lesbian establishes and affirms herself. . . . The coming-out story is the lesbian myth of origins, the explanation of how we came to be lesbians, how our consciousness formed and our identity developed.[33]

Unlike lesbianism, bisexuality doesn't seem to generate myths of origin. While the 'first timers' sessions at bisexual conferences are invariably packed, as are workshops on 'developing a bisexual identity', there is no bisexual fiction equivalent to the lesbian *Bildungsroman*. One explanation I've heard mooted among bisexuals is that there is rarely a single moment of 'coming out' for the bisexual.[34] Yes; but this is surely also true for lesbians, and I agree with Zimmerman's appraisal that '[c]oming out is process', a view which is emphasized by her synonym for coming-out novels, 'the lesbian novel of development'.[35] Perhaps lesbians are more inclined than bisexuals to construct their coming out as an epiphanic moment.

Yet there are contemporary novels which are akin to lesbian coming-out fiction in their depiction of 'positive' and 'realistic' sexual attraction to both women and men.[36] Where they differ markedly from coming-out novels is, I think, less in the form of representation of women's sexuality than in the reception of such novels. Although bi lists and paperbacks are passed around the bisexual community with as much enthusiasm as texts within a lesbian exchange of fiction, somehow bisexual books never attain the same kind of status.[37] There are no 'classic stories of bisexual love'. And, connectedly, bi books, unlike lesbian texts, haven't become part of the creation of a sexual community. The relationship of fiction to bisexual identity is much less vigorous and much less established than that within lesbian (and also, significantly, gay and queer) communities.

I shall pursue these connections now through returning to the beach, to Sandy, and to that shiver. Could the shiver animate a bisexual 'myth of origins'? Could the shiver provoke a way of reading ourselves, of 'explaining how we came to be bisexuals, how our consciousness formed and our identity developed'? I shall stay with the image of the shiver, following its effect on both Jenny and Sandy (and on a bisexual reading).

The shiver runs 'through' Sandy's body. Not 'over' or 'round' but 'through'. The shiver fragments Sandy's body and pierces her sense of self. She is depicted as figuratively penetrated and mutilated by bisexuality: it's a kind of psychic assault. But where does the metaphor come from? Why is it powerful? The notion of being wounded by a tiny but dynamic piece of evil is embedded in 'western' folklore, as this passage from *The Snow Queen* indicates:

> One day Kay and Gerda sat looking at a book full of pictures of animals and birds, and then just as the clock in the tower struck twelve, Kay said, 'Oh! something has struck my heart!' and soon after 'There is something in my eye.'
> The little girl put her arm around his neck, and looked into his eye, but she could see nothing.

'I think it is gone,' he said. But it was not gone. It was one of those bits of the looking glass – that magic mirror, of which I have spoken – the ugly glass which made everything great and good appear small and ugly, while all that was wicked and bad became more visible, and every little fault could be plainly seen. Poor little Kay had also received a small grain in his heart, which quickly turned to a lump of ice.[38]

One reason for the potency of this folk story is the narrative play on fears that being good and true and honest is not enough, that even the purest can be contaminated – randomly – by evil. In *Choices* there is an element of this fear of indiscriminate contamination by a bisexuality which is 'evil' (translated in the secular and less absolute discourse of 1970s US culture as 'a crock of shit' (p. 132)). Toder seeks to prioritize agency as a large component of sexual orientation, favouring the term 'sexual *preference*' over 'sexual *orientation*'. Yet, as I've pointed out, only two sexual options are prescribed, homosexuality and heterosexuality: the option of a bisexual identity is not developed. Sandy, whose voice functions as the main narrative thread of *Choices*, thinks of bisexual behaviour as, at best, confusing:

Jenny, who Sandy suspected was really a lesbian, was with a man, and Julie, who Sandy had been sure was straight, was now experimenting with women, and Sandy was beginning to wonder what the hell it was all about anyhow. (p. 169)

At this point in the story, Sandy is lucky; the fragment of bisexuality which enters her consciousness doesn't stay. On this beach, the shiver runs through her body. Even so, the bisexual penetration has left its mark on her, and she feels cold. This isn't quite as intense as the 'ice' of Kay's sliver of glass, but the power of the bisexual fragment is such that Sandy's body is chilled and, as with the troll's mirror, the world of the victim is no longer harmonious and 'good'. Despite her femaleness (and her name) Sandy cannot feel her usual peace by the ocean: she's unsettled by the bisexual shiver.

Unknown legend

This image returns in a more palpable form towards the end of the novel. Jenny, Barry, Sandy and Shelly have coincidentally booked into the same holiday apartments in Hawaii, and Jenny and Sandy take a walk on the beach together: it is a tumultuous encounter, with each woman feeling angry with and attracted to the other. At the point in the text I'm entering here, Sandy is finally revealing her long-repressed rage towards Jenny, and, in particular, her fury at being coerced by Jenny into attending her wedding. Jenny retorts:

'Are you saying that you would have preferred that I ignore you or make believe you didn't exist?'

> Sandy was just about to answer when she stepped down on something slimy and soft. A burning sensation shot up her foot and calf. (p. 244)

It is at this precise moment, when the loved bisexual woman is demanding recognition, and acknowledgement of her attraction to men, that Sandy is wounded.

What's to be made of this incident? It is part of the lesbian crisis of the novel, which allows Sandy to resolve her anger with Jenny and to turn to Shelly with more commitment. Yet it is Sandy who is stung, and it's possible to read this section for its resonances of powerful bisexuality and an ambivalent lesbianism. Sandy has been wounded; the jellyfish sting which literally pierces her is (in this reading) a fragment, a bisexual shiver. Sandy is aroused by her closeness to Jenny, and her foot is punctured by something unknown, stung by a shiver from something 'slimy and soft' (one could almost, in this novel of symbolic names, read 'Jenny' as 'Jelly' here, and compare the nebulousness of the bi woman's image with the containment symbolized in the lesbian 'Shelly'). At first Sandy ignores the pain, but once she realizes her foot is swollen and very sore, she needs help, joking 'This is obviously a case for Wonder Woman' (p. 247). Jenny turns (and turns and turns) into a super heroine as she races for help, and then back to her friend. Bisexual woman as lesbian hero? At a stroke or, rather, a spin, Jenny's femininity is exaggerated and parodied, her power magnified, her 'otherness' materialized, her ability to pass made ironic. And Sandy? She no longer has the burden of whole(some)ness, and is able to come closer to Jenny. She at last recognizes the strength of Jenny's college words: '"Sandy, I'd like to kiss you". That was probably the most important thing any person has ever said to me. It changed my life' (p. 250). Sandy, the lesbian, at last values Jenny, the bisexual 'I owe you an awful lot, Jenny' – and reverses the discourse of their adolescence to take the initiative and say 'I'd like to kiss you' to her friend (p. 250).

And so?

The les/bi embrace is not quite the end of the novel. Sandy returns to Shelly, more certain of her relationship. Jenny is left not knowing, wanting Barry *and . . .?* But Sandy has accepted Jenny's worth, and finally allowed her 'difference' space within her. The bisexual shiver is no longer something which must be eliminated from the lesbian body: it can be embraced.

Notes

Many thanks to Jo Eadie and Merl Storr for their careful and challenging readings of this article. Thanks are also due to Trev Broughton for her insightful and inspiring comments when I was writing an earlier version of this piece. And thanks to Neil Young for the headings.

1. Nancy Toder, *Choices* (Boston: Alyson Publications, Inc., 1991) (first published 1980), p. 7. Further page references to this novel will be made in the main text, where no further expansion is necessary.
2. JK, '*Choices*: A Novel about Lesbian Love', review in *Off Our Backs* (December 1980), p. 17.
3. *Ibid.*
4. *Ibid.*
5. For a fuller exploration of the connections between gender, sexual identity politics and reader-response theorizing, see Elizabeth A. Flynn and Patrocinio P. Schweickart (eds), *Gender and Reading: Essays on Readers, Texts, and Contexts* (Baltimore and London: Johns Hopkins University Press, 1986); and Karla Jay and Joanne Glasgow (eds), *Lesbian Texts and Contexts: Radical Revisions* (New York and London: New York University Press, 1990).
6. The reasons for changes in the meanings of bisexuality over the past two decades are too complex to enter into here, and involve a large number of cultural movements. In the hope of encouraging more research in this area, I would throw into the theoretical ring: women's and gay liberation, feminism, increased lesbian politicalization, lesbian chic, the dissemination of postmodern thought which has helped legitimize notions of multiple selves, the rise of the 'New Right' with its emphasis on individual morality and freedom of choice, the popularizing of Freudian and Jungian notions of bisexuality, and the proliferation of 'Green' and 'mystic' philosophies which incline towards integration and wholeness.
7. I write *lesbian/feminist* with a slash to indicate their joint and related critical histories, the differences between the two theoretical areas and the connections I wish to assume – strategically – in this work between lesbian critical theory and feminist critical theory.
8. The term 'a bisexual reading' is deliberately ambiguous, deliberately awkward, even. Is *bisexual* a noun or an adjective? Is *reading* a noun or a verb? I intend the term to operate through both possible meanings, and to highlight the interconnectedness of text, reader and culture.
9. Not all critics would agree with my assertion that coming-out fiction is lesbian/feminist in its cultural and historical moment. For instance, Bonnie Zimmerman mentions 'prefeminist' examples in her analysis of coming-out novels (Bonnie Zimmerman, 'Exiting from Patriarchy: The Lesbian Novel of Development', in Elizabeth Abel, Marianne Hirsch and Elizabeth Langland (eds), *The Voyage in Fictions of Female Development* (Hanover and London: University Press of New England, 1983)). Nevertheless I think my position is upheld even in the case of Zimmerman, as few pre-1969 examples are used, and – more importantly – all are read in the light of lesbian/feminist theories.
10. Elizabeth Wilson, 'I'll Climb the Stairway to Heaven: Lesbianism in the Seventies', in Sue Cartledge and Joanna Ryan (eds), *Sex and Love: New Thoughts on Old Contradictions* (London: Women's Press, 1983).
11. *Ibid.*, p. 192.
12. Judith Butler's much quoted theory of gender identity – as produced through the repetitive performance of that gender – opens up ways of also understanding the replaying in the coming-out genre as a radical (series of) act(s) (Judith Butler, *Gender Trouble: Feminism and the Subversion of Identity*, London: Routledge, 1990).
13. Not that there was much mainstream lesbian literary theory around, as suggested by the title, as well as the content, of Bonnie Zimmerman's 1981 article, 'What Has Never Been: An Overview of Lesbian Feminist Literary Criticism', first published in *Feminist Review,* and later in Elaine Showalter (ed.), *The New Feminist Criticism: Essays on Women, Literature and Theory* (London: Virago, 1986), pp. 200–24. Publications from this period worth looking out for are *Sinister Wisdom, Fireweed, Trivia* and *Gossip*. Another useful text is Catharine Stimpson's 'Zero Degree Deviancy: The Lesbian Novel in English', in Elizabeth Abel (ed.), *Writing and Sexual Difference* (Chicago: University of Chicago Press, 1982), pp. 243–59.
14. Bonnie Zimmerman, 'Exiting from Patriarchy', pp. 244–57.

15. Gabriele Griffin, *Heavenly Love? Lesbian Images in Twentieth-Century Women's Writing* (Manchester and New York: Manchester University Press, 1993), p. 62.

16. Nicki Hastie, 'Lesbian Bibliomythography', in Gabriele Griffin (ed.), *Outwrite Lesbianism and Popular Culture* (London and Boulder, Col.: Pluto Press, 1993).

17. This particular comment is, as Jo Eadie pointed out to me, 'astonishing', indicating a rather ghostly les/bi alliance which has slipped (into the) past unnoticed. Paulina Palmer, *Contemporary Lesbian Writing: Dreams, Desire, Difference* (Buckingham and Philadelphia: Open University Press, 1993), p. ix. See also the chapter on lesbian fiction in Palmer's *Contemporary Women's Fiction: Narrative Practice and Feminist Theory* (Hemel Hempstead: Harvester Wheatsheaf, 1989).

18. Bisexuality' and 'Bisexual Movement' are indexed, and it is pleasing to note eleven page references. In contrast, however, 'lesbian' is classified with more subtlety (as, for instance, 'lesbian, the' or 'lesbianism'), and more precisely (as 'lesbian art', or 'lesbian as monster' and so on), a total of 102 references, many of two or more pages.

19. Palmer, *Contemporary Lesbian Writing*, p. 8.

20. *Ibid.*

21. Rita Mae Brown, *Rubyfruit Jungle* (London: Corgi, 1978) (first published 1973); Jeanette Winterson, *Oranges Are Not the Only Fruit* (London: Pandora, 1985).

22. *Choices*, Introduction to 1991 edition, pages unnumbered.

23. *Ibid.*

24. *Ibid.*

25. The relationship between bisexuality and femininity is, I think, intriguing and largely unexplored. Within lesbian lore, both attributes are depicted as traitorous, and as inhabiting women who pass as heterosexual, who are 'really' heterosexual, who will (re)turn to heterosexuality when the lesbian going gets tough. See Fran Michel, 'Do Bats Eat Cats?: Reading What Bisexuality Does', unpublished essay, Department of English, Williamette University Salem, OR, USA; my own work in 'The Bisexual and the Femme', part of my unpublished thesis, University of York, England; and the exchange between Clare Hemmings and myself – about bisexuals and femmes – in the Roundtable conclusion of this volume.

26. One of my favourites is Rita Wilde, *Two-Way Street* (El Cajon, CA: Publisher's Export Co., Inc., 1970). I picked the book up in a queer bookshop in Amsterdam, and was intrigued by the blurb: 'She was torn between the security of her husband and her love for the gorgeous girl named Martha', and the promising last line, 'Love was a three way word'. I should have left my dreams of a bisexual romance intact! The plot, of course, involves an increasingly passionate and psychopathic lesbian – Martha – and a dramatic rescue by the husband – Bill. The wife realizes: 'sex wasn't merely a physical thing, but a spiritual thing, and without the spiritual side of it there wasn't much left. It took the blending of all three to make a beautiful thing out of the relationship of a man and a woman making love. Love was a three way word' (p. 159). As well as the ironic pleasure afforded by the extreme language, I am also struck by the similarities in the plots of both *Two-Way Street* and *Choices*. In particular, I'm fascinated by the implications of the last line of *Choices*, 'Maybe there were some things they couldn't take away from you' (p. 258); where 'they' refers to patriarchal society, and 'some things' alludes to the 'passion' which Jenny has seemingly given up. In both the het and lesbian narratives lesbians are passionate, sexual women and bi/het women are seen to refuse this passion for 'security' (in *Choices)* and 'protection' (in *Two-Way Street*).

27. Interview with Nancy Toder, *Off Our Backs*, 16 (December 1980), p. 16.

28. *Ibid.*

29. This point is one I have thought long about: is there something about the experience of bisexuality which is *more* 'partial' than, say, that of a lesbian? I have to say that I don't know, but I point the reader to the work of Clare Hemmings in this volume, and to my own (unpublished) thesis where I suggest that a reading which speaks to a bisexual sense of self is one that tolerates not-knowing, flux, postponement and transition, and is aware of, but continually attempts to mediate between, multiple subject positions and the multiple relationships between them.

30. Judith Fetterley, Introduction to *The Resisting Reader* (1977), in Robyn R. Warhol and Diane Price Herndl (eds), *Feminisms: An Anthology of Literary Theory and Criticism* (New Brunswick, NJ: Rutgers University Press, 1991), pp. 492–508.
31. *Ibid.*, p. 493.
32. See, for instance, Ara Wilson's witty and quite vicious attack on bisexuals and the politics of bisexuality, which begins by unpacking the name of a bisexual magazine. Wilson writes: 'One explanation of what the [bisexual] "movement" is about can be found in the premiere issue of a new bisexual magazine. On the inside cover a six-part dictionary definition of "move" accompanies the publication's clever name, *Anything That Moves*. The final instance of the last meaning, "to set in motion," is emphasized: "STIR OR SHAKE." Not advance, progress, change, or take action, but movement pure and simple. And, from the perspective of an embattled lesbian, this emphasis indeed seems to be appropriate for the bisexual movement's political practices and endeavour thus far: movement and shaking, not direction and vision.' Ara Wilson, 'Just Add Water: Searching for the Bisexual Politic', *Out/Look*, **16** (4): 4 (Spring 1992).
33. Zimmerman, 'Exiting from Patriarchy', p. 244.
34. See, for example, the section on 'Personal Stories', in Sharon Rose, Cris Stevens *et al.*/ the Off Pink Collective (eds), *Bisexual Horizons: Politics, Histories, Lives* (London: Lawrence & Wishart, 1996), pp. 83–157.
35. Zimmerman, 'Exiting from Patriarchy', p. 244.
36. This may be a lie. My readers strongly disagree with my view of Sarah Schulman's *People in Trouble* (New York: Sheba Feminist Publishers, 1990) as a bi-positive book.
37. See, for instance, the fiction book list in Sharon Rose *et al.* (eds), *Bisexual Horizons*.
38. Hans Christian Andersen, 'The Snow Queen', in *The Golden Treasury of Stories for Boys and Girls* (London: Victor Gollancz, 1959).

6

'Two Loves I Have': Shakespeare and Bisexuality

Kate Chedgzoy

Two loves I have, of comfort and despair,
Which like two angels do suggest me still.
The better angel is a man right fair
The worser spirit a woman coloured ill.
To win me soon to hell my female evil
Tempteth my better angel from my side,
And would corrupt my saint to be a devil,
Wooing his purity with her foul pride;
And whether that my angel be turned fiend
Suspect I may, yet not directly tell;
But being both from me, both to each friend,
I guess one angel in another's hell.
Yet this shall I ne'er know, but live in doubt
Till my bad angel fire my good one out.[1]

With these words the male persona who utters Shakespeare's Sonnet 144 describes what looks to a modern reader very much like a bisexual scenario. Yet while the poem powerfully articulates the pain of erotic conflict, and the intensity of erotic longing, it bears no trace of the shame or unease which conventional attitudes to both Shakespeare and sexuality might lead us to expect. Critical discussion of this poem has tended to focus on its use of theological discourse in a distinctly secular context, or has seen it as one stage in the gradual triumph of heterosexuality over the 'passing phase' of homosexuality – a triumph which is supposedly narrated over the course of Shakespeare's entire sequence of 154 poems.[2] Only recently has the possibility of bisexuality been mooted, most notably in important and enabling works by Marjorie Garber and Joseph Pequigney to which I shall have occasion to return more than once in this chapter.[3] Here, I want not merely to make a case for a bisexual reading of Shakespeare's texts but to ask what it means to speak of Shakespeare and bisexuality in the same breath. Or to put it another way: what aesthetic, historical, and political effects are produced by thinking about those plays and poems in terms of modern conceptualizations of bisexuality? These are, of course, ideas which were not available to Shakespeare when he composed those words in the 1590s; and so I want to explore both the historical specificity of categories of sexual identity and representations of desire in his texts.

Sonnet 144 stages a violent erotic conflict between a 'fair' young man and a 'foul' woman for possession of the speaker, body and soul. The persona who speaks in this poem – as he apparently does in all the Sonnets – is an enigmatic figure named 'Will', whose relationship to the Will (Shakespeare) who authored the Sonnets has been a subject of intense debate for two centuries. The identification of the Will in the Sonnets with the Will who wrote them has often turned on anxieties about the unconventional sexuality apparently represented in these poems. To date, such anxieties have generally focused on the homoerotic liaison between the speaker and the young man: but I want to join Marjorie Garber in suggesting that it may now be time to begin reading the Sonnets as a document not of homosexuality but of bisexuality.

Garber's witty and erudite work on Shakespearean bisexuality has been a vital resource for the present chapter. But I also want to mark some areas of difference from her position on these poems. Garber's case in *Vice Versa* is that the erotic content of the Sonnets is self-evidently bisexual, but that this fact has long been suppressed because 'a bisexual Shakespeare fits no one's erotic agenda' (p. 515). As the present chapter makes clear, I have reservations about the unproblematic identification of Shakespeare with the persona who speaks in the Sonnets, an identification which Garber perpetuates here. The critical history of the Sonnets certainly tells us a great deal about cultural perceptions of Shakespeare's sexuality. But the poems themselves remain a literary work whose relation to their author's life is unguessable. Moreover, I disagree with Garber's assumption that the biseuxal nature of the Sonnets has been deliberately and ruthlessly repressed over the centuries. Rather, I would say that just as the homoerotic reading of the Sonnets was brought into focus in the 1890s, at the moment when modern homosexual identities and politics were crystallizing,[4] so it is the emergence in the 1990s of a theoretically and politically confident discourse of bisexuality that now allows us to read the poems as instantiating a 'bisexual imaginary'.[5] The practice of bisexual revisioning of culture can now disclose that, if we accept that plot which many readers have found in the 1609 sequence, we are also of necessity constructing it as a bisexual narrative, because it is a plot which in juxtaposing the speaker's love for the young man and the dark woman insists on the co-presence of both these erotic possibilities.

Sonnet 144 has often been adduced as evidence for Shakespeare's supposed *homo*sexuality; yet the numerous studies of Shakespeare and sexuality written in the last decade or so almost never take seriously the *bi*sexuality which this poem would appear more obviously to evoke. More generally, in the recent burgeoning of work on historical constructions and literary representations of sexualities in the early modern period, the category of bisexuality has been almost entirely elided.[6] I propose that it is premature to exclude bisexuality from the analysis of Renaissance culture and society. It has become a commonplace of work in the field to claim that exclusivity of sexual preference was in no way at issue during the early modern period.[7] Nevertheless, the debate about whether sexual subjectivities existed as such in the period, and if so what range of forms they took, continues more often than not to be couched in terms of the binary opposition of homo- and heterosexuality. This is particularly problematic for historians of female sexuality, given the crucial importance in the early modern period of the institution of marriage, and the extremely limited opportunities which women had to achieve economic independence or exercise erotic autonomy in a social context outside of marriage. Emma Donoghue has demonstrated with reference to the period after 1660 the usefulness of the notion of bisexuality in evaluating the range of erotic possibilities open to women.[8] In the present chapter, I am mainly concerned to make a case about the representation of male bisexuality; but I want to note that a similar project could facilitate our understanding of female sexuality as it is represented in earlier texts. Such work might be particularly illuminating in relation to those plays by Shakespeare whose persistent life in twentieth-century culture helps to endow early modern sexualities with continued significance in the present.[9]

I have already suggested that in Sonnet 144 bisexuality is figured in terms of struggle and conflict. This conflict, it seems, is twofold. It is located in the speaker's psyche, in his inability or reluctance to choose one love rather than the other. Yet it also exists outside him, in a battle between the other man and the woman which apparently centres on possession of the speaker, but which in fact is still more complex than this. For the sexual puns which saturate the poem clearly indicate that the traffic of desire in this sexual triangle circulates in every possible direction. The speaker wants the young man and the woman; the young man and the woman both desire each other as well as the poet. It is an oddly volatile and over-determined contest: the young man is presented as angelic and saintly, in the tradition of the idealized beloved of courtly love poetry, while the woman is ugly, dark, demonic – the fact that 'hell', amongst various other slang meanings, could refer to female genitals gives a tang of misogyny to this erotic division. Yet the woman is no less compelling for this; indeed, her sexual magnetism appears strong enough to corrupt the angelic boy's purity. Meanwhile, the speaker's place in this tormented erotic cosmology remains troubled and uncertain.

The language of sexuality in this and other poems in the sequence makes it very clear that the desire which circulates in this fraught situation is not potential but actual. In other words, it is implied that the various erotic liaisons possible between the speaker, the woman, and the younger man have been consummated. As Stephen Booth's magisterial edition demonstrates, the language of the entire sequence is dense with what he calls 'incidental and incidentally bawdy nnuendo' (p. 548), creating a thoroughly sexualized atmosphere which is quite unlike the erotics of distance and delay typical of other Renaissance sonnet sequences. In Sonnet 144, for instance, the last three lines are dense with sexual metaphor. Line 12, 'I guess one angel in another's hell' plays on the slang sense of 'hell' as female genitals noted above to imply the consummation of the relationship between the woman and the young man. But it also refers to the rules for playing the popular Elizabethan game of 'barley-break', which often provided both a pretext and a euphemism for sexual play.[10] Finally, the last line implies both the possibility of the young man's sexual rejection by the woman and that she might infect him with venereal disease.

Other sonnets, such as 129 and 135, also bear out this almost obsessive focus on sexual experience. Sonnet 129 ('Th'expense of spirit in a waste of shame') powerfully evokes the speaker's sense of being immersed in a troubled and complex sexual situation, while 135 ('Whoever hath her wish, thou hast thy will') is enabled to take a more sardonic view by taking the punning technique to an extreme which is both comic and scathing. In the sixteenth century the word 'will' could refer to sexual desire or to the male or female genitals: moreover, some commentators have suggested that the young man, like the persona, is called Will. Sonnet 135 repeats the word 'will' thirteen times, creating a dizzying impression of the boundless promiscuity of this woman's sexual life.[11]

This emphasis on the accomplishment of passion makes Shakespeare's Sonnets unusual among Elizabethan sonnet sequences. Conventionally, these reveal the influence of the Italian poet Petrarch in being structured around the speaker's attempt to use poetic eloquence to seduce a beautiful but unobtainable woman.[12] Shakespeare is highly self-conscious about the un-Petrarchan nature of his sequence: Sonnet 130 ('My mistress' eyes are nothing like the sun'), for example, works through many of the classic tropes used to praise the female beloved's beauty, neatly reversing them one by one. But clearly this is not the only respect in which Shakespeare's sequence is unusual. Linked to this atypical focus on what happens to desire and love in a consummated relationship is another deviation from traditional practice – and one which may appear more obviously striking to modern eyes: many of the poems appear to be addressed not to a female but to a male beloved. As a result the Sonnets have come to occupy a crucial but problematic position in Shakespeare's canon of writings, in that they are taken by many readers to tell a story of love between men which reveals things about Shakespeare's own desires and identity which are otherwise obscured. Indeed, it is often felt that these things would have been better kept hidden: in the mid nineteenth century Henry Hallam – father of the Arthur Hallam for whom Tennyson wrote *In Memoriam* – lamented 'it is impossible not to wish Shakespeare had never written [the Sonnets]'.[13] The work which seems to offer the reader the most direct and privileged access to the reality of Shakespeare's emotional life has the regrettable effect of disclosing that life as sexually scandalous.

In order to consider how far Sonnet 144 – taken with other poems in the sequence – can be seen as a literary inscription of the bisexual imaginary, I want now to flesh out the literary and historical contexts in which these poems need to be read. There is an ironic and important contrast between the private nature of the Sonnets' original composition and circulation in Elizabethan and Jacobean England, and the public reasons for our interest, as modern readers, in decoding the sexual subjectivity we find inscribed in them. Our understanding of the relation between public and private is crucial to the terms on which we consider the construction of sexual identity in the past, but runs the risk of forcing poems like Shakespeare's Sonnets into anachronistic moulds. Shakespeare's Sonnets were not published during his lifetime in what we might call an authorized edition, but this is assuredly not because he was ashamed of their supposed homosexual content. Rather, this reflects his conformity as a poet to the practices of manuscript circulation and patronage relations which prevailed in literary Britain until well into the seventeenth century. Arthur Marotti offers a succinct outline of this context for early modern literary production:

> In the English Renaissance, the composition of lyric poems was part of social life, associated with a variety of practices in polite and educated circles. Read aloud to live audiences or passed from hand to hand in single sheets, small booklets, quires, or pamphlets, verse typically found its way into manuscript commonplace books rather than into printed volumes – though, of course, printers often eventually gained access to manuscripts preserving the work of single writers or groups of authors and exploited them for their own economic and social purposes.[14]

This was almost precisely the fate of Shakespeare's Sonnets. Initially they circulated privately – his contemporary Francis Meres informs us that his 'sugared sonnets' were being read 'among his private friends' by 1598[15] – before being printed by Thomas Thorpe in 1609, in essentially the form and order in which we know them today. The next edition of the Sonnets appeared in 1640, rearranged by the publisher John Benson in a curious form which may signal homophobia, or simple puzzlement. By 1640 the vogue for extended sequences of fourteen-line sonnets was over, and Benson responded to shifts in poetic fashion by running a number of sonnets together to create longer poems, reordering others, and omitting eight poems altogether. More salient, for our purposes, was his transformation of all the masculine pronouns used in the first 126 sonnets to feminine ones – a move which heterosexualized all these texts at a stroke. He also took the further precaution of adding titles to many poems which emphasized their 'heterosexual' nature.

This was the form in which the Sonnets circulated for the next century and a half. During this period they had few readers, however, although the cultural stock both of Shakespeare's plays and the author himself was rising steadily. It was only when Edmond Malone, in 1790, produced an edition which reverted to the ordering of the 1609 sequence that the conditions which made possible an autobiographical reading of the Sonnets fell into place. There are two key aspects to this new way of reading the Sonnets: first, the focusing of attention on the emotional and sexual plot which was suddenly revealed by the re-ordering; and, second, the coincidence of Malone's edition becoming available at the moment when the Romantic creed of poetry which is still so influential was being formulated. Shakespeare's Sonnets came to be read in terms of a particular Romantic analysis of lyric poetry which locates the subject's self-present interiority as knowable in and through the language of his text. Although such conjectures had been by no means self-evident before Malone produced his edition, by the time James Boswell came to revise it in 1821 he could note that 'it seems to be generally admitted that the poet speaks in his own person'.[16] The swift assimilation of this understanding of the Sonnets into the general culture is signalled by Wordsworth's declaration, that 'with this key / Shakespeare unlocked his heart'.[17] The possibility that this identification could lead to worrying speculation about Shakespeare's private life was also articulated – and firmly refuted – by Malone: 'Such addresses to men, however indelicate, were customary in our author's time, and neither imparted criminality, nor were esteemed indecorous' (*Plays and Poems*, p. 191).

It is clear, then, that the tracing within the Sonnets of an erotic plot which acknowledges as fully sexual the speaker's desires for both the young man and the woman has always been entangled with anxieties about Shakespeare's own sexual identity. Thus the history of homophobic readings of the Sonnets has made the positing of a bisexual element in that plot impossible, because any evidence of heterosexual activity has been seized upon enthusiastically as that which redeems Shakespeare from the charge of homosexuality. Attempting to displace this stress on biography, Gregory Bredbeck insists that these poems are not 'about' a particular sexual narrative which can be pinned down and used to read Shakespeare's life, but rather embody the fissured, multiple nature of poetic writing.[18] I agree with Bredbeck that univocality is counter to the nature of the Sonnets' linguistic and rhetorical texture. But I would also argue that the desire to find in these poems an exploitation of the rich ambiguities of poetic language is not necessarily incompatible with the interpretation of the sequence as a narrative of sexual desire: or, perhaps better, as an intertwining of multiple narratives of love and desire asserted, acted on and frustrated. These are poems dense with metaphor, puns, ambiguity, charged with a freight of equivocal sexual meaning. Might it be that not merely the situation described, but also the poetic substance of the Sonnets, is best labelled as 'bisexual'?

Bredbeck's emphasis on a non-biographical reading of the Sonnets is both persuasive and salutary. For it reminds us that if we treat the past as our mirror, to borrow a phrase from Derek Jarman,[19] the image we find there will be the one we seek. That is, we will be producing Shakespeare in our own image, as an intervention in the cultural politics of our own day, rather than holding an accurate glass up to the past. But Shakespeare's cultural power means that there are good reasons for doing this, and Bredbeck's argument is unlikely substantially to change the ways in which the Sonnets are read and used. I have argued elsewhere that anxieties about the nature of Shakespearian sexuality have a peculiar intensity because of the playwright's unique status in English-language culture.[20] This point is also emphasised by Simon Shepherd:

> Discussion of homosexuality in Shakspeer [*sic*] seems to be motivated not by an interest in Renaissance sexuality but by Shakespaire's [*sic*] national status. Criticism's task is to discover a fitting sexuality for the National Bard. The task is specifically taken up by and shaped by *literary* criticism, for the literature is what is to be protected. The literature belongs to the nation.[21]

Bredbeck's analysis of the Sonnets is thus limited in its effectiveness because it treats in purely intellectual and aesthetic terms what is in fact a primarily socio-cultural phenomenon. However, it remains important in so far as it draws our attention to the insistent presence in the sequence not only of linguistic instability but also of gender ambiguity. The relations between bisexuality and gender ambiguity are complex and volatile, but also highly relevant to a consideration of the possible meanings of bisexuality in Renaissance culture. I therefore want now to explore some aspects of these relations, and their implications for a bisexual reading of Shakespeare.

Malcolm Bowie outlines three crucial ways of defining 'bisexuality': as biological hermaphroditism, psychological androgyny, and a tendency on the part of an individual to find both men and women sexually attractive.[22] As Clare Hemmings notes elsewhere in this volume, these three definitions – and particularly the latter two – are often mutually reinforcing. An understanding of bisexuality as androgyny has played a persistent role in Shakespeare studies. Cross-dressed, ambiguous characters such as Rosalind/Ganymede in *As You Like It* and Viola/Cesario in *Twelfth Night* appear to evoke the possibility that the figure who unites both masculine and feminine within one body may both incarnate androgyny, and be the object of bisexual desire from both men and women. The teasing and pleasurable erotic ambiguity of these figures is an important aspect of Shakespearian bisexuality. But the notion of androgyny has also been deployed in order to occlude the possibility of finding bisexuality as erotic potential inscribed in Shakespeare's texts. As Marjorie Garber notes, one way of approaching Shakespeare's bisexuality has been to see him as the possessor of a bisexual mind, or an androgynous aesthetic sensibility (*Vice Versa*, p. 515). The earliest instance of this is offered by Margaret Cavendish, writing less than half a century after Shakespeare's death of his ability to enter imaginatively into the psychic life of female as well as male characters: 'one would think that he had been Metamorphosed from a Man to a Woman, for who could Describe *Cleopatra* Better than he hath done, and many other

Females of his own Creating.'[23] Later, Coleridge asserted that 'myriad-minded' Shakespeare was like women in being 'characterless', and therefore endlessly able to sympathize or identify with others.[24] Post-Romantic criticism takes up this vision of a polymorphously sympathetic, but by no means perverse, Shakespeare capable of imaginatively transgressing gender boundaries in terms of identification rather than desire. Virginia Woolf's suggestion that psychic androgyny is essential to the 'creative, incandescent and undivided' functioning of the mind invokes Shakespeare as an ideal model: 'one goes back to Shakespeare's mind as the type of the androgynous, of the man-womanly mind, though it would be impossible to say what Shakespeare thought of women.'[25] Here, androgyny as the higher impersonality and the source of great writing evokes a Shakespeare remote indeed from the persona of Sonnet 144, wrestling with a bisexual triangle of desire and jealousy. Psychoanalytically influenced accounts of Shakespearean bisexuality as creative potential also rely on the notion of mental androgyny, as Garber points out in reference to both Freud (p. 516) and Hélène Cixous (p. 515).[26]

More recently, however, the critic Joseph Pequigney has adopted the Freudian theorization of bisexuality to argue for a fully eroticized understanding of the bisexual dynamics apparently represented in the Sonnets. Chapter 5 of his study of the Sonnets, *Such is My Love*, is entitled 'The Bisexual Soul'. Here, Pequigney joins the tradition of commentators since Wordsworth who have seen the Sonnets as the 'key' with which 'Shakespeare unlocked his heart', and puts Freud into play in order to explicate Shakespeare's sexual identity, noting the existence of 'a remarkable coincidence between Freud's theories of inversion and the bisexual psychology adumbrated in the Sonnets.'[27] He goes so far as to propose an identification of Shakespeare as an 'amphigenic invert', a member of the rather specialized category outlined in Freud's taxonomy of inverts in the 'Three Essays on the Theory of Sexuality': 'They may be *amphigenic inverts*, that is psychosexual hermaphrodites. In that case their sexual objects may equally well be of their own or of the opposite sex. This kind of inversion thus lacks the characteristic of exclusiveness.'[28] It is, I think, important that Freud does not insist on exclusivity as a defining factor of inversion – the bisexual is still an invert in his account. This is crucial for an understanding of the possible location of bisexuality in terms of early modern sexual and social practices. Freud thus opens the possibility of seeing bisexuality – or, to use his term, amphigenic inversion – not as a state of transition or indecision between heterosexuality and homosexuality but as a distinct form of libidinal existence. Moreover, in combining 'psychosexual hermaphrodit[ism]' as a charcteristic of the invert's emotional life with an inclusiveness of sexual object-choice, Freud destabilizes the restrictive taxonomy of bisexuality outlined by Malcolm Bowie. Pequigney illustrates this point by weaving together fragments from Freud's essay and Sonnet 20 so that Freud analyses Shakespeare's sexuality, and Shakespeare provides evidence for Freud's theory:

> Freud finds that a goodly proportion of 'alleged inverts' are 'by no means insusceptible to the charms of women' and that 'in their sexual object' they seek 'feminine mental traits' ('a woman's heart') and 'physical resemblance to a woman' ('a woman's face' and 'eye'), together with a masculine 'body (i.e. genitals)' ('a man in hue . . . pricked'), so that they look for 'not someone of the same sex but someone who combines the characters of both sexes', and 'the sexual object is a kind of reflection of the subject's own bisexual nature'. (p. 82)

In effect, then, Pequigney is producing an account of Shakespearean bisexuality which conflates all three of the definitions outlined by Malcolm Bowie: the combination within one person of masculine and feminine characteristics of the mind and body, with a tendency to desire both men and women.

According to this scenario, the ideal object of desire for the persona who speaks of his love for both the 'man right fair' conventionally identified as the addressee of the first 126 poems, and the 'woman coloured ill' of the remaining group might well be the ambiguous, androgynous figure described in Sonnet 20 ('A woman's face, with nature's own hand painted'). This, of course, is the poem Pequigney uses to illustrate Freud's theory of the 'amphigenic invert'. It might therefore be suggested that the 'lovely boy' (Sonnet 126) depicted here constitutes the ideal erotic object for bisexual men. Eva Cantarella and James Saslow have both discussed the valorization of the figure of the lovely and somewhat effeminate boy in cultures which appear to endorse male–male sexual activity without enforcing sexual exclusivity.[29] Despite her title – *Bisexuality in the Ancient World* – Cantarella's subject is not bisexuality in any of the terms in which it has been defined in the current chapter, and in which it is generally understood. Rather, she is principally concerned with tracing and interpreting evidence concerning sexual contacts between adult men and young boys, which she chooses to describe as bisexuality rather than homosexuality because, as she says,

> For the Greeks and Romans . . . homosexuality was not an exclusive choice. Loving another man was not an option falling outside the norm, a different or somehow deviant decision. It was just one part of the experience of life: the manifestation of an impulse which could be either a matter of feelings or of sexuality. (p. vii)

Cantarella is at pains to emphasize that this perception of same-sex desire does not testify to an extraordinary permissiveness or liberality of attitude in the ancient world so much as it reveals the importance of constructions of gender identity in shaping the meanings of sexual practices. In so far as women, boys and slaves all come short of the full subjectivity and citizenship which, in these societies, were accorded only to adult males of a certain class, the gender of the sexual object chosen by an adult man is irrelevant. What is important is the preservation of hierarchy within the sexual situation such that the man always takes the 'active, masculine' role *vis-à-vis* his 'passive, feminine' partner; who may be female, youthful or enslaved.

This way of organizing sexual relations may well, as Bruce Smith has recently suggested,[30] have had some pertinence in Shakespeare's England, and as such it is important in contextualizing Shakespearian images of male homoeroticism, and fleshing out a sense of the conventions which the Sonnets respond to and test. But it does not seem to me to be an entirely fruitful way of describing the bisexual situation of these poems. Following the narrative I sketched earlier, we might reasonably assume that the speaker, as a mature man, would be more powerful in Renaissance society than either of his lovers. But what the Sonnets make very plain is that erotic power follows its own laws, whose relation to the power dynamics of society in general is often complex and unstable. And in these poems the persona is often effectively in a relatively powerless position because he finds himself, in various ways, at an erotic and emotional disadvantage *vis-à-vis* either the young man or the woman.

The Shakespearian bisexuality of which I have spoken so far is essentially masculine, in two key senses. First, it echoes as it problematizes Cantarella's delineation of a world in which adult men are required to found their sexual identity not on object-choice but on a position of mastery in the sexual relation. Second, it is masculine in the very practical sense that the cast of the Sonnets' erotic drama consists of three persons, of whom two – both men – are represented as the subjects of bisexual desire. Since no woman other than the 'dark lady' is mentioned in the Sonnets, and she only as object, there is no possibility of articulating a woman's bisexual desires. However, I want briefly to suggest that gender ambiguity also opens up the possibility of a feminine bisexuality being represented elsewhere in Shakespeare's work. Staying with the Sonnets for a moment, we might for example ask: if we perceive the fair youth as feminized, what is at stake in the dark lady's desire for him? To recall the terminology of Sonnet 20: is it the femininity of his 'woman's face', the masculinity of the 'one thing added' or the deliciously ambiguous conjunction of the two that she finds attractive?

Just such a desire on the part of a woman for a lovely, androgynous youth can be traced in both *Twelfth Night* and *As You Like It*. James Saslow, as I mentioned earlier, places the 'lovely boy' as an ideal object of desire for adult men. But why should such a figure not be attractive to women too? Saslow makes his remarks in a book, *Ganymede in the Renaissance*, which explores the enduring appeal of Jove's cup-bearer as an image of the homoerotically desirable boy. In Shakespeare's *As You Like It*, Rosalind declares when she adopts male disguise in order to go into exile, 'I'll have no worse a name than Jove's own page / And therefore look you call me Ganymede'. This, assuredly, is no coincidence: and neither is it mere chance that Rosalind/ Ganymede proves erotically irresistible to both men and women. Similarly, in *Twelfth Night*, the androgynous figure of Viola/Cesario is desired by both men and women. As a member of the audience at modern productions of these plays, I have often been aware that these sexually ambiguous figures offer particular pleasures to the women who watch them. The possibility that such pleasures might also have been available to Shakespeare's female contemporaries should not be dismissed lightly.

I began this chapter with Shakespeare's Sonnet 144, a poem which seems to offer a particularly clearly delineated outline of one bisexual situation. I want to end by taking another look at that situation, recontextualizing it in relation to recent works which articulate the bisexual potential of Shakespeare's texts in new ways. There is no other poem in the sequence which juxtaposes quite so dramatically the competing desires which make the triangle involving the poet, the young man and the woman a bisexual one. But it would also, I think, be legitimate to suggest that the entire sequence might be seen as representing bisexuality, simply in so far as it depicts the speaker's desire for, and emotional and erotic involvement with, both a woman and a man. We need not only locate bisexuality at/as the point of conflict between heterosexual and homosexual loves; it may equally be found in the co-existence within one life or one psyche of diverse erotic possibilities. Perhaps surprisingly, one work which offers a rich source for thinking about bisexuality in this way is Derek Jarman's film based on Shakespeare's Sonnets, *The Angelic Conversation* (1985), which juxtaposes homoerotic visuals with a reading of some of the Sonnets by Judi Dench. Fragmentary and kaleidoscopic, the film, made on a tiny budget and with minimal equipment, is typical of much of Jarman's work in resisting narrative drive, embodying an aesthetics of fracture and openness, and demanding the spectator's active engagement in the construction of its meanings. In thinking about film, we are accustomed to privilege the visual over the aural; but Jarman's last completed feature film, *Blue* (1993), attempts to disrupt this hierarchy of response and to destabilize the relation between these two elements by pairing a plain blue screen with a densely textured script. What, then, is at stake when we hear Judi Dench read the Sonnets and see young men embracing? In this strange and beautiful film, that resonant voice, rich in connotations of acceptable middle-class English femininity, combines both with the words of Sonnet 144 or 126 ('O thou, my lovely boy, who in thy pow'r') and with the spectacle of young men whose healthy, muscular bodies represent one of the erotic ideals of modern gay male culture, to offer the spectator considerable cinematic pleasure at the same time as unsettling the easy assumptions about gender and sexuality which we all too often bring to Shakespeare.

Bisexuality need not, therefore, be conceptualized in terms of conflict or cleavage but rather as the co-existence of diverse erotic possibilities. Nevertheless, the terms in which it is figured in the Sonnets do often seem to revolve around struggle, pain and jealousy. Towards the end of 1992, the Swansea-based physical theatre company, Volcano, toured a production based on Shakespeare's Sonnets which endowed this aspect of the sequence with viscerally powerful and vivid theatrical form. The show was called *L.O.V.E.*, and its emphasis was on the obsessive, violent side of desire – the mood was set by the opening sequence, in which individual, disconnected words drawn from Shakespeare's Sonnets were chanted: canker, couldst, didst, bemoaned, wanton. The production was unusual in its approach to the Sonnets in that it did not seek to interpret them in terms of the usual narrative. The bisexual story that emerged over the course of the performance was not one that others have teased out from the Sonnets, but one that the three performers used the Sonnets to construct. Throughout, the text was fragmented, dislocated and often subsumed by the extraordinary energy and commitment which the Volcano performers bring to their movement-based work; but certain Sonnets featured prominently, and indeed were in some cases repeated insistently. 'Two loves I have', for example, was predictably important, although the company's handling of it was surprising: the young man was left to stand alone to one side of the stage, gazing angrily across to where the other, older man and the woman kissed violently. An analysis of the performance which took gesture to be illustrative of meaning would have to read this in terms of the young man's rage and resentment that the two people whom he is used to consider his admirers have turned away from him, to find erotic gratification in each other. But in Volcano's complex, multi-layered shows it is not always possible to be confident that this particular relationship between language and movement is what is in play. In this show as in *The Angelic Conversation*, a transformation of the relation between form and content also serves to challenge and transform the social and sexual meanings which can be made from Shakespeare's texts.

Commentary on bisexuality has often presumed the prior existence of the categories of homo- and heterosexuality, with bisexuality being produced subsequently as a third term, occupying a relation to the other two which may be characterized in a number of ways. I have argued elsewhere that the project to produce a history of same-sex desires has occluded the extent to which the category of heterosexuality is problematic in the early modern context. By way of offering a conclusion which is effectively a beginning – a marker for work yet to be done – I want briefly to pursue that point here.[31] The foreclosure of bi- or homoerotic possibilities by means of comic closure in marriage should be treated not necessarily as celebrating heterosexual love but rather as marking the power of the institution of marriage. Outside that bulwark of compulsory heterosexuality, I am not sure that it is always helpful, when discussing Renaissance culture, to distinguish between bi- and homoeroticism. The key distinction for the early modern period may not be one which has to do with the modern categories of sexual identity which go by the labels of bi-, homo-, hetero-, but one which differentiates licit married sex from everything else, including certain kinds of heterosexual activity, or particular articulations of heterosexual desire. Similarly, Alan Bray in his influential *Homosexuality in Renaissance England*, and more recently Valerie Traub have both argued that sexual activity which does not trouble marriage may be winked at, if not endorsed, regardless of factors like the gender of the participants.[32] It is my view that in early modern culture, bisexuality cannot easily be defined or located, in that it is both a phenomenon which, according to prevailing gender arrangements, can co-exist within or alongside the institution of marriage, and one which needs to be seen in terms of its occupation of a category of illicit sexual activity which it shares with all forms of sexuality which are not marital and reproductive. For me, this means that bisexuality is a crucial concept for thinking about early modern sexualities in ways which simultaneously acknowledge and bridge the divide between our twentieth-century understandings of desire and those which prevailed in Shakespeare's time. But it also means that the notion of bisexuality cannot be used to assert the early modern existence of a position as the subject of a particular sexual identity which could be occupied by an individual. That is, it may enable us to read the textualization of bisexual desire in Shakespeare's poems in ways which speak to our own concerns at the same time as recognizing the four centuries of historical difference which lie between us and the moment in which they were written; but it does not allow us to claim that Shakespeare 'was' bisexual. Earlier, I cited Paula Bennett's article 'Gender as Performance: Shakespearean Ambiguity and the Lesbian Reader', in which she movingly describes the ways in which her youthful engagement with the ambiguities of Shakespeare's desire provided her with some of the resources she needed to survive a lesbian adolescence, and the ways in which feminist and queer theory subsequently enabled her to critique the sexual politics of Shakespeare's plays. I hope and believe the as-yet scarcely begun project of reading Shakespeare in terms of a bisexual imaginary will similarly prove illuminating of both the texts which come to us from the past, and the concerns which shape our reading of them in the present.

Notes

1. All quotations from the Sonnets are taken from Stephen Booth (ed.), *Shakespeare's Sonnets* (New Haven and London: Yale University Press, 1977).
2. For an overview of this critical history, see Joseph Pequigney, *Such Is My Love: A Study of Shakespeare's Sonnets* (Chicago: University of Chicago Press, 1985).
3. Pequigney, *Such Is My Love*; Marjorie Garber, *Vice Versa: Bisexuality and the Erotics of Everyday Life* (New York: Simon & Schuster, 1995).
4. On this topic, see ' "Strange Worship": Oscar Wilde and the Key to Shakespeare's Sonnets', Chapter 4 of my *Shakespeare's Queer Children: Sexual Politics and Contemporary Culture* (Manchester: Manchester University Press, 1996).
5. See the Roundtable discussion in this volume for further consideration of this point.
6. It is gratifying that it is no longer feasible to provide a bibliography of such work in a single footnote. Apart from works mentioned elsewhere in the present article, for useful starting points see, for example, Jonathan Goldberg (ed.), *Queering the Renaissance* (Durham, NC: Duke University Press, 1994), Claude J. Summers (ed.), *Homosexuality in Renaissance and Enlightenment England: Literary Representations in Historical Context* (New York: Harrington Park Press, 1992), Susan Zimmerman (ed.), *Erotic Politics: Desire on the Renaissance Stage* (London: Routledge, 1992).
7. This assumption derives, of course, from the hugely influential work of Michel Foucault, most obviously *The History of Sexuality, Volume 1: An Introduction* (London: Allen Lane, 1979). For one example of a Foucauldian approach to early modern sexuality, see Jonathan Goldberg, *Sodometries: Renaissance Texts, Modern Sexualities* (Stanford: Stanford University Press, 1992).
8. Emma Donoghue, *Passions Between Women: British Lesbian Culture 1668-1801* (London: Scarlet Press, 1993).
9. For an article which accomplishes a similar task from a lesbian perspective, see Paula Bennett, 'Gender as Performance: Shakespearean Ambiguity and the Lesbian Reader',

in Susan J. Wolfe and Julia Penelope (eds), *Sexual Practice/Textual Theory: Lesbian Cultural Criticism* (Oxford: Blackwell, 1993), pp. 94–109.

10. The rules for barley-break are explained in Booth's edition, p. 499.

11. See Eve Kosofsky Sedgwick's discussion of the sexual politics of this poem in her *Between Men: English Literature and Male Homosocial Desire* (New York: Columbia University Press, 1985).

12. Another interesting counter-example is Lady Mary Wroth's *Pamphilia to Amphilanthus* (1621), which inverts the conventional Petrarchan structure and imagery by using them to record a woman's longing for her faithless male lover.

13. Hallam made the comment in his *Introduction to the Literature of Europe*; it is quoted in Alfred Tennyson, *The Poems of Tennyson*, ed. Christopher Ricks (London: Longman, 1969), p. 861.

14. Arthur F. Marotti, *Manuscript, Print, and the English Renaissance Lyric* (Ithaca, NY: Cornell University Press, 1995), p. 2.

15. See the Introduction to John Kerrigan (ed.), *William Shakespeare: The Sonnets and A Lover's Complaint* (Harmondsworth: Penguin, 1986), p. 10. The following brief account of Benson's edition is also indebted to Kerrigan.

16. Quoted in Margreta de Grazia, *Shakespeare Verbatim: The Reproduction of Authenticity and the 1790 Apparatus* (Oxford: Clarendon Press, 1991), p. 154.

17. William Wordsworth, 'Scorn Not the Sonnet', *Poems*, ed. John O. Hayden, 2 vols (Harmondsworth: Penguin, 1977), vol. II, p. 635.

18. Gregory W. Bredbeck, *Sodomy and Interpretation from Marlowe to Milton* (Ithaca, NY: Cornell University Press, 1991); for substantiation of his argument about the interrelation of linguistic and sexual ambiguity, which is too dense and complex to summarize here, see especially pp. 167–85.

19. The full phrase used by Jarman is, 'Without our past the future cannot be reflected, the past is our mirror'. Letter to *The Independent*, 20 May 1993.

20. See the final two chapters of *Shakespeare's Queer Children: Sexual Politics and Contemporary Culture*.

21. 'Shakespeare's Private Drawer: Shakespeare and Homosexuality', in Graham Holderness (ed.), *The Shakespeare Myth* (Manchester: Manchester University Press, 1988), p. 97.

22. Malcolm Bowie, 'Bisexuality', in Elizabeth Wright (ed.), *Feminism and Psychoanalysis: A Critical Dictionary* (Oxford: Blackwell, 1992), p. 26.

23. Letter 113, from *CCXI Sociable Letters* (1664), quoted in Brian Vickers (ed.), *Shakespeare: The Critical Heritage*, vol. I, *1623-1692* (London: Routledge & Kegan Paul, 1974), p. 43.

24. Quoted in Jonathan Bate (ed.), *The Romantics on Shakespeare* (Harmondsworth: Penguin, 1992), pp. 147, 161.

25. *A Room of One's Own* (London: Grafton, 1977), p. 94 (first published 1929).

26. On the complex relations between notions of bi- or homosexuality and androgyny, see Catharine Stimpson, 'The Homosexual and the Androgyne', in *Where the Meanings Are: Feminism and Cultural Spaces* (New York: Methuen, 1988).

27. *Such Is My Love*, p. 81.

28. Sigmund Freud, 'Three Essays on the Theory of Sexuality', I, 'The Sexual Aberrations', in *The Standard Edition of the Complete Works of Sigmund Freud*, vol. 7 (London: Hogarth Press, 1953), p. 136.

29. Eva Cantarella, *Bisexuality in the Ancient World* (New Haven: Yale University Press, 1992); James M. Saslow, *Ganymede in the Renaissance: Homosexuality in Art and Society* (New Haven: Yale University Press, 1986).

30. Bruce Smith, *Homosexual Desire in Shakespeare's England: A Cultural Poetics* (Chicago: University of Chicago Press, 1991).

31. Kate Chedgzoy, ' "True Love 'tween Maid and Maid": Theorising "Lesbian" Desire in Early Modern Writing', unpublished paper, 1994.

32. Alan Bray, *Homosexuality in Renaissance England* (London: Gay Men's Press, 1982); Valerie Traub, 'The (In)significance of "Lesbian" Desire', in Zimmerman (ed.), *Erotic Politics*, pp. 150–69.

7

'Queer Shoulders to the Wheel': Whitman, Ginsberg and a Bisexual Poetics

Nick Selby

It has become a critical commonplace to view the two American poets Walt Whitman and Allen Ginsberg as gay poets whose works demonstrate and develop a gay poetic.[1] Indeed, their homosexuality and their radical poetic agendas are seen as inseparably bound together with their status as rebel heroes whose visions of America challenge mainstream American ideology and culture. Robert K. Martin's notion of a (male) homosexual tradition in American poetry starts with Whitman, and describes him as an heroic father-figure against whom subsequent gay American poets have measured themselves. Whitman's position as the hero-poet of American romantic democracy is, argues Martin, a direct result of his oppositional sexuality. 'No other poet, until the present time', writes Martin,

> has so clearly defined himself in terms of his sexuality and so clearly defined his poetic mission as a consequence of his homosexuality. This remains true despite the attempts Whitman made, late in his own lifetime, to conceal his homosexuality from outsiders. It may be, of course, that in part he was telling the truth: that he never gave physical expression to his love for men. The textual evidence makes that seem unlikely, however; Whitman was fully aware of the possibilities of sexual expression between men, and he celebrated them not only as an end in themselves but also as a means to a mystic penetration of the universe and a more democratic vision of the American future.[2]

It is the assumed clarity of such a connection between the production of Whitman as radical American poet and Whitman as the site for the production of a specifically gay poetic which this paper seeks to challenge. My aim is to ease the work of Whitman and Ginsberg away from a poetic that places them exclusively within the canon of gay writing by emphasizing their importance in the theorization of a bisexual poetics. This can be seen by turning, initially, to two examples from Whitman. Both examples show how the operation of desire in Whitman's text becomes a site in which claims for America as a poetic democracy are contested. The first example records the type of same-sex desire which Martin designates homosexual, whilst the second records opposite-sex desire commonly designated heterosexual. Clearly, such designations of desire would not have been understood by Whitman, and in fact both could be seen as bisexual. However, they provide a convenient shorthand for opening up an investigation of the constitution of desire in Whitman's text. The poetic fluidity of desires, then, and how this is a product of Whitman's America is the ground upon which I will investigate Whitman's mobilization of a bisexual poetics.

In the above quotation from Martin, for instance, the assumed clarity with which Whitman defined his sexuality and his poetic mission serves to illustrate Martin's desire to categorize Whitman within a gay aesthetic rather better than it illustrates the experience of reading Whitman's poetry. 'Textual evidence' does indeed show Whitman's awareness of 'the possibilities of sexual expression between men'. The poem 'When I Heard at the Close of Day' from the 'Calamus' section of *Leaves of Grass* clearly defines the poet's desire for the return of his male lover: 'And when I thought how my dear friend my lover was on his way coming, O then I was happy'.[3] The poem's conclusion is a clear celebration of homosexual love:

> For the one I love most lay sleeping by me under the same cover in
> the cool night,
> In the stillness in the autumn moonbeams his face was inclined
> toward me,
> And his arm lay lightly around my breast – and that night I was
> happy.[4]

Whitman's declaration of his homosexual desire becomes here (as throughout the 'Calamus' section generally) the means by which he generates his 'vision' of a 'more democratic . . . American future'. The play of poetic, homosexual and political desires in the poem make it the site from which the terms of Whitman's democratic Romanticism emerge. The poem itself mobilizes and satisfies those desires. In terms of poetic logic, the desire for completion, for narrative closure, that is set up in the opening line's 'still it was not a happy night for me' is satisfied by the final line's 'and that night I was happy'. It is thus that the poem is structured out of desire and its satisfaction. By making his poem into such a structure of desire Whitman is allowed to conflate his homosexual and his democratic desires. Not only does the poem, finally, satisfy the desire for the anticipated embrace of the poet's male lover, but in that embrace it engages Whitman's romance of American democracy. The poem's lovers are themselves held by the embrace of a primal romantic scene of 'autumn moonbeams', in a gesture that mirrors the comradely love described in the poem 'For You O Democracy' from earlier in the 'Calamus' section:[5]

> I will plant companionship thick as trees along all the rivers of
>   America, and along the shores of the great lakes, and all over the
>   prairies;
> I will make inseparable cities with their arms about each other's
>   necks,
>   By the love of comrades,
>   By the manly love of comrades.[6]

Whitman's homosexual desire is thus legitimized because it is seen, as here, to form the basis of his democratic conception of America.

The 'manly love of comrades', as with the two lovers earlier who incline towards each other in the moonlight, articulates a desire to embrace that which is not other. To desire, and thence to embrace, that which is the same produces the ideal of union that lies at the heart of Whitman's ideal of America. Whitman's generic notion of The Poem, in its embodying of such a principle of 'companionship', constitutes, and is constituted by, the constellation of desires that shape America into the *United* States. His poetic embracing of America thus renders cities 'inseparable', the 'continent indissoluble' in the poem's first line, and is underscored by a Romantic reaching after a union of individual and democracy, of poem and nation. Whitman acknowledges this in his Preface to the 1855 edition of *Leaves of Grass* where he writes, 'The United States themselves are essentially the greatest poem.'[7] He thus provides a clear link to Emerson's transcendental romance of America and its poetry. Though Emerson writes that 'America is a poem in our eyes', it is crucially important to note that his conception of the American Poet is very different from that of Whitman.[8] Emerson's poetics relies upon a Romantic model of subjectivity with an assumed unity of self, *through* which will pour universal meanings: 'Doubt not, O Poet, but persist. Say "It is in me, and shall out".'[9] In effect, the transcendental desire for the annihilation of self so sought after by Emerson relies, paradoxically, upon a confirmation of that self even as it becomes the conduit through which pass the universe and its symbols. Self and universe, inner-nature and Nature (that which lies 'out there') are undifferentiated as they all partake of the one subjectivity. This paradox, wherein a mystic penetration of the universe destroys the subject–object opposition upon which it is raised, is expressed in the famous passage from Emerson's essay 'Nature' (1836), where

> Standing on the bare ground, – my head bathed by the blithe air, and
> uplifted into infinite space, – all mean egotism vanishes. I become a
> transparent eyeball; I am nothing; I see all; the currents of the Universal
> Being circulate through me; I am part or particle of God . . . I am the
> lover of uncontained and immortal beauty.[10]

This 'pinnacle of selfhood', as it has been described by Cary Wolfe, which disappears 'at the very moment of its attainment', does so at a point of realization that the self cannot be differentiated from the forces of a universal totality.[11] Selfhood, for Emerson, is no different from Universal Being: it is therefore (albeit paradoxically) assured, total, a lover unified with 'unconditional and immortal beauty'.

For Whitman, however, selfhood is never so assured or unified. This is precisely because it is raised on a poetics of desire, or more accurately, as I shall go on to argue, it is raised upon a bisexual poetics of desire. Thus, despite Robert K. Martin's insistence upon the clarity with which Whitman defines himself in terms of his homosexuality, what does become clear is that Whitman's poetics engages the idea of the self as fluid. This is reflected, as we shall see, in the embracing of both homosexual and heterosexual desire by his text. The pinnacle of selfhood for Whitman, the source of his poetic vitality and seeming radicalism, stems from the fact that his poetic self is always on the point of *becoming* something else. This is unlike Emerson, where self *is* the other and therefore excludes any possibility of differentiating between Self and Universal Being. Whitman's text seeks actively, poetically, to mark the differentiations between which its desiring subject can flow in its act of adhesive union. Whitman's Poet, his subjectivity, renders America the greatest poem as it flows within an American scene, not like Emerson's 'bare ground', but of sharply differentiated objects. His poetic self must distinguish between, in order to flow between, 'the great lakes' and 'the prairies'; between 'rivers', 'trees' and 'cities'; between desire for men and desire for women.

I am thus arguing that, counter to traditional (i.e. Freudian) theories of bisexuality that are predicated upon a notion of undifferentiated desire, Whitman's bisexual poetics is one peculiarly reliant on acts of differentiation. The Freudian model of a primary 'full bisexuality' is built from an idea of essential similarity, not difference, wherein, as Martin Duberman notes, 'bisexuality . . . [is] a biological universal'.[12] According to Judith Butler, Freud's theory of bisexuality abolishes difference by asserting 'the coincidence of two heterosexual desires within a single psyche'.[13] Freud's privileging of heterosexual desire abolishes homosexuality, as Butler notes, by asserting that 'only opposites attract'.[14] Initially this notion of the attraction of opposites may seem to go against the grain of undifferentiated desire at the heart of Freudian formulations of bisexuality. However, we should note that the force of Butler's '*only* opposites attract' implies that in Freud's model the possibility of same-sex (i.e. 'homosexual') attraction is excluded. Differentiation of desires is thus effectively precluded by Freud's bisexual model. This is not the case with Whitman's bisexual poetics: its very fluidity between positions is an attempt to embrace the 'full range of sexual attitudes of his day' described by David Reynolds.[15] Whitman's bisexual poetics does not, then, see men and women as all essentially the same, undifferentiated. What it does display, though, is how such a poetic emerges from, indeed is produced by, an America in which sexuality was a relatively fluid concept able to embrace a range of differing and (to late twentieth-century minds) contradictory emotional, psychological and sexual attitudes. Reynolds has further noted that Whitman's poetry is the product of a culture in which 'gender roles . . . were fluid, elastic, [and] shifting in a time when sexual types had not yet solidified' into the rigid categories demanded by increasing urbanization, commercialism and the expansion of capitalism in the latter part of the nineteenth century.[16] Whitman's bisexual poetics is radical precisely because its fluidity represents an attempt not to surrender to a coercive universalism which (like that of Emerson, or Freud) abolishes difference at the same time that it seems to be being proclaimed. Yet to see Whitman's bisexual poetics working in these terms paves the way for a consideration of how that poetics is a product of capitalist discourses of exchange emerging in nineteenth-century America, and therefore offers a substantially less radical version of America than Whitman would have us believe.

When we turn to the poem 'A Woman Waits for Me' we find clear expression of heterosexual desire, a desire, moreover, that expresses the 'mystic penetration' at the heart of Whitman's vision of American democracy. The poem relies upon the productive interpenetration of various oppositions – 'containing all'/'lacking'; 'bodies'/'souls'; active poet/passive woman waiting; male/female – which are set up in its opening lines. Such interpenetration is not to be found in the comradely poems of the 'Calamus' section. It signals a desire for the embrace of otherness and difference in order to produce its democratic vision of America as a sexual melting-pot. The man and woman of the following lines are caught in a poetic interplay of similarity and difference: 'without shame' both avow 'deliciousness' whilst the gender roles which underpin this democratic vision are, despite Reynolds's claims for fluidity noted above, fixed pretty firmly. The passivity of the woman's waiting is matched by a depiction of her sexuality as something so passive that it has to be assumed in grammatical parallel to that of the man:

A woman waits for me, she contains all, nothing is lacking,
Yet all were lacking if sex were lacking, or if the moisture of the
   right man were lacking.

Sex contains all, bodies, souls,
Meanings, proofs, purities, delicacies, results, promulgations,
Songs, commands, health, pride, and maternal mystery, the seminal
   milk,
All hopes, benefactions, bestowals, all the passions, loves, beauties,
   delights of the earth,
All the governments, judges, gods, follow'd persons of the earth,
These are contained in sex as parts of itself and justification of
   itself.

Without shame the man I like knows and avows the deliciousness of
   his sex,
Without shame the woman I like knows and avows hers.[17]

Given the expression of heterosexual desire here, as well as the sense of rapidly shifting perspectives in poetic subjectivity, it is simply not possible to read Whitman as clearly as Martin's model of him as the gay American poet-hero *par excellence* demands. Martin's (re)production of Whitman assumes, insists upon, a unity of self and sexuality where in fact there is seen to be flux. Thus Martin's model resolves Whitman's sexuality into a state of undifferentiated oneness, whereas Whitman's own model of unity is a state of combined differences, the 'en-mass' of his democratic 'song'. Although Martin goes so far as to acknowledge the fluidity of Whitman's sexual persona – 'This remains true despite the attempts he made, late in his lifetime, to conceal his homosexuality' – he can only close down his argument again before considering the implications of such fluidity. He thus fails to register the degree to which Whitman, as poet of democracy, is a product of the flow of cultural, political and social debates which dominated the discourses of mid-nineteenth-century America.[18] Such fluidity is, however, attested to by the rapid shifts from object to object, abstraction to abstraction, which mark the above passage and are inscribed within a discourse of the sexual, wherein all is 'contain'd in sex as parts of itself'. The trope of egalitarian containment here blunts Whitman's radical edge somewhat because of its complicity with images of America as a melting-pot of equality.

Reading on further in the poem shows how such a complex of sexual, poetic and political discourses is increasingly (as in American culture generally at this time) the subject of a capitalist discourse of production. Whitman's poem becomes a reproductive economy based on heterosexual desire. Within such a system, America, its poetry and especially its sexualities become cultural commodities. The mystic penetration of the universe that will engender a new American sense of nationhood becomes a matter of saving and capital, of deposit and withdrawal. Semen, like money, is spent and thus Whitman's democratic vision realizes itself as a product of America's burgeoning commercialism.

> I pour the stuff to start sons and daughters fit for these States, I
>   press with slow rude muscle,
> I brace myself effectually, I listen to no entreaties,
> I dare not withdraw till I deposit what has so long accumulated
>   within me.
>
> Through you I drain the pent-up rivers of myself,
> In you I wrap a thousand onward years,
> On you I graft the grafts of the best-beloved of me and America,
> The drops I distil upon you shall grow fierce and athletic girls, new
>   artists, musicians, and singers,
> The babes I beget upon you are to beget babes in their turn,
> I shall demand perfect men and women out of my love-spendings,
> I shall expect them to interpenetrate with others, as I and you
>   interpenetrate now.[19]

Here the fluidity of poetic exchange that is deeply rooted in Whitman's sexuality begins to give way to a fixing of meaning within a capitalist discourse of exchange. The process witnessed in the poem thus mirrors the claim of John D'Emilio and Estelle B. Freedman that 'sexuality . . . moved into the world of commerce' over the course of the nineteenth century in America.[20] Such elision of Whitman's discourses of sexuality and reproduction by that of commerce witnesses also what Stephen Heath has described as the way in which, in the Victorian age, '*sexuality*' and 'the sexual' were 'beginning to be named, and realized and pulled into a hesitant focus'.[21] It is against such a pulling into focus that the fluidity of poetic and sexual personae that mark Whitman's bisexual poetics attempts to work. In this sense Whitman's bisexual poetics, with its fluidity of exchange between the objects of its desired America, between poetic selves, and between desire for men and for women, can be seen to set the terms for Camille Paglia's definition of bisexuality as 'a liberation from false, narrow categories'.[22] Whereas Paglia's model of liberation seems grounded in free market capitalism, Whitman's historical position means that his bisexual poetics emerges at the start of such discourses. Although it was a site for a radical critique of consumer capitalism as it was emerging in the nineteenth century, its reliance upon a model of exchange, and the way in which the reproductive economy of the passage above turns from the sexual to the financial, indicate the degree to which it is a product of the increasingly dominant discourse of capitalism at the time. What we witness therefore in Whitman's bisexual poetics is not only the 'production of sexuality', as Foucault would have it but also the production of the idea of 'American poet' as a kind of rebel-hero out of the capitalist discourses it seeks to challenge.[23]

In the hundred years between the publication of the first edition of Whitman's *Leaves of Grass* (1855) and the publication of Allen Ginsberg's *Howl and Other Poems* (1956) the production of sexuality within capitalism solidified. Indeed sexuality in the 1950s was, superficially at least, expressed in terms of rigidity and conformity to mainstream ideals of consumer desire. This culture is one which, according to D'Emilio and Freedman, 'has regulated sexuality in both overt and subtle ways', a culture where 'the media, for instance, are saturated with sexual images that promise free choice but in fact channel individuals toward particular visions of sexual happiness, often closely linked to the purchase of consumer goods.'[24] Allen Ginsberg's depiction of Whitman as rebel poet and sexual hero is conducted within a site that makes ironic the mass consumer capitalism of 1950s America. In the poem 'A Supermarket in California', from the collection *Howl and Other Poems* (1956), Whitman figures ambiguously. Amongst the supermarket shelves he becomes a poetic commodity, an image, consumed by the dominant culture of America. At the same time, though, this occurs because of his rebellious sexuality. His homosexual desire, which goes against the grain of American supermarket culture, is discovered in the act of desiring the products of that culture:

> What thoughts I have of you tonight, Walt Whitman, for I walked
>   down the sidestreets under the trees with a headache self-
>   conscious looking at the full moon.
> In my hungry fatigue, and shopping for images, I went into the neon
>   fruit supermarket, dreaming of your enumerations!
> What peaches and what penumbras! Whole families shopping at
>   night! Aisles full of husbands! Wives in the avocados, babies in
>   the tomatoes![25]

Whitman is here less of a rebel outsider than a poetic father-figure who declares a curious allegiance to an America of fathers, families and fruit. Whitman's heroism here, the sense of him as culturally important, becomes a model for the rhetoric of production and consumption of popular, commercial, American culture of the 1950s. This takes place within the recognizable utopian discourse of America as the land of bountiful riches. The text produces its poetic heroes within a landscape – a supermarket – which in turn represents a commercial appropriation of discourses which have, even before its discovery, associated America with material riches and fruitfulness. In this America the natural has succumbed to the commercial, as we see it regimented into stacks of cans, cuts of meat, regulated desires and unanswerable questions. The rather surreal imagery of 'neon fruit'; of being 'together' whilst 'solitary'; and of 'frozen delicacies' marks Ginsberg's language with an irony not seen in Whitman's poetry. Such ironies emerge from the poem's expression of oppositional sexuality:

> I saw you, Walt Whitman, childless, lonely old grubber, poking
>   among the meats in the refrigerator and eyeing the grocery boys.
> I heard you asking questions of each: Who killed the pork chops?
>   What price bananas? Are you my Angel?
> I wandered in and out of the brilliant stacks of cans following you,
>   and followed in my imagination by the store detective.
> We strode down the open corridors together in our solitary fancy
>   tasting artichokes, possessing every frozen delicacy, and never
>   passing the cashier.[26]

The desire for freedom, for an unregulated satisfaction of desires, signalled by the wish not to pass the cashier is ironically undercut by the imaginary policing of that desire by the store detective. Ginsberg asserts here that Whitman, his poetics, and his sexuality are commodities which we consume in Ginsberg's new poetic text. Whitman is neatly packaged as the poet of homosexual desire: 'I saw you, Walt Whitman, childless, lonely old grubber, poking among the meats in the refrigerator and eyeing the grocery boys'. Any threat he may pose as a 'childless', thus non-productive, father-figure is swiftly consumed by the desire to assert his role as poetic hero presiding over a mythical America. Ginsberg's much-vaunted rebellious sexual heroism, of which Whitman is the model, is not a liberation but a myth. It takes place within the discourses of conformity and commodity which dominated the capitalist enterprise of 1950s America. Poet becomes popular hero only through the conspicuous consumption of old myths of heroism that, in turn, reinscribe the idea of America as having lost its way, passed into forgetfulness:

> Will we stroll dreaming of the lost America of love past blue
>   automobiles in driveways, home to our silent cottage?
> Ah, dear father, graybeard, lonely old courage-teacher, what
>   America did you have when Charon quit poling his ferry and
>   you got out on a smoking bank and stood watching the boat
>   disappear on the black waters of Lethe?[27]

This poetic odyssey ends in a new mode of conformity, a romanticized sexuality of rebellious heroism.

Ginsberg's bisexual poetics emerges from these discourses of consumer capitalism. The ironic and ambiguous figuring of Whitman in this poem is at the heart of this emergence. For if it is fluidity that is the defining characteristic of Whitman's bisexual poetics, then it is rigidity which defines Ginsberg's. His bisexual poetics is the product of the sets of binary oppositions that characterized American conformity in the 1950s: American or un-American; capitalist or communist; mainstream culture or counterculture; heterosexual or homosexual, etc. Ginsberg's bisexual poetics may thus be defined in much the same way as Martin Duberman has defined bisexuality, as that which suggests 'each of us may contain within ourselves all of those supposed opposites we've been taught to divide humanity into'.[28] However ironic Ginsberg's bisexual poetics may appear, though, it is clear that it is produced out of the sexual discourses of the dominant culture. At the time of the publication of *Howl and Other Poems* such discourses mobilized an ethos of family, conformity, and consumption by recourse to a rapidly expanding advertising industry which provided white middle-class America, especially, with images 'designed' as D'Emilio and Freedman note 'to stimulate male erotic fantasies' about women, or 'to persuade women to spend by emphasizing the personal allure which consumer items would obtain for them'.[29] Such exclusively heterosexual imagery recognizes the power of sexual discourses at the time whilst also marking the limited sense of desire that they encompass. The ironies implicit in such sexual discourses are marked by Ginsberg's poetry. Its language of ironic juxtapositions demonstrate how it operates within heterosexual models of American popular culture in order to articulate its sense of radical homosexuality.

For both Ginsberg and Whitman their respective bisexual poetics is at the heart of their radical poetic agendas. This is because it allows them to explore the constellation of personal and national identities within the concept, and production, of America as heroic poem. This process is by no means uncomplicated for them. It becomes an extended meditation upon the fluidity of selfhood in Whitman's 'Song of Myself', and a troubled and parodic set of confessions in Ginsberg's 'America'. I shall turn briefly to these poems, then, as a means of examining how a bisexual poetics can become the site for challenging the dominant discourses of America, even as it is produced out of such discourses.

Throughout 'Song of Myself' Whitman's bisexual poetics becomes the site for an exploration of the complex and fluid interpenetration of ideas of personal identity, American democracy and sexuality. The poem's opening lines present poetic and personal identities in problematic relation as they seek to unfix ideas of stable identity and easy categorization:

> I celebrate myself, and sing myself,
> And what I assume you shall assume,
> For every atom belonging to me as good belongs to you.
>
> I loafe and invite my soul,
> I lean and loafe at my ease observing a spear of summer grass.
>
> My tongue, every atom of my blood, form'd from this soil, this air,
> Born here of parents born here from parents the same, and their
>   parents the same,
> I, now thirty-seven years old in perfect health begin,
> Hoping to cease not till death.[30]

Coming at the start of the poem, these lines set up the terms by which the poem invents its poetic persona. The poem invites the reader into a radical investigation of selfhood. It is not clear who is speaking, or what terms of reciprocity between poem and reader are being established. What seems initially simple – a loafing invitation – is revealed on closer inspection as complex and ambiguous. This is reflected in the precarious balance set up between 'I' and 'you' in the first three lines, in the ambiguity of the repeated word 'assume', and in the use of the word 'spear' as a metaphor for grass-blade. These difficulties represent less of a bullying or coercive tactic than one that is designed to include the reader in the production of the text itself. The body of the text becomes a space in which a debate about the embodiment of personal and political identity is enacted with the reader. We are asked to consider who 'myself' might be, and how that identity springs from 'this soil, this air' and is born 'here'. Again America as text and as soil is the ground for a reproductive economy similar to that of 'A Woman Waits for Me'. The invention of this poetic identity is thus intimately, and textually, interwoven with a search for a specifically American identity.

What is assumed – that identity is stable – is here undercut by the very slipperiness of selfhood in its act of self-creation. The poet, America as a poem, is not located in any one solid body but in the continually shifting body of the text that is in front of us as we read. The poem asks us to assume, not in the sense of taking something for granted, but in the sense of our being willing to become something else, to desire change.[31] 'Song of Myself' thus sets up the desire for an identity that it recognizes as fluid, that sees the body as the site in which apparently conflicting desires can reside to radical and liberating effect:

> I am the poet of the Body and I am the poet of the Soul,
> The pleasures of heaven are with me and the pains of hell are with
>   me
> The first I graft and increase upon myself, the latter I translate into
>   a new tongue.

> I am the poet of the woman the same as the man,
> And I say it is as great to be a woman as to be a man
> And I say there is nothing greater than the mother of men.[32]

The identity of the poet is built here, as in the earlier passages from Whitman, not from a hopelessly universalist poetics of desire but from the fluid interpenetration between seeming opposites. Whitman here becomes the poet of a radical re-vision of America because his bisexual poetics allows, or even demands that, his identity as the 'poet of the Body' is in fluid and productive exchange with the body of his text, and with America's body politic. When the poet finally names himself more than a third of the way through 'Song of Myself', the constellation of somatic, poetic and democratic concerns is marked by Whitman's radical construction and voicing of sexuality in the poem.

> Walt Whitman, a kosmos, of Manhattan the son,
> Turbulent, fleshy, sensual, eating, drinking and breeding,
> No sentimentalist, no stander above men and women or apart from
>   them,
> No more modest than immodest.

> Unscrew the locks from the doors!
> Unscrew the doors themselves from the jambs! . . .

> Through me the afflatus surging and surging, through me the
>   current and index.
> I speak the password primeval, I give the sign of democracy,
> By God! I will accept nothing which all cannot have their
>   counterpart of in the same terms. . . .

> Through me forbidden voices,
> Voices of sexes and of lusts, voices veil'd and I remove the veil,
> Voices indecent by me clarified and transfigur'd.[33]

The poetic self here opens up the poem as a discursive and desiring site through which surge many different voices that, taken together, constitute 'the sign of democracy'. Whitman's fluidity of language and voice, his poetic lists and his radical defiance of rigid patterns of thought all point to a bisexual poetics that conforms to Paglia's fluidity model of bisexuality. In this sense, then, his poetics struggles with his concept of American democracy. Whilst seeking to preserve difference, to plot a range of desires, it seems also to be at the point of surrendering to the erasure of social, ethnic and sexual difference implied by America's ideological conception of itself as melting-pot.

Such fluidity of identity and sexual desire is explicitly presented in section 11 of the poem. The poet watches the desiring woman in her 'fine house by the rise of the bank' as she watches, desires and (in her imagination) passes her hand over the 'Twenty-eight young men [who] bathe by the shore'. The desire of the lonesome woman and the desire of the poet become one within the poem's imagery of fluidity:

> The beards of the young men glisten'd with wet, it ran from their
>   long hair,
> Little streams pass'd all over their bodies.
>
> An unseen hand also pass'd over their bodies,
> It descended tremblingly from their temples and ribs.
>
> The young men float on their backs, their white bellies bulge to the
>   sun, they do not ask who seizes fast to them,
> They do not know who puffs and declines with pendant and
>   bending arch,
> They do not think whom they souse with spray.[34]

Whitman's bisexual poetics thus becomes the means through which can flow a complex of meanings which extend outwards from the purely sexual. It is possible to see the woman as a figure of fate, or death; she is the figure for women's emancipation; and she signals male desires, or female. The spermatic imagery of her being 'soused with spray' represents the creative poetic act, the procreative sexual act, as well as signalling a wasted 'expenditure' on pleasure of Whitman's precious 'fatherstuff of nations'. The passage also generates a specifically American political meaning, by representing the admitting of the twenty-ninth state, Texas, into the Union in 1845. As a rich and complex vehicle of several interpenetrative meanings Whitman's poetics thus allows him to sing and celebrate his democratic American self. His allegiance is to a radicalized vision of America that, like his bisexual model, 'contain[s] multitudes'.[35]

In his poetic efforts to 'contain multitudes', though, Whitman can be seen very much to be the white man. In the passage above the woman's role (as in 'A Woman Waits for Me') is passive. Her desire to escape the class-bound decorum by which she finds herself contained in her 'fine house' is radical only in her imagination. She remains contained by images of her status and sex: 'She hides handsome and richly drest aft the blinds of the window'. And blind, too, seems Whitman to the full implications of the whiteness of the twenty-eight young men. His vision of American democracy is severely limited if what it contains is multitudes of white men surprisingly similar in looks, with their beards and flowing hair, to Walt himself as he appears in the daguerreotype frontispiece to the 1855 edition of *Leaves of Grass*. Even though Whitman details his harbouring of a runaway slave in lines immediately preceding these, the radicalism of this gesture is somewhat undercut by its sentimental paternalism: '[I] gave him some coarse, clean clothes, / And remember well his revolving eyes and his awkwardness, / And remember putting plasters on the galls of his neck and ankles'.[36] Thus Whitman's bisexual poetics registers a radicalism that its production out of the discourses and ideology of white nineteenth-century America violates.

Ginsberg's pledge of allegiance to America takes the form of a series of troubled confessions in the poem 'America' from the *Howl* collection. At the same time that the House Un-American Activities Committee (HUAC) acted as confessor to square America, Ginsberg's text confesses allegiance to a hip America of sexual bravado. 'America' is the flipside to the McCarthyist conformity of which it is a curious product. The poem leads Ginsberg to a realization of his assimilation by America; he is consumed by it just as he is its product: 'America I've given you all and now I'm nothing. . . . / . . . America I used to be a communist when I was a kid I'm not sorry. . . . / . . . It occurs to me that I am America.'[37] To see Ginsberg, therefore, as an 'oppositional sign' to the dominant ideology of America in the 1950s is to miss the point slightly.[38] The oppositional stance of Ginsberg's poetic disguises a troubled allegiance to American culture. The final line of 'America', an ironic nod to Emerson, demonstrates the contingency of discourses of sexuality and of American identity: 'America, I'm putting my queer shoulder to the wheel'.[39] This line develops the language of ironic juxtaposition seen in 'Supermarket in California' and upon which Ginsberg's bisexual poetics is raised. As there, where the manufactured and the natural are brought together in the 'neon fruit supermarket', such imagery seeks to combine perceived opposites. The 'queer' outsider who puts his shoulder to America's wheel is thus assimilated by the mainstream ideology because of, rather than in spite of, his oppositional sexuality.

Such a fascination with the consumption and deployment of sexuality is a dominant feature of American culture of the time. The bestseller status achieved in the 1950s by the two Kinsey reports into sexual behaviour further confirms the fascination of American popular culture with accounts of the 'nightmare world' of sex.[40] Advertisers used the name of Kinsey to promote novels and plays, music and film on the assumption that sex sells. Another aspect of this fascination was the proliferation of 'Kinsey imposters' demanding intimate sexual details over the telephone from unsuspecting housewives. One woman victimized in this way said of her fraudulent Kinsey investigator that 'He seemed awfully scientific and sounded just like a doctor'.[41]

In the case of the Kinsey reports, then, interest in sex is legitimized by recourse to a language of scientific rationality in which sexuality is described and treated as a commodity produced and consumed by the dominant ideology.

Howl and Other Poems was itself legitimized at its 1957 trial for obscenity in San Francisco by the words of Judge Clayton Horn. The trial, thus, ironically marks the process of assimilation of marginal cultures into and by the mainstream in 1950s America. Daily news coverage of the trial propelled Allen Ginsberg into the national consciousness and transformed him from rebel poet to popular hero, thereby assuring sales of the book, which sold out its first edition of forty thousand copies immediately after it was exonerated by Judge Clayton Horn.[42] Horn's summing-up at the trial demonstrates neatly how the tensions between cultures of the margin and of the centre, tensions which Ginsberg's poetic seeks to exploit, are effectively obliterated in a dominant language of quasi-scientific rationality:

> I do not believe that 'Howl' is without redeeming social importance. The first part of 'Howl' presents a picture of a nightmare world; the second part is an indictment of those elements in modern society destructive of the best qualities of human nature; such elements are predominantly identified as materialism, conformity, and mechanization leading toward war. The third part presents a picture of an individual who is a specific representation of what the author conceives as a general condition.[43]

It is through such language that the rebel poet is redeemed as popular hero. He is seen as an heroic figure because of his poem's anguished and detailed confessions from the 'nightmare world' of postwar American society. However, such legal justifications place Ginsberg as popular hero squarely within the discourses of the mainstream, rather than at its margins. The redeeming social importance of the poem is seen to result from its atmosphere of confession and repression, an atmosphere which it shares with the 'general condition' of the America from which it springs.

The ironies and ambiguous allegiance to America that mark Ginsberg's bisexual poetics are the product of a culture that is deeply bifurcated, that is grounded in division and the promulgation of binary oppositions. Though the tension between confession and repression which characterizes American culture of the time is also seen to produce Ginsberg's poetics, it is possible to see, however, that such a poetics attempts to re-envision an America of poetic heroism and radicalism out of those very structures of repressive rigidity. The harsh conformities of the Cold War and the McCarthy hearings, the demands for public confession of the HUAC committee alongside the execution of the Rosenbergs and the conviction of Alger Hiss, all contributed to a dominant culture of secrecy and suspicion which in turn generated the need, as Michael Davidson has noted, for 'oppositional heroes'.[44] Ginsberg's role as a kind of poet-hero is therefore not entirely surprising: not only does it arise out of the dominant culture but its rhetoric of confession stems directly from the demands of that culture. *Howl and Other Poems* complicates the act of rebelling against that culture by deploying its rhetoric.

Ginsberg arises as a popular hero, a poet struggling to rewrite the text of America, out of the tensions, fears and social conformities of postwar America. To assert that the fabrication of Ginsberg's status as Whitman-like poet-hero is deeply enmeshed within a poetics of bisexuality is to assert that *Howl and Other Poems* is far from being a clear-cut text of radical sexual liberation. Despite its explicitly sexual material, and its apparent declaration of sexual independence, it conforms deeply to a model of the construction and deployment of sexuality within the discourses of capitalism. Its fascination both with popular heroes and with sexuality mark it clearly as a product of 1950s America. In effect, it is a text which exemplifies the production and consumption of sex and heroism as commodities of American popular culture. What we see in the text is the way in which marginalized discourses are absorbed into the mainstream. As in so many other 1950s texts, we see in it the figure of the sexual rebel become popular hero. This, then, marks the beginnings of what Stephen Heath has described as 'The Sexual Fix'. He writes that:

> The much-vaunted 'liberation' of sexuality, our triumphant emergence from the 'dark-ages', is . . . not a liberation but a myth, an ideology, the definition of a new mode of conformity (that can be understood, moreover, in relation to the capitalist system, the production of a commodity 'sexuality').[45]

Ginsberg's text, with its descriptions of 'The tongue and cock and hand and asshole holy' and its litany of heroic homosexual lovers – 'Holy Peter holy Allen holy Solomon holy Lucien holy Kerouac holy Huncke holy Burroughs holy Cassady holy the unknown buggered and suffering beggars holy the hideous human angels!'— seems triumphantly to herald such an 'emergence' into liberated sexuality in the 1950s.[46] The myths that sustain a 'new mode of conformity' in Ginsberg's sexual-heroic text are precisely those upon which Ginsberg's bisexual poetic can be seen to rest.

Ginsberg's bisexual poetic thus allows him to address questions of American identity, because of American popular culture's reliance on discourses of sexuality. Ginsberg's appeal is that of the transgressor: he's a rebel, he's queer. This demonstrates how a marginalized subculture is absorbed into, contained by, mainstream ideology in which his desire to 'contain' America ends with his containment by America. However, it also shows, as we shall see, how such containment can become a site, albeit tentative and ironized, for a turning of straight America's myths against themselves. The play between dominant and marginalized cultures embedded in Ginsberg's poetics creates an ambiguous space in which 'queer shoulders' can be 'put to the wheel'. Thus the gay heroes that appear in Ginsberg's text, like Whitman in a supermarket, are absorbed into the popular heroisms of straight America, whilst that process of absorption leaves traces that disturb the superficial equanimity of that vision of America. The sexual heroism of Ginsberg's text, his declaration of sexual independence, exposes in a particularly Foucauldian way the dependence of straight, 'square', America's popular culture upon the discourses of its sexual dissidents.[47]

We are catapulted into an America of just such sexual and linguistic appropriation in the opening lines of the poem 'Howl'. Ginsberg's Beat argot provides the site within which discourses of power and pleasure become co-extensive with a search for a 'true' America. The protagonist is seen as a representative American hero because of the overlapping and reinforcement between the mythologies of 'square' America and its 'hip' subcultures:[48]

> I saw the best minds of my generation destroyed by madness,
>   starving hysterical naked,
> dragging themselves through the negro streets at dawn looking for
>   an angry fix, angelheaded hipsters burning for the ancient
>   heavenly connection to the starry dynamo in the machinery of
>   night,
> who poverty and tatters and hollow-eyed and high sat up smoking
>   in the supernatural darkness of cold-water flats floating across
>   the tops of cities contemplating jazz.[49]

Paradoxically the voice of conformity speaks through that of a representative rebel hero. This voice speaks consciously for a new generation on an heroic quest through a ravaged America. It bears witness to a 'destroyed' and 'hysterical' American urban landscape and declares allegiance to a mythical America, a transcendental new world of youths 'burning for the heavenly connection to the starry dynamo in the machinery of the night'. However rebellious this may seem, it is rebellious in a very traditional way. The sentiments are Emersonian, they employ a Whitman-like verse form, and are expressed in a scientific language that conflates sexual desire and electromagnetic power much like that which proved so entrancing to the prototypically modern American Henry Adams.[50]

It is in its proliferation of sexual discourses that the poem reflects most strongly its search for a mythical American connectedness. This, in turn, helps to demonstrate Foucault's 'repressive hypothesis' whereby a culture of seeming sexual repression invests much of its cultural and economic power in discourses and representations of sex and sexuality.[51] The heroes of 'Howl' are described as sexual rebels

> who let themselves be fucked in the ass by saintly motorcyclists, and
>   screamed with joy,
> who blew and were blown by those human seraphim, the sailors,
>   caresses of Atlantic and Caribbean love,

> who balled in the morning in the evenings in rosegardens and the
>   grass of public parks and cemeteries scattering their semen freely
>   to whomever come who may,
> who hiccuped endlessly trying to giggle but wound up with a sob
>   behind a partition in a Turkish Bath when the blond & naked
>   angel came to pierce them with a sword.[52]

Yet such language, though rebelliously sexual, is again traditionally American. The models for Ginsberg's heroes are established as traditional icons of American identity and popular culture. Frontiersmen are translated into 'saintly motorcyclists' pushing back sexual boundaries, and the uniting of the continent, north and south, is realized in the 'caresses of Atlantic and Caribbean love' of heroic sailors. This is an America of myth where sexual encounters are described in terms usually reserved for the conqueror heroes of its popular culture. We should not forget, however, that these were indeed *conqueror* heroes. The myths of freedom which are articulated in the image of the frontiersman disguise a history of the displacement of America's native peoples. The deployment of sexuality within the discourse of American popular heroism which is no more apparent than in the poem's description of Neal Cassady is thus fraught with an ambiguity that Ginsberg's bisexual poetics can raise but cannot resolve. Cassady is presented as an American Adonis, the 'secret hero of these poems', because his sexual conquests come to represent the conquest of the American landscape. He is seen as a great hero of the west, blazing a sexual trail into the heart of America. Sexuality and American myth are united in this figure

> who sweetened the snatches of a million girls trembling in the
>   sunset, and were red eyed in the morning but prepared to
>   sweeten the snatch of the sunrise, flashing buttocks under barns
>   and naked in the lake,
> who went out whoring through Colorado in myriad stolen night-
>   cars, N.C., secret hero of these poems, cocksman and Adonis of
>   Denver – joy to the memory of his innumerable lays of girls in
>   empty lots & diner backyards, moviehouses' rickety rows, on
>   mountaintops in caves or with gaunt waitresses in familiar
>   roadside lonely petticoat upliftings & especially secret gas-
>   station solipsisms of johns, & hometown alleys too.[53]

This is exactly the sort of popular hero who deserves, according to Ginsberg, poetic accolades. Sexual and poetic heroism are clearly linked when, three lines later, the protagonist declares of his rebel heroes 'their heads shall be crowned with laurel in oblivion'.[54] However, any suggestion of Cassady's gay sexuality (or even bisexuality) is almost totally subsumed by such vehemently heterosexual heroism. America itself is feminized at the hands of its conqueror hero as he prepares to 'sweeten the snatch of the sunrise'. Archetypal images of the American landscape such as sunset, sunrise and distant horizons operate, as Annette Kolodny argues, through metaphors of the sexual exploration of the female body.[55] As heroic poem, then, America is traditionally a text of heterosexual male desire. Thus Ginsberg's confession of sexual otherness, of the homosexual undercurrent to Beat life in the 1950s, and his portrayal of it as heroic, is couched in a language of tantalizing secrecy. Cassady is thus 'N.C., secret hero of these poems' who indulges, in between his heroic heterosexual conquests, in 'secret gas-station solipsisms of johns'. To write of Cassady and himself as popular heroes, Ginsberg's sexual dissidence, his gay identity, is absorbed into the discourses of mainstream America in his deployment of a bisexual poetics. We may notice, though, that Cassady's heroism is 'especially' apparent in the scenes of his secret homosexual encounters. Ginsberg's bisexual poetics is, thus, raised upon a language and an imagery of ironic juxtaposition that acknowledges the sets of oppositions by which it is constituted and which it finds, ultimately, troubling because such oppositions reconfirm mainstream myths of American identity. Like Whitman's loneliness in the Californian supermarket, from which America can learn 'courage', perhaps Ginsberg is suggesting that America's sexual and political desires, its conspicuous consumption, are marked by discourses of its sexual outsiders. It is in his bisexual poetics that Ginsberg attempts therefore to reradicalize Whitman's democratic vision of America as heroic poem whilst recognizing his complicity with mainstream American ideology.

The poems of *Howl* thus contribute to a litany of displacement in which the heroism of Ginsberg's desire to confess his sexual identity is complicated by his attempt to define himself as a prototypical American hero. Rather than simply valorizing his gay identity in opposition to the repressive structures of American society of the 1950s, as argued by Catharine Stimpson, his poetry reveals far deeper entanglements between sexuality, popular culture and American identity. Stimpson's argument allows no differentiation between America as ideal and as reality – something which Ginsberg's text continually struggles to express. For Stimpson the Beats, like Walt Whitman a century before them, entertain a vision of an utopian American society and culture that is attainable through acts of rebellion. This, she argues, is a result of their sexual dissidence which challenges cultural conformism. She writes: 'The Beats remind us of the value of free speech as a weapon against taboos; of the force of culture itself in the struggle against social, political, psychic, and cultural constrictions . . . their language must become our vision.'[56] Such easy romanticizing of the Beats as rebel heroes rests heavily upon this elision of 'language' and 'vision'. The Beat vision, implies Stimpson, liberates our language from America's harsh conformities. Yet it is precisely those conformities which we have seen to provide Ginsberg with the terms for his sexually rebellious text; as Stimpson herself notes: 'He [Ginsberg] both transgresses against and accepts tradition'.[57] Ginsberg's language, then, is not so much a 'weapon against taboos' as that which is defined by, and has force, precisely because of those taboos. By embracing his status as rebel hero he is, albeit ambivalently, accepting the terms and the force of mainstream American culture itself. But in such an act of poetic acceptance are traced the terms for the subversion of that America, even as it traces the terms of his bisexual poetics: 'America I'm putting my queer shoulder to the wheel.'

Notes

1. It is necessary to make clear that, in line with the usage of Whitman and Ginsberg, 'America' throughout this chapter designates 'The United States of America'. It should not, therefore, be confused either with North America (which includes Canada) or with the continents of America. Such conventional shorthand conveys a sense of the power of America's political presence over and above the mere fact of its geographical presence in the world.
2. Robert K. Martin, *The Homosexual Tradition in American Poetry* (Austin and London: University of Texas Press, 1979), pp. xvi–xvii.
3. Walt Whitman, *The Complete Poems*, ed. Francis Murphy (1975; rpt London: Penguin Books, 1986), p. 155. Subsequent references to Whitman's work will be to this edition, unless otherwise stated.
4. *Ibid.*, p. 156.
5. An interesting parallel to this same-sex embrace as a model for the romantic embrace of American democratic idealism is found in the fourth chapter of Melville's *Moby Dick*, 'The Counterpane'.
6. Whitman, *Complete Poems*, p. 150.
7. *Ibid.*, p. 741.
8. Ralph Waldo Emerson, 'The Poet' (1844), in Sherman Paul (ed.), *Emerson's Essays* (London: J. M. Dent, 1980), p. 224. The essay is also reprinted in Paul Lauter *et al.* (eds), *The Heath Anthology of American Literature*, second edition, vol. 1 (Lexington: Heath, 1994), pp. 1566–81.
9. Emerson, 'The Poet', p. 226. And Lauter *et al.* (eds), *Heath Anthology*, p. 1580.
10. Emerson, 'Nature' (1836), in Lauter *et al.* (eds), *Heath Anthology*, p. 1504.
11. Cary Wolfe, *The Limits of American Literary Ideology in Pound and Emerson* (Cambridge: Cambridge University Press, 1993), p. 5.
12. Martin Duberman, *About Time: Exploring the Gay Past* (rev. ed. New York: Meridian, 1991), p. 289. The essay (pp. 288-304) from which this quotation is taken is an informative discussion of the history and changing theories of bisexuality. See also Jonathan Dollimore, *Sexual Dissidence: Augustine to Wilde, Freud to Foucault* (Oxford: Clarendon Press, 1991), p. 217, for a discussion of Freud's theory of the 'polymorphous perverse' and its relation to his notion of 'full bisexuality'.
13. Judith Butler, *Gender Trouble: Feminism and the Subversion of Identity* (London: Routledge & Kegan Paul, 1990), p. 61.
14. Butler, *Gender Trouble*, p. 61. See also Dollimore, *Sexual Dissidence*, p. 255.
15. David S. Reynolds, *Walt Whitman's America: A Cultural Biography* (New York: Alfred A. Knopf, 1995), p. 199.
16. *Ibid.*, pp. 198–9.
17. Whitman, *Complete Poems*, p. 136.
18. This is the basic assumption of Reynolds's *Walt Whitman's America*.
19. Whitman, *Complete Poems*, p. 137.
20. John D'Emilio and Estelle B. Freedman, *Intimate Matters: A History of Sexuality in America* (New York: Harper & Row, 1988), p. 111.
21. Stephen Heath, *The Sexual Fix* (Basingstoke: Macmillan, 1982), p. 16.
22. Camille Paglia, *Sex, Art and American Culture: Essays* (Harmondsworth: Viking Penguin, 1992), p. 11.
23. Michel Foucault, *The History of Sexuality: Volume 1: An Introduction*, trans. Robert Hurley (1979; rpt Harmondsworth: Penguin, 1990), pp. 113–14, especially, details the production of sexuality within capitalism.

24. D'Emilio and Freedman, *Intimate Matters*, p. xvii. See also John D'Emilio, 'Capitalism and Gay Identity', in Ann Snitow, Christine Stansell and Sharon Thompson (eds), *Powers of Desire: The Politics of Sexuality* (New York: Monthly Review Press, 1983), pp. 100–13.

25. Allen Ginsberg, *Collected Poems, 1947-1980* (Harmondsworth: Viking Penguin, 1984), p. 136.

26. *Ibid.*

27. *Ibid.*

28. Duberman, *About Time*, p. 300.

29. D'Emilio and Freedman, *Intimate Matters*, pp. 279 and 278. See also John D'Emilio, 'Gay Politics and Community in San Francisco since World War II', in Martin Duberman, Martha Vicinus and George Chauncey (eds), *Hidden from History: Reclaiming the Gay and Lesbian Past* (Harmondsworth: Penguin, 1991), pp. 456-73, which analyses the emergence of San Francisco's gay subculture from the discourses of mainstream, straight America of the post-war years.

30. 'Song of Myself' (1891–2 version), Section 1, in Whitman, *Complete Poems*, p. 63.

31. See M. Jimmie Killingsworth, *Whitman's Poetry of the Body: Sexuality, Politics, and the Text* (Chapel Hill: University of North Carolina Press, 1989), who writes of 'Song of Myself' (p. xvii): 'In an effort analogous to social revolution, the poet subverts the accepted conventions of poetic practice to reveal a new literature whose rhetorical strength is founded in a figural representation of bodily forces that overwhelm the rational, self-defensive tactics of conventional thinking and writing.'

32. 'Song of Myself' (1891–2 version), Section 21, in Whitman, *Complete Poems*, p. 83.

33. 'Song of Myself' (1891–2 version), Section 24, in Whitman, *Complete Poems*, pp. 86-7. The 1855 version of the poem makes even more explicit the interpenetration of Whitman's poetic and American identities within the sexual and somatic. He writes there: 'Walt Whitman, an American, one of the roughs, a kosmos, / Disorderly, fleshly and sensual . . . / Through me many long dumb voices, / Voices of the interminable generations of slaves, / Voices of prostitutes and of deformed persons . . .' etc. See Whitman, *Complete Poems*, 'Appendix 4', pp. 698–9.

34. 'Song of Myself' (1891–2 version), in Whitman, *Complete Poems*, p. 73.

35. The quotation is from Section 51 of 'Song of Myself' (1891–2 version), in Whitman, *Complete Poems*, p. 123.

36. 'Song of Myself' (1891–2 version), in Whitman, *Complete Poems*, p. 72.

37. Ginsberg, *Collected Poems*, pp. 146–7.

38. Michael Davidson, *The San Francisco Renaissance: Poetics and Community at Mid-Century* (Cambridge: Cambridge University Press, 1989), describes (p. 27) the impact of the writers of the San Francisco Renaissance in the political arena as stemming from their 'collective role as a kind of oppositional sign'.

39. At the close of his essay 'Self-Reliance' (1841) Emerson calls for Americans to put their shoulders to the wheel of chance. Their strength of self-reliance will still its turning and herald 'the triumph of principles'. In Lauter *et al.* (eds), *Heath Anthology*, p. 1558.

40. Alfred C. Kinsey, Wardell B. Pomeroy and Clyde E. Martin, *Sexual Behavior in the Human Male* (Philadelphia: W. B. Saunders, 1948); and Alfred C. Kinsey, Wardell B. Pomeroy, Clyde E. Martin, and Paul H. Gebhard, *Sexual Behavior in the Human Female* (Philadelphia: W. B. Saunders, 1953). The impact and reception of these reports are discussed in Jerome Himelhoch and Sylvia Fleis Fava (eds), *Sexual Behavior in American Society: An Appraisal of the First Two Kinsey Reports* (New York: W. W. Norton, 1955), esp. Section X, 'The Reaction of Public Opinion and Mass Media to the Kinsey Studies', pp. 364-85. Ginsberg himself was interviewed in New York by Kinsey: see Barry Miles, *Ginsberg: A Biography* (New York: Simon & Schuster, 1989), p. 73.

41. See Himelhoch *et al.* (eds), *Sexual Behavior*, p. 383.

42. Miles, *Ginsberg*, p. 228.

43. Quoted from J. W. Ehrlich (ed.), *Howl of the Censor* (San Carlos, CA: Nourse Publishing Co., 1961), p. 119.

44. Michael Davidson, *The San Francisco Renaissance*, pp. 24–31. Alger Hiss, a high-ranking State Department official, was convicted in 1950 of perjuring himself in his denial of allegations that he had allowed documents to be passed to the USSR. His case precipitated much Cold War paranoia. See Mari Jo Buhle, Paul Buhle and Dan Georgakas (eds), *The Encyclopedia of the American Left* (Chicago: University of Chicago Press, 1992), pp. 314–17. Ethel and Julius Rosenberg, communists, were executed on 19 June 1953, having been found guilty of conspiracy to commit espionage by passing information to the Soviets about America's A-bomb programme. Their innocence or guilt is still hotly debated. See Buhle *et al.* (eds), *The Encyclopedia of the American Left*, pp. 658–61; and William E. Leuchtenburg, *A Troubled Feast: American Society since 1945*, rev. edn (Boston: Little, Brown and Company, 1979), p. 29.
45. Heath, *The Sexual Fix*, p. 3.
46. The quotations are from 'Footnote to Howl', in Ginsberg, *Collected Poems*, p. 134.
47. See Foucault, *Introduction*. The first two sections of this text, 'We "Other Victorians"' and 'The Repressive Hypothesis' are particularly useful when considering the relationship of sexual dissidence to the discourses of the mainstream. See also D'Emilio, 'Gay Politics and Community in San Francisco since World War II'; D'Emilio and Freedman, *Intimate Matters*; and Catharine R. Stimpson, 'The Beat Generation and the Trials of Homosexual Liberation,' *Salmagundi*, 58 (1983), pp. 373–92.
48. This kind of overlapping and reinforcement is described in Foucault, *Introduction*, p. 48. The division of America into 'Hip' and 'Square' is found in Norman Mailer's 1957 essay for *Dissent* magazine, 'The White Negro'. This is reprinted in Ann Charters (ed.), *The Penguin Book of the Beats* (Harmondsworth: Penguin, 1993), pp. 582–605. Mailer writes (p. 585): 'One is Hip or one is Square (the alternative which each new generation coming into American life is beginning to feel), one is a rebel or one conforms, one is a frontiersman in the Wild West of American night life, or else a Square cell, trapped in the totalitarian tissues of American society, doomed willy-nilly to conform if one is to succeed.'
49. Ginsberg, *Collected Poems*, p. 126.
50. See Henry Brooks Adams, 'The Virgin and the Dynamo (1900)', in *The Education of Henry Adams: An Autobiography* (Boston and New York: Houghton Mifflin, 1918), pp. 380–1. Adams (1838-1918), the great-grandson of America's second president John Adams, was a novelist, teacher, and social commentator. The ironic idealism of his eccentric and most famous works *Mont-San-Michel and Chartres* and *The Education of Henry Adams* provides a model for the modernisms of his compatriots T. S. Eliot and Ezra Pound. See D. L. Kirkpatrick (ed.), *Reference Guide to American Literature*, 2nd edn (Chicago: St James Press, 1987), pp. 39–40.
51. See Foucault, *Introduction*, pp. 17–49, esp. pp. 43–5 and p. 49.
52. Ginsberg, *Collected Poems*, p. 128.
53. *Ibid.*
54. *Ibid.*
55. See Annette Kolodny, *The Lay of the Land: Metaphor as Experience and History in American Life and Letters* (Chapel Hill: University of North Carolina Press, 1975), *passim*, esp. pp. 136–7 which explore the notion that 'the West was a woman, and to it belonged the hope of rebirth and regeneration'.
56. Stimpson, 'Beat Generation', p. 392.
57. *Ibid.*, p. 389.

THREE

Visual Cultures

8

'That's Why She Is Bisexual': Contexts for Bisexual Visibility

Jo Eadie

On the back cover of *Bisexual Politics: Theories, Queries and Visions*, Pat Califia tells us that 'this is the next generation. Ignore it at your peril.'[1] Another recent book on bisexuality, *Dual Attraction*, states on its flyleaf that it addresses 'what is perhaps the most mysterious – and potentially illuminating – variation of human sexual expression, bisexuality', and its first chapter is titled 'The Riddle of Bisexuality'.[2] In this focus on the mystery of bisexuality – and the attendant promises of its explication – it is striking that the assumed audience is not itself bisexual. They are, in Califia's quote, those who 'ignore it at [their] peril' – the nameless others for whom bisexuality is news. Bisexuality, then, appears as fascinating because it says something about strangers, it is the sexuality of the Other which teaches about those experiences which are somehow both beyond the normal range of human experience ('most mysterious') and central to it ('potentially illuminating'). My argument in this chapter is that the presence of a bisexual figure in film is an indicator that a cultural tension is being broached, whose contours the bisexual enables the audience to negotiate, and whose dangers the bisexual always embodies. As an outsider s/he is the one who is seen as going beyond the limits, and who thereby serves to teach a lesson about what those limits are. The bisexual is therefore a marker, whose bisexuality signals that there is something – or rather, something else – of interest about them. For what interests me about these figures – and what makes them of interest to their non-bisexual audiences – is that it is not their bisexuality in itself that is significant, but rather those concerns which their bisexuality *stands for*.

If it sounds like such films denigrate bisexuality, we might want to label such a process 'biphobia'. This is a neologism coined by the bisexual community to describe attitudes and emotions of hostility towards the fact of bisexuality in the abstract, and the lives of bisexual people in particular. 'Biphobia', writes Kathleen Bennett, 'is the denigration of bisexuality as a valid life choice.'[3] It is common for bisexuals to class as forms of denigration: the refusal to recognize or address bisexuality, its being subordinated to other ssues, and its prejudicial association with myths and stereotypes. The reason or this hostility has generally been seen as resentment and fear at bisexuality's efusal to conform to the existing division of desire into heterosexual and omosexual. Thus in a representative formulation of the roots of biphobia, Amanda Udis-Kessler claims that:

> Community-oriented individuals [both heterosexual and homosexual], protective of the essentialist view of sexuality that seems to give rhyme and reason to their communities, equate the fluidity and apparent choice-making of bisexuality with that of constructionism, and see only a threat to that which they hold dear.[4]

While these emotions play a role in representations of bisexuality, such an nswer reduces any enquiry into the range of determinants for such images nd thereby narrows our grasp of the social contexts within which bisexuality s made visible. I believe it is essential to link the appearance of bisexual igures to wider social, ethical and philosophical debates; I want to suggest ot that bisexuality is being marginalized, or stereotyped in such contexts ut rather that we may learn something here about the discursive regulation f bisexuality. By this I mean not merely how non-bisexuals represent it in ncorrect, or prejudiced ways, but how bisexuality is made socially meaningful and therefore how as bisexuals we construct and understand ourselves. For t is both defensive and naive to argue that there are two sets of beliefs about isexuality: the false ones (held by those in the grip of biphobia) and the true nes (held by bisexuals).[5] Rather, I shall be arguing that there is a set of egemonic conceptions of what bisexuality means which structure for all of s the perception of bisexuality, but which may be inflected, according to he different agendas in which they find themselves, in very different ways.

Concerns such as the moral restraint of appetite, monogamous commitment nd excessive desire figure strongly in the films I will be studying here. But t is clear enough that these are issues whose cultural import ranges far beyond isexuality and which precede, however much they may be intertwined with, he figure of the bisexual. The role of the bisexual in these films is to mark ut what is at stake in these other debates for whom s/he is useful. Hostility owards bisexuality is the result of the specific ways in which it is made meaningful through its being located within these other discourses. I am oncerned therefore to distance myself from a reading of these figures in which it is bisexuality *itself* that provokes concern, hostility or horror.[6] What makes these bisexuals dangerous is their place within other debates about imit and constraint, the cultural ambivalence around which they are obliged o bear.

As a comment on supposed biphobia and the malleability of bisexuality, wish to turn briefly to perhaps the key film in this debate, *Basic Instinct*, nd Catherine Tramell, the bisexual killer played by Sharon Stone. Questioned bout the role of Tramell's bisexuality, director Paul Verhoeven announced hat 'Catherine is the devil – that's why she is bisexual', and by this he said he meant that: 'God created man in his image – male and female. So that's why I think God is male and female. And that's why I think the devil is male and female, and that's why I think bisexuality is appropriate to Catherine's character.'[7] Here bisexuality seems to mean something more like hermaphroditism – as it so often has:[8] Catherine must be universal to be the Devil, she must be both male and female. And yet there is another sense behind Verhoeven's phrase, which is that to be the Devil Catherine must be *attractive and available* to both men and women. The perfect object of temptation cannot be a lesbian, or a heterosexual woman – she must be a woman whom anyone could desire. Catherine's bisexuality, then, is a structural requirement – as Marjorie Garber has noted of stardom: 'all great stars are bisexual in the performative mode', for in order to elicit maximum attention from the audience, stars must make themselves desirable to both men and women.[9] Verhoeven's syntax is essential here, yet in his much-quoted statement it is often overlooked. Catherine is bisexual *because* she is the Devil: not the other way around. She is not the Devil because she is bisexual – bisexuality does not make her evil – rather, because she is evil in a certain way (universal, archetypal, eternal, metaphysical, seductive), it is necessary that she be bisexual in order to allow that other, dominant meaning (the Christian notion of sin as temptation) the fullest possible scope.

I shall be analysing two films whose bisexual figures are required by the texts they inhabit. I do not take these films to be instances of biphobia but rather read them as instances of pre-existing debates, which find the bisexual figure functionally useful. This is not to deny that bisexuals face prejudice but is an attempt to open up the question of why and how we face it into the territory of the very precise social conflicts through which it is imagined and to which it provides a map. Reading this way, we may begin to see more clearly where, and how, bisexuals are made visible, why we come to occupy those places, and what we may do from them.

Crush (Alison Maclean, New Zealand, 1990)

Synopsis: *Two women, Lane (Marcia Gay Harden) and Tina (Donogh Rees) are driving across New Zealand. Tina is on her way to interview an author Colin Iseman (William Zappa). Momentarily distracted when speeding, Lane crashes the car, and Tina ends up in hospital with horrific injuries. Abandoning Tina, Lane goes to Iseman's house where she meets his fifteen-year-old daughter, Angela (Caitlin Bossley), who quickly forms an intense crush on her, which Lane seems to enjoy manipulating. She begins an affair with Iseman, to which a jealous Angela responds by starting to visit Tina in hospital. Angela becomes central to Tina's slow, painful recovery, while Lane refuses to visit. Lane, bored and angry, leaves Iseman, who quickly breaks down, unable to bear the loss, and is only too glad to take her back when she returns. Lane, Angela and Iseman go on holiday, a reunited but uncomfortable family, and while at their holiday house are interrupted by*

Tina. She has been invited, unbeknownst to them, by Angela, who enjoys the guilt and discomfort this causes Lane. The film ends with Tina rising from her wheelchair to push Lane over a cliff to her death.

A woman staggers from the wreckage to pick up three objects: first a novel, then the private notebook of her companion, and lastly a wing-mirror, broken off in the crash. She looks into it, to notice blood running from her temple. If the mirror is the privileged signifier for female vanity, and also for the threat of hidden doubleness, then the conjunction of the two themes is no coincidence. It is as if – as in their repeated circulation in *film noir* [10] – the desire to gaze into the mirror is itself a sin, suggesting as it does both an irresistible beauty whose appeal threatens male autonomy, and an unhealthy desire to appreciate that beauty. Hence, for the woman who looks, the act of looking is a crime. To look is to be revealed as too interested in oneself.

It is Lane, in *Crush*, who looks into the mirror, but with an obvious distaste. At the most mundane level, this is for the blood, which mars a beauty that she is otherwise so scrupulous to maintain. But the look of disgust invites the audience to look at her in the same way – and the mixture of doubt and dislike which plays over the face in the mirror makes her seem uneasy at the audience's gaze being directed on that face. We are looking at her and frowning. She frowns too. None of us likes what we see.

Why then, should we dislike Lane?

In the course of the film our dislike will be generated around the meanings attached to these three objects collected by Lane. While the mirror denotes selfishness, the other two objects prove equally to be clues to Lane's unhealthy desires. The novel is by Colin Iseman, whom Tina (who may or may not be, or have been, Lane's lover) had been going to interview – and whom, Lane implies, Tina desires. [11] It is this novel, and Tina's desire for its writer, which intrigue Lane and draw her into an affair with Iseman. The taking of the book from the wreckage marks, as we shall see, an excessive and unchecked appetite (when we first see Lane, she is eating, licking her fingertips with glee). The notebook signals a second transgression, violating as it does Tina's privacy. When Lane tries to read it in the car, Tina snatches it away, angrily. Her subsequent visit to Iseman is an encroachment on Tina's territory, as in a sense her unconsummated flirtation with Angela is an encroachment on the territory of her father, whose paternal authority she disregards. Lane likes other people's property. Indeed, it seems to be the fact that something is linked to another which draws her to it. It is only when she starts to see that Angela and Tina have grown close that her interest in Tina returns. Were we pop psychologists – and as we shall see, this is just what the film invites us to be – we would say (as we would of all bisexuals): 'she has no boundaries'.

It is around these three objects that I want to structure the explanations for Lane's status in the film – in particular, how she comes to be offered to us as an object for contempt. But, as one last sign of her dangerous status, I want to point out Lane's nationality. Her attributes are clearly linked in the film to her being a US American, an identity here constructed as overbearing and aggressive.[12] In her nationality her other three attributes come together. We are encouraged to read her, as a US woman, as self-obsessed – with brash, stylish clothes which distinguish her from the drab, conventionally dressed New Zealanders around her. As a US woman she has an excessive appetite, marked in the film by the references to McDonald's as the sign of American desire to eat. And as a US woman she is depicted as unable to respect the rights and boundaries of others: when Angela takes her past Maori burial sites, Lane casually comments that 'our Indians bury their dead in trees', the 'our' a powerful reminder of American colonial ambitions.

Her American-ness links to another defining trait: that she moves. Lane has crossed the sea to be here, although it is not clear when she did so, or how often she may have repeated that crossing. But it is clear, as I have already noted, that boundaries – geographical, proprietary or sexual – mean little to her. The capacity to move easily defines her, for the mobility of Lane's desire is what drives the narrative. At one point, she and Angela come home together to Iseman's house. Uncomfortable with their intimacy, he is nervous and excluded, a fact which the camera marks by cutting between shots of Iseman, alone on the sofa, and Angela and Lane in shot together. But by the time Angela has been to the kitchen to get a drink, Lane has moved to join Iseman. Lane and Iseman are now in shot together, while Angela is on screen alone. The swiftness of the movement, and the ease with which the camera shifts the structure of couple/hanger-on from one object of Lane's interest to another, marks her own unsteady affections – whose course has already led her away from Tina, as they will ultimately lead her back to Tina in the closing sections.

None of the other characters is any more steady in their affections, however. Iseman switches all interest from his daughter to his new lover; Angela switches affections from Lane to Tina; Tina switches affections from Lane to Angela. What distinguishes Lane's mobility, in this landscape of mobile desires, is that it is seemingly arbitrary, while for the others it is provoked. While others are drawn away because they are seduced or hurt, Lane's changes have no discernible motive. Having arranged to meet Angela to go out for the night, Lane arrives with another man at her side, unable to keep the commitment of desire from shifting. *Crush* thereby constructs Lane's fickleness as innate: she *embodies* a failure of fidelity, made motiveless precisely in order to figure it as a defining character trait, rather than, as it is in the others, incidental or situational.

Lane's mobile affections provoke strong reactions. Grief in Iseman, hatred in Angela, and in Tina a murderous fury signalled in the moment when Lane begs her forgiveness. As she hugs Tina, we see her face, furious, over Lane's shoulder, and the music sounds a loud, discordant crash. The strength of those reactions is a testimony to the badness of the object which incites them: she cannot arouse healthy or moderate passions; she cannot arouse manageable love. After cutting Iseman's hair she offers him, instead of a mirror, a toaster, in whose dented silver surface a distorted image swirls. It suggests that the blame for the dangerous emotions which surface lies with

Lane – for it is she who provides the mode of reflection which produces distortion. It is her mirrors which show back the unhealthy side of the observer. It is in effect *her* mirror into which Angela looks when she applies her make-up, transformed – at Lane's insistence – from comfortable tomboy into uneasy femme by Lane's offer of lipstick and a new dress. As she recoils from Lane, Angela will return to her boyish attire (dungarees, baseball cap and duffel coat) so that the film closes with her wearing exactly the clothes that we first saw her wearing, purged of Lane's influence, no longer the image which Lane's mirror would return.[13] So it is she – the bad object – who generates obsession in her admirers. What, we might ask, is wrong with her?

The easy answer – and the answer which I will be disputing – is 'her bisexuality'. Raising again the spirit of Catherine Tramell in order to exorcize it, we should remember that it is not the *bisexuality* of the gorgeous, deadly bisexual woman which is so dangerous. Bisexuality here is one element in a network of signifiers of pathology. Why should this film be taken as an indictment of bisexuals, any more than an indictment of Americans, or of femininity (which is not to rule out the possibility that it might be an indictment of all three)? *Crush* pathologizes Lane via her restlessness, intrusiveness and selfishness, indicating its use of a very conventional standard of mental health within popular psychology: commitment, unselfishness and what counsellors like to call 'healthy boundaries' (a phrase which should alert any bisexual). All three ethical-psychological terms are variations on a theme: that of *self-discipline*. To stay with one person, to give indefinitely and to resist temptation are how we might rephrase these three missing traits. They are a recognizable form of Protestant asceticism. This is an ethic ruled by moderation of the passions, in the name of hard work. Max Weber is the figure most associated with the formulation that Protestantism is the conjunction of Christian abstinence with capitalist labour, whose goal is a workforce that defers its immediate gratification in order to produce more commodities.[14] In Bryan Turner's succinct summary of Weber:

> Appetite and sexuality became the principal threat to the religious vocation, but also to a more general rational control of the instinctual life. Weber noted, in passing, that the answer to religious doubts and sexual temptation was the same – 'a moderate diet and cold baths'.[15]

That observation on the necessary conditions for spiritual and physical self-control finds its corollaries in *Crush*. The baths that Lane takes are hot – she luxuriates in geysers and hot springs. Eyes closed, and head back, her face recalls her expression when she makes love with Iseman: self-absorbed pleasure. The warmth and heat associated with her sensual activities cast her in the role of the temptress who will thaw the ice-man. 'Why would I come and see you?', he asks. 'Blind impulse – isn't that what you're famous for', she replies. 'Used to be', he says, limply – but under her influence it seems inevitable that he will be again.[16] It is therefore appropriate that her death should see her plunging over a cliff and into a cold, icy lake – her ardour quenched at last, her excessive passion cooled off.

Nor is her diet likely to calm her appetites. With venom, Angela describes Lane: 'I saw her once in the fridge – she was sticking her spoon into everything and licking it in between'. Unable to commit ('sticking it into everything'), unable to give (taking from another's fridge) and refusing to respect boundaries ('licking it in between'), Lane personifies the woman who goes beyond – whose energy cannot be contained.[17] It is no coincidence that she, like Catherine Tramell, should drive so recklessly. Nor, as the woman who will not stay within the boundary, is it any coincidence that she meets her death by being pushed over the fence at a cliff-edge, a bitterly ironic comment on her refusal to keep within other bounds in the course of the film.

It would be premature to assume that it is *because* she is bisexual, that these other signifiers of excess are heaped upon her. Lane's bisexuality is a *function* of her instability, and the importance of her bisexuality becomes clear if we put her three traits together. For what bisexuality makes possible is the conjunction of these traits: *restless*, because the bisexual is presumed faithless and fickle; *selfish*, because the bisexual is presumed a slave to their predatory appetite; and *intrusive* because the bisexual is unable to respect normal boundaries. Why, in the face of such persistent links to bisexuality, should I wish to claim that the key to Lane's pathology lies elsewhere? It is because these violations of rules are all intimately related to larger social structures which the film explores. The 'normal boundaries' in question are the rules of marital heterosexual monogamy, for the demonization of excessive desire has its roots in the regulation of the couple.

The west's attempt to maintain the sexual and economic centrality of the reproductive unit of the monogamous heterosexual couple finds its object beleaguered by temptations which it will not easily accommodate. Warning of the incompatibility of such desire with 'stable' (i.e. marital, monogamous and heterosexual) relationships, one 'marital therapist' advises: 'We all have an understandable desire to live life as children . . . we want to walk out the back door and pluck a handful of grapes . . . and it is the cause of much of the world's unhappiness.'[18] This representation of restless appetite, with its concomitant misery, might serve as a fine epitaph or diagnosis for Lane, with its invocation of irresponsibility: for what is implied by 'we want' if not 'but we shouldn't'? The use of 'we' returns us to the risk which Lane poses to others – that she releases these unacceptable desires in those around her and makes us recognize the extent to which Iseman, Tina and Angela share her 'understandable desire', but had somehow contained it.

What we are moving towards here is a recognition that bisexuality may be *central* to a film, without being what a film is *about*. That is, *Crush* explores the terms of stability and relationships via the figure of a bisexual, rather than exploring bisexuality through figures of stability and relationships. Lane is bisexual *because* it fits so well with her other defining characteristics, characteristics which she is called on to incarnate because they enable the film to engage with the construction of the monogamous couple. Bisexuality is an available trope to hold together these other characteristics because it so often seems a potential violation of these structures. This is not, it is important to stress, because it *is* in fact a necessary violation of them – monogamous, bounded relationships between bisexuals, between bisexual men and gay men, between bisexual women and lesbians, and so on, are entirely possible. Rather, it is because the bisexual is able to incarnate the social dangers of the sort of person who cannot fit into a marriage, without suggesting that the sort of people who *do* marry will exhibit any of these alarming tendencies. As Richard Dyer so ably expresses it, the point of stereotypes is to 'insist on boundaries exactly at those points where in reality there are none'.[19] Good heterosexuals, thoroughly monogamous, will – without the distractions of bisexuals and their distorting mirrors – be able to assume their places in this structure. As indeed will good homosexuals – the lesbian couple which Lane and Tina could have been, if Lane were not so twisted.

In this film the bisexual burden is to represent both lack and excess – the failure to live up to these standards and the refusal to be contained within them. The bisexual cannot function within the rules of moderation which (supposedly) define the sexual contract – and to which, crucially, all others seem able to adhere.[20] What I want to stress one last time is that while bisexuality enables *Crush* to explore the notion of the 'healthy' relationship, it is these other assumptions which are at stake: how to maintain commitment, how to respect boundaries, how to moderate appetites. In its production of a film about disruption and obsession, what is necessary is the graphic display of the violation of these guidelines, and here Lane is exemplary in that she provides such a violation. That is why she is bisexual.

The Hunger (Tony Scott, USA, 1982)

Synopsis: *Miriam and John Blaylock (Catherine Deneuve and David Bowie) are vampires living in New York. Miriam is immortal, converting new lovers of both sexes over the millennia. John, however, begins to age suddenly and finds that Miriam's lovers do not stay forever youthful, as she does, but eventually grow old. John visits Sarah (Susan Sarandon), an expert in ageing, but she refuses to believe him, and he returns to Miriam who seals him, forever undying, in a crate alongside her previous lovers. Miriam selects Sarah as a new companion, draws Sarah to her, seduces her, and converts her into a vampire. Sarah's lover pursues her, but Sarah kills him. She then tries to kill herself, but, when Miriam carries her up to join the other past companions, these animate corpses break free and push Miriam to her 'death'. Released from her power they crumble away to dust, while Miriam ages rapidly to become, as they had been, a living corpse. The film ends with Sarah now alive, having taken over Miriam's position, while Miriam is sealed in a coffin of her own, forever living.*

The Hunger clearly marks itself as a film about bisexuality. Miriam has male and female lovers during the film and in her past; in the closing scene Sarah is ensconced in a new apartment, having taken on Miriam's role as confident, cultured vampire, with both a man and a woman in attendance on her. Its bisexual interest also lies in its choice of performers. As Marjorie Garber notes in her reading of *The Hunger*, the bisexual elements are set in place by the choice of Bowie – famous for his (first proclaimed, then denied) bisexuality – and Sarandon, 'who had earlier fallen prey to the seductions of bisexual Transylvanian heartthrob Tim Curry in the *Rocky Horror Picture Show*'.[21] Yet readings of the film manage to skirt this. Sarah's new male lover finds himself erased from Shameen Kabir's recent account of the film, which refers solely to 'a kiss between a young girl and Sarandon in the penultimate scene'.[22] Equally bizarrely, Barbara Creed erases the woman: 'the final scene re-establishes the vampire as a heterosexual'.[23] Rather than reading this simply as a biphobic blindness in these critics, I want to link this oversight to the role in the film of appetite – that of bisexuals, and that of vampires.

Elaine Scarry observes that 'the interior states of physical hunger and psychological desire have nothing aversive, fearful or unpleasant about them if the person experiencing them inhabits a world where food is bountiful and a companion is near'.[24] Yet that dream of easy contentment belies the way that desire resists satisfaction – Miriam, driven by just such twin desires (for companionship and sustenance), will serve as an illustration of how the problems posed by both make hunger *always* fearful and unpleasant. In his analysis of human appetite, Pasi Falk explores the combined force of modern capitalism's insistence that we consume without limit, and the oral obsession at the heart of the Freudian unconscious. In his synthesis of the two, Falk suggests that the human subject experiences itself as forever empty 'with an inside to be filled up, completed'.[25] This leads to his suggestive formulation that 'hunger is not only hunger', but rather marks the need for a satiety which will never come, and therefore an appetite which will never be satisfied.[26]

The Hunger marks this fear about inexhaustible appetite with a striking motif. It comes when Miriam and John have finished the film's first kill. Each has cut the throat and drunk the blood of one half of a mixed-sex couple. Cautiously heterosexual, he devours the woman while she devours the man. They wash: we see trails of blood and water disappearing into a plughole. The sound of the bloody water rushing down is amplified to a roar on the soundtrack. With that sound the insistent desires of this first sequence end, and we cut to a night scene of the New York skyline, as a more relaxed score replaces the screams and electronic notes of the first five minutes. That deep, sucking, gurgling sound concludes the sequence, highlighting a supplementary devouring of the last remnants of blood, necessary to finish the consumption of the precious liquid. Yet, crucially, one last act is required to consume all the remains: the incineration of the corpses. Those thematically opposed means of consumption – fire and water – suggest both the finality of the act of devouring, and also, paradoxically, the deferral of its completion: the body is not gone when eaten; nor quite gone when the blood has been washed away; nor quite gone until consumed by flames – and maybe, still, not gone then.

The difficulty of finishing the job of devouring a body resonates throughout the text. Speaking of the eternal life-in-death which is the fate of her lovers, Miriam contrasts them with humans: 'their end is final, ours is not'. These bodies cannot be finished off. They – like any bad meal – will come back up, returning in the final scene to take their revenge. And just as the objects of desire refuse to be washed – or wished – away, so too hunger is never quite satisfied. The vampire needs another body a week after the first: 'you will feed one day in seven', Miriam explains. Climactic though the consumption of blood may be, its satisfaction can never last. To bring home this point, Sarandon's blood-lust is figured in terms recognizable as a popular image of drug-addiction: she sweats; she shivers; her skin is pale; her eyes shadowed; she curls up on the bed, shaking with need. Hunger, the film reminds us, is the state of never being able to get *enough*, the all-consuming appetite; but at the same time it is an appetite which can never succeed, which this film represents as unable to subdue its objects adequately. Profoundly threatening, it is thus simultaneously fated to fail. What makes this appetite so dangerous that it needs to have this inbuilt safety-device of inevitable failure?

What is most dangerous about this appetite is its lack of limits. The vampire's need is distinguished by its lack of differentiation: it can be satisfied with anyone. Appetite transforms the body from an erotic object to the object of a less discriminate desire, the vampire's gaze offering an almost Whitmanesque democratic vision of all flesh as equally desirable, but equally undifferentiated.[27] It is the film's concern with this mode of desire that makes bisexuality a convenient cultural shorthand. Not only are bisexuals unable ever to get enough, but one other accusation commonly made is that in their lack of preference they evince an indiscriminate desire, which is oblivious to the specificity of the partner, and concerned only with finding a suitable orifice: concerned only with the body as meat.[28]

The defining image for this bisexuality in the vampire's desire follows the love-scene between Miriam and Sarah. We cut to a rare steak on a plate, sliced by Sarah's knife. As she opens the meat, and the juice runs out of it, she parts it into a provocatively vaginal V, the two dripping slabs meeting at an apex suggestive of two labia. It is, we might say, a meat shot.[29] The cutting of the meat contains two important visual echoes, both from the opening sequence. During their sex scenes with the couple picked up at the club, we cut between John and Miriam. As Miriam pulls open her partner's shirt, we cut to John who, as he kisses his partner, pushes open her legs. The two acts of parting, of opening up the V of the body's exposure, mark the similarity of the two bodies, which will both, in due course, be opened up in exactly the same way when they are cut open and eaten. This visual chime then links meat and sex via a moment where male and female bodies are interwoven. The vampire's appetite is ungendered: just as the meat on the plate has no sex (and yet is all sex), we might say that *The Hunger* is a film in which the most sexual act is also the moment where the sex of its participants ceases to matter. There is no sex in sex.

And so we return to the plughole: we do not know whose blood it is that runs into it – male or female? It hardly matters – 'it could be either'.[30] More than that, there is no need even to distinguish between the different liquids that disappear into that black maw – water, blood, sweat, soap, vomit. The drainage system of the city can contain all substances, the definitive image of an undifferentiating and inexhaustible appetite. But we might also recall here how often the image of the blocked drain indicates some aberration which society can no longer contain. This is the lesson that Gene Hackman's Harry Caul learns in *The Conversation*,[31] where similar gurgling noises from a blocked toilet precede a rush of blood from a concealed corpse. That which will not disappear down the drains is that which must, ultimately, be dealt with.[32] The film's insistent imbrication of these two themes again grounds itself in bisexuality: the figure of insatiable bisexuals who get their come-uppance through the vengeance of their discarded lovers (their left-overs) is a revenge-fantasy which might find many takers.

As a marker of its need to make these vampire passions different from the passions of its audience, the film strives to make them both alien and undesirable. 'For ever' intones Miriam throughout the film, 'for ever and ever' – a litany not, I suggest, of eternal love or eternal life, but eternal *need*, a burden which the audience would not want. Underscoring that undesirability, what the vampire foregrounds about such a state is its ethical dimension: s/he cannot feed without killing. While discourses of human diet are based on the assumption that, with some modification, there is an acceptable way to eat, for the vampire there is no such option. All feeding is immoral. Kabir reads this challenge as structuring the film:

> The value system in operation in the film is generated by Sarandon, whose desire we share, whose seduction we enjoy, but whose ambivalence and resistance we also identify with as morally right. . . . Sarandon cannot become a vampire without validating destruction and the nihilism of murder.[33]

Nor can she become a vampire without overcoming disgust, for the film emphasizes the physical disgust of vampirism, with Sarah's first sight of Miriam at prey represented in a jarring succession of close-ups, which show her elegant face smeared with blood, her hair disordered, her mouth snarling. What then makes possible the transformation into vampire is the suspension of this disgust – the same suspension which supposedly brings about bisexuality: popularly figured as undiscriminating, it is the desire for 'anything that moves'. Roger Clarke proposes that 'What people have always found baffling about the concept of bisexuality' – and we should note the casual universalizing gestures of 'people' and 'always' – 'is that there appears to be no disgust in it'.[34] There seems to be some qualitative difference between the desires of the bisexual, and the desires of everyone else. The passions of both vampires and bisexuals are not containable within acceptable social structures. Between the two of them, they mark out the marginality of hunger which, in spite of an attempt such as Scarry's to define its apparent safety, remains risky.

If bisexuality is such an insistent presence grounding these other meanings of hunger, how does it come to be overlooked? Again, rather than read this in terms of biphobia, it is bisexuality's role as the figure for hunger which necessitates its erasure. In the ethical terms by which Kabir reads it, the film itself would seem, at one level, to want to end the vampire's feeding, using Sarah as a check to Miriam's appetite. Although it is not clear how and why Miriam's former lovers get out of their coffins at that very moment of Sarah's 'death', it seems connected to – or even provoked by – her suicide attempt. Her 'death' acts as the catalyst for the resurrection of Miriam's past lovers, and their vengeance against her, so that Sarah effectively heads the revolution of the devoured. It is thus crucial that we link Sarah back to the chain of unfinished meals, whose logical conclusion she represents. Of all that refuses to be digested, assimilated, finished off, she is the one whose return is so strong that she displaces the one who tried to consume her, and thereby introduces a limit to this dangerous appetite: its failure to conquer what it consumes.

But while the film might thus seem to want to punish and contain hunger, the closing scene of Sarah and her two lovers is a coda which seems to promise absolute repletion: hunger rewarded. The romantic music suggests the happy ending for the happy couple – or in this case, the happy triad. So too the soft lights, the billowing curtains and the careful pattern of peaches-and-cream colours make the scene an object of – albeit slightly cloying – aesthetic appeal. If our attention on Sarah-as-heroine motivated our desire for her not to sacrifice her morality by becoming a vampire, it now motivates our satisfaction at her triumphant survival. The loss of her previous two lovers has left a gap which we are now satisfied to see fulfilled. As she walks to the balcony to look out over the city, her position of spectatorship suggests not only mastery (of all she surveys) but also appetite: she is looking out on her feeding ground. Underneath this triumph, then, is the start of a new cycle of murders and, presumably, discarded lovers.

In this conclusion the film marks its ambivalence. On the one hand, as the meal which fights back, Sarah precipitates the death of Miriam, the end of her reign of consumption. But the film also wants her to survive, thereby exposing its own structure of addiction. This is a film that cannot get enough of vampirism, that is hungry for hunger. Even as it makes Sarah the vehicle for a punitive closure of illicit appetite, it simultaneously restores her as the vampire-queen whose reign of desire it adores, and for which it is still hungry. Audiences frequently find the film's ending confusing – and this can be partly ascribed to its ending twice, with each ending motivated by an opposite impulse: once to punish hunger, once to celebrate it. What is validated here is not 'the nihilism of murder' but the inevitability of need, for which the indiscriminate bisexual is the ambivalently alluring figure.

If these two ideas – hunger as curse, and the problem of the return of the consumed – come together in the all-devouring drain, it is because it is not human. Indiscriminate, as we have seen, it is also the threatening black hole into which *everything* might disappear. Any reworkings of vampirism which suggest that its appetites may be legitimated – not unlike those refigurings of bisexuality which stress its potential for monogamy, stability and lifelong commitment – attempt to wish away the fear that it rests upon: that this hunger will consume everything. The convenience of imagining this through the figure of the bisexual returns us to the fact that the problem of appetite will not disappear merely by insisting that it can be managed. *It cannot be managed.* And we all know this. *The Hunger* articulates a problem about a certain desperation that lines the stomach.

It is as a solution to this problem that consumed food insists on coming back up: as a wishful guarantee of the finality of that appetite, an almost built-in safety measure. Like Scarry's domestication of desire, *The Hunger* requires its invoked terrors to be bounded by a promise of the failure of digestion, necessary because *there is no other form of closure for appetite.* Eating merely makes it pause, and restraint is unworkable: John's protracted decision about whether or not to kill his young friend Alice, and Sarah's attempt not to eat her husband, end in failure, as they must. Hunger, not being manageable from within, must be managed from without in order to be safe. Ultimately this is why Creed and Kabir erase the bisexual woman from their accounts. They read this as a film which finishes off its meal by destroying Miriam and thereby tidying up its two sets of dangerous desires. In order to conclude, as the film does, with appetite's closure, the uncontainable bisexual must be imagined to have vanished, taking this hunger with her.

In this sense, vampirism is not a metaphor for bisexuality, any more than bisexuality is a metaphor for vampirism. This is not a film with one 'real' subject and one ostensible subject. Rather, it is a film whose concern with forms of hunger and appetite is well served by the copresence of vampirism and bisexuality: a copresence which operates not by a stigmatization of bisexuality but by an exploitation of the erotic/horrific frisson which an unquenchable appetite produces. Clearly celebratory of *all* these appetites, and equally clearly structured by a fear and revulsion towards those appetites, the film reminds us that the conventional distinction between need and greed requires figures who will police its boundary, whose refusal to respect its (untenable) protocols make them comprehensible to all others. Sarah, standing on the balcony, is just such a figure.

Conclusion

It might seem perverse to refuse to read these films as instances of biphobia. The iconography and thematics of *The Hunger* are never far from those of *Crush*: hot baths, food, emotional obsession, jealous triangles. It would be easy enough to read in the two the contours of a general – and negative – cultural attitude towards bisexuality. But what is lost in such a reading is the specificity of the form of desire which each film explores. Where *Crush* is concerned to explore the tensions at the limits of the rules of monogamy, *The Hunger* addresses, in an almost existential form, the struggle between the appetite and its objects.

It might seem doubly perverse to attempt such a reading on two films whose subject matter is so very close: appetite, passion, excess. But if bisexual scholarship is to advance it must attend to the minutiae of difference: when bisexuality appears, what are the contexts that shape it? Lesbian and Gay Studies once asserted vast continua of stereotyping which revealed identical lesbian and gay identities, facing identical oppressions, across the centuries.[35] It now challenges even the most provisional of stabilities – Judith Butler, for instance, phrases her politics very carefully: 'This is not to say that I will not appear at political occasions under the sign of lesbian, but that I would like to have it permanently unclear what precisely that sign signifies.'[36] Against such scrupulously postmodern formulations, the bisexual search for transhistorical predecessors seems naive and old-fashioned.[37] Will bisexual scholarship recapitulate these stages in brief – moving rapidly through its essentialist phase before catching up with the deconstructive and ironic suspicion with which our queer comrades regard their sexuality? Will we always be the late guests at this particular sexual-political-theoretical feast?

This chapter is meant to offer a model for a more discriminate bisexual scholarship. My concern is to locate the specific ways in which bisexuality is made meaningful through its deployment in contexts where its representation is produced not out of a general emotion of 'biphobia' but through its implication in very particular discourses of anxiety. This is not to say that *no* similarities exist amongst these deployments. It is not as if bisexuals find themselves recruited to represent any and every social anxiety (although perhaps the very underdeveloped nature of systematic bisexual stereotyping does make us open to this). I wish to close by indicating briefly what those similarities are, and what they might suggest about the future of a bisexual politics.

First, unconfined figures. These are figures who will not stay within the confines of what is acceptable. The vampires of *The Hunger* fall in the most striking way outside the bounds of what is normal, but Lane, too, is over the edge (as her death reminds us). Furthermore these figures are marked by the reference to an other place, to which they more properly belong, but which they have left behind. Lane's origins in the USA, and Miriam's in the distant past (pictured in a series of flashbacks), suggest that they, along with their desires, are out of place, belonging to another set of customs which make them impossible to place within the communities in which they find themselves.[38] Insisting that Lane has no place in her world, Angela declares that 'America's history'.

Second, trying to fit in. At the same time as being outsiders they are also shown trying to make themselves belong. Their wanderings mark them as homeless, uncomfortable with each new place they occupy: but they are also *pretenders*. Discourses on bisexuality return constantly to the idea that the bisexual is a deceiver, who disguises same-sex desires under the façade of marriage, or opposite-sex desires under a gay façade.[39] The bisexual then joins well with these other pretenders: vampires, whose human form belies inhuman desires; and Lane, whose mirror is the surface in which she provides a superficial gloss to conceal her instability. These dangerous creatures threaten to take up a place amongst us if they are not detected and destroyed. The bisexual thus suggests a need for vigilance, chiming well with the ascetic discourses of restraint which play so large a role here.

Third, disruption. In their different ways, these are characters who disrupt the stability of a settled situation. The disruption that they bring with them indicates the radically alien nature of the feelings which these figures experience and arouse, whose absence until their arrival is the necessary condition for that stability. But at the same time this capacity to blend in or (to borrow a telling verb from queer culture) to *pass* suggests the possibility that the disruption is caused by the uncomfortable proximity of these alien figures to those whom they lead astray. Bisexuality, as we have seen with Catherine Trammel, is a useful signifier for a universally desirable object – and a universally tempting one.[40] It therefore makes possible the representation of the desires of these figures as a risky potential in all its characters, which is nevertheless contained until the bisexual brings it out – a position which draws on Freudian formulations of bisexuality as a latent potential within all subjects. A dangerous outsider, the bisexual carries the stigma of passions for which there is no place in anyone, and yet which find in everyone a place prepared for them.[41] The capacity of Lane or Miriam to pass is also a reminder that anyone might be made over to conceal an other presence under the skin. The bisexual makes everyone into a deceiver, whose normality is transformed from authentic self to inauthentic mask.

If the halo of bisexuality helps to make these figures seem foreign (quite literally, for the English Bowie, the French Deneuve and the American Harden all create a sense of distance from the cultures in which the films take place), this helps to distance the audience from the emotions which they embody. This is no surprise in films whose project is to incite, and then (unsuccessfully) allay, desires which the audience must share. Bisexuality is useful here, since it is seen as outside the heterosexual/homosexual binary, and hence outside the domain of the acceptable. It therefore functions to distance the rather common, and mundane, problems of troublesome pleasure by locating them in these alien lovers. Rather than being unique to the bisexual, the disruptive force they bring is an embodiment of the social tensions that emerge at these cultural flashpoints, out of the impossibility for anyone of meeting these strictures. Clearly the threats of unchecked appetite and joyful promiscuity do not originate with the bisexual: s/he is only the vehicle for this anxiety.

The emotional states implied by the titles of *Crush* and *The Hunger* are states of intense desire and need whose very familiarity belies the distancing strategies which the films deploy. Bisexuality makes a useful alliance with other distancing devices in making these passions seem remote – able therefore to be condemned and rejected.

Our role as critical readers should be to define the limits and rules against which they acquire that character. Whether as container or object of excessive passion, what we must resist is the figuring of the bisexual as alien and insist instead that what these bisexuals signify is a problem that is not in itself a bisexual concern. For a bisexual politics this must, I think, make us pause. It is a reminder that bisexuality can become a positive presence only to the degree that it addresses these other issues of which it has become symptomatic. To engage with these issues we cannot insist that they are myths, but must look at how we too understand our bisexuality through these terms. One response to this new framing of the bisexual problematic would be a conservative one: to argue that, in so far as we are stigmatized because we are perceived as *going too far* in various ways, we must prove that we are in fact decent, responsible citizens, with suitably restrained appetites. Such a position goes on requiring such figures as the 'bad' bisexual in order to define the limits of a supposedly healthy society.[42]

While attempting to appease the authorities with promises of our authentic, loving selves is no solution, neither is the option offered by queer politics: to celebrate these transgressions as liberatory. The pull between uncontainable appetite and dour asceticism cannot be resolved by choosing one over the other. It is the production of the conflict between the two which is the social context that we should challenge. By producing appetite as saturated by anxiety, torn between conflicts, and riven by contradictions, we are clearly in a situation which is problematic in itself, rather than caught in a battle between good and evil.

If we can read these texts not as misrepresenting us but as accurately locating tensions which we, along with all those other subjects constructed through them, must live with, then we can refuse to refuse them. Rather than banishing Lane, or moralizing about Susan, we should identify with their struggles. A committed, radical reading of the possibilities which this understanding of bisexual oppression opens up is that we are located within rather than simply misrepresented by certain key ethical and philosophical debates. This puts us in a powerful position from which to disrupt them. We can achieve this best not by claiming that these images are myths or stereotypes and asserting some positive bisexual reality: these images *are* the reality of the threat which excess poses – and again, crucially, which bisexuals do not experience in any unique or separate way. The fact that bisexuality is used to represent these hungers, these crushes, is a strategy for separating them from all those non-bisexual subjects who also experience them, but who are less likely to identify with them if they are framed in those terms – or else will identify with them only in order to identify also with their dissolution.

As bisexual critics we may be in a position to trace back the uncomfortable social structures whose burden we are made to bear, and for whose failings we are the scapegoats. If bisexual politics is to challenge the systems which benefit from our stigmatization, then it must insert itself into these places – against, for instance, the laws which uphold monogamy, and the structures of capitalism which generate and then condemn appetite. And if bisexual scholarship is to assist, then its role is to chart the points of conflict where such intervention is possible. Rather than reducing the explanation to 'biphobia', we should be expanding it to a thorough analysis of the anxieties which we are able to embody.

Notes

1. Naomi Tucker (ed.), *Bisexual Politics: Theories, Queries and Visions* (New York: Harrington Park Press, 1995).
2. Martin S. Weinberg, Colin J. Williams and Douglas W. Pryor, *Dual Attraction: Understanding Bisexuality* (New York: Oxford University Press, 1994).
3. Kathleen Bennett, 'Feminist Bisexuality: A Both/and Option in an Either/or World', in Elizabeth Reba Weise (ed.), *Closer to Home: Bisexuality and Feminism* (Boston: The Seal Press, 1992), p. 207.
4. Amanda Udis-Kessler, 'Bisexuality in an Essentialist World: Towards an Understanding of Biphobia', in Thomas Geller (ed.), *Bisexuality: A Reader and Sourcebook* (Ojai, CA: Times Change Press, 1990), p. 58.
5. For such a claim see Sharon Forman Sumpter, 'Myths/Realities of Bisexuality', in Lorraine Hutchins and Lani Ka'ahumanu (eds), *Bi Any Other Name: Bisexual People Speak Out* (Boston: Alyson Publications, 1991).
6. Similar objections have been raised to the term *homophobia*: it is not that homosexuality in itself produces any psychological disgust, but rather its social meaning as non-procreative, as not contained by a heavily gendered couple, as not a part of official cultural heritage. Its mobile location within *a number of* discourses on gender, the family and the nation makes it a source of anxiety and revulsion to a heterosexual culture for which those values are paramount. See for instance Simon Watney, *Policing Desire: Pornography, Aids and the Media* (London: Methuen, 1987), who suggests that '[i]t is still probably more helpful than not to retain the notion of "homophobia" . . . as long as this does not lead us to assume a single underlying and all determining factor at work behind every example of irrational anti-gay prejudice' (p. 56). Similarly Jonathan Dollimore calls for a materialist analysis of 'homophobia's several interconnected and enabling conditions', *Sexual Dissidence* (Oxford: Oxford University Press, 1991), p. 246.
7. *Time Out* (22 April 1992).
8. See the chapter by Merl Storr in this collection.
9. Marjorie Garber, *Vice Versa: Bisexuality and the Eroticism of Everyday Life* (London: Hamish Hamilton, 1995), p. 140. In Garber's reading, the entire audience is attracted to a star because, in her world of simple Freudianism, we are all bisexual already: what we require is only a star whom we believe would be responsive. I would suggest that there are segments of the audience for whom Catherine's bisexuality does not make her automatically desirable: gay men, and heterosexual women. But here too, Catherine has been carefully constructed as an object of identification: for heterosexual women she can be a figure of (stereotypically) ideal beauty; for gay men she is the tough woman, in the Joan Crawford mode, whose hyper-femininity, combined with a masculine savagery, has made her into a camp icon.
10. See for instance Janey Place, 'Women in Film Noir', in E. Ann Kaplan (ed.), *Women in Film Noir* (London: BFI Publishing, 1978): 'the woman gazes at her own reflection in the mirror, ignoring the man she will use to achieve her goals' (p. 47).

11. When Tina says that her interview will only last an hour or two, Lane spits that 'it doesn't give you long to fuck him'. An ambivalence haunts their relationship: since the film is marketed in many quarters as a lesbian film, much of the audience (and certainly most of my acquaintances) assumed from Lane and Tina's physical closeness, lengthy history and emotional volatility that they were lovers. Maclean herself, however, stresses the ambiguity of their relationship: 'I've been asked whether they are lovers but I don't want to spell that out, and I've been told that's a cop-out. But for me it's exciting to be in a film where you're not sure exactly where you stand. Once you say that they were lovers, you close as many doors as you open' (Lizzie Francke, 'Dark Side', *Sight and Sound*, 3(4) (April 1993), pp. 18–19).

12. According to Francke 'the brash American becomes an obvious object of others' infatuation in such a way that the film can almost be read as an allegory of New Zealand's relationship with the US' (*ibid.*).

13. Iseman too, once exposed to Lane's influence, begins to look at himself in mirrors.

14. This key component of western subjectivity has become increasingly problematic as capitalism shifts from a production-based economy to a consumption-based economy. See Chris Shilling, *The Body and Social Theory* (London: Sage, 1994), pp. 35–6.

15. Bryan Turner, *Regulating Bodies* (London: Routledge, 1992), p. 178.

16. Indeed, all the names of her three admirers suggest a purity which she despoils: *Angel*-a, and *Christ*-ina. Their holy connotations provide little protection against their lapse into sins of Anger, Vanity, Gluttony and Lust at her incitement.

17. We could link her to another unrestrained bisexual, Eunice in *Butterfly Kiss* (Michael Winterbottom, UK, 1994), driven mad by her inability to keep inside appropriate boundaries.

18. Harville Hendrix, *Getting the Love You Want* (London: Simon & Schuster, 1993), pp. 118–19.

19. Richard Dyer, *The Matter of Images* (London: Routledge, 1993), p. 16.

20. One graphic example of this bisexual burden is the bisexual character Camille, in *When Night Is Falling* (Patricia Rozema, Canada, 1995). Torn between her lesbian desire for a lesbian lover and her heterosexual desire for a heterosexual lover, Camille gets drunk and lies down in the snow on an isolated hill, willing herself to die, unable to shoulder the burden of nonconformity. It is as if her decisions are *unliveable*, while those of her lovers are merely hard – involving as they do the choice of *how to* manage a monogamous pair-bond (i.e. what sort of relationship will they have with her once they convince her to settle down), rather than *whether* to submit to its logic. The bisexual is here a figure of the limit, representing an experience which quite literally has no place in society. Camille eventually leaves for San Francisco with her lesbian lover, thereby dissolving both her bisexuality and her other excessive passions.

21. Marjorie Garber, *Vice Versa*, p. 102–3.

22. Shameen Kabir, 'Lesbian Desire on the Screen: *The Hunger*', in Liz Gibbs (ed.), *Daring to Dissent* (London: Cassell, 1994), p. 187.

23. Barbara Creed, *The Monstrous Feminine* (London: Routledge, 1993), p. 71.

24. Elaine Scarry, *The Body in Pain* (Oxford: Oxford University Press, 1987), p. 166 .

25. Pasi Falk, *The Consuming Body* (London: Sage, 1994), p. 29.

26. *Ibid.*, p. 160

27. See Nick Selby's chapter in this volume for a different reading of Whitman's poetic strategy.

28. Against this, humanist bisexuals have asserted the alternative reading: that bisexual desire must be *more* genuine, because it is not fixated on sex organs as, by definition, the love of a heterosexual or homosexual must be. 'The clearest way for me to understand lesbians and straight women is to accept them as fetishists', argues Jane Litwoman: fetishists because their desires are fixated on biological sex – just as the desires of any other fetishist might be fixated on leather or high heels – as the particular physical presence without which sexual arousal is impossible. Quoted in Hutchins and Ka'ahumanu, *Bi Any Other Name*, p. 5.

29. According to Linda William's definition, 'this is the quintessential stag-film shot: a close-up of penetration that shows that hard-core sexual activity is taking place'; Linda Williams, *Hard Core* (London: Pandora Press, 1991), p. 72.

30. This is the title of a bisexual autobiography by Marie King, in Sharon Rose, Cris Stevens *et al.* (eds), *Bisexual Horizons: Politics, Histories, Lives* (London: Lawrence & Wishart, 1995), pp. 105–10.

31. Francis Ford Coppola, USA, 1974.

32. The mysterious object lodged in a drainage system is also a favoured trope of that drama of concealment and exposure, hunger for the truth, and frustrated desire, *The X Files*.

33. Kabir, 'Lesbian Desire on the Screen: *The Hunger*', p. 186.

34. *The Independent Weekend*, p. 9, in *The Independent* (20 January 1996).

35. Judy Grahn, for example, traces 'bull-dyke' back to 'Boadicea', and 'faggot' back to witch-burnings. See Judy Grahn, *Another Mother Tongue: Gay Words, Gay Worlds* (Boston: Beacon Press, 1984).

36. 'Imitation and Gender Insubordination', in Diana Fuss (ed.), *Inside/Out* (London: Routledge, 1991), p. 14.

37. See for instance Guy Chapman, 'Roots of a Male Bisexual Nature', and Emma Donoghue, ' Divided Heart, Divided History: Eighteenth-century Bisexual Heroines', in Rose, Stevens *et al.* (eds), *Bisexual Horizons*. The former traces back '[q]ueerness in more than 40,000 years of human history' (p. 68) from a bisexual perspective, while the latter challenges 'the distinct impression that bisexuality is a twentieth-century invention' (p. 75).

38. While in these cases this makes them dangerous, it can also be transcoded to make the bisexual the bearer of a utopian promise. I am thinking of those feminist science-fiction texts where the bisexual is the representative of an alien, or futuristic, civilization which, freed from gender, is necessarily unbound by heterosexuality or homosexuality: see for instance Marge Piercy, *Woman on the Edge of Time* (London: The Women's Press, 1987).

39. See Mariam Fraser's chapter in this collection for a discussion of the inauthenticity imputed to the bisexual.

40. *Teorema* (Pier Paolo Pasolini, Italy, 1968) is an important source here for the bisexual who enters and disrupts a settled community. It too draws on religious connotations, with its angel/devil bisexual protagonist seducing every member of a household, his bisexuality again a testament to the universal availability of the feelings he arouses.

41. One thinks also of figures such as Milton's Satan, or David Thewlis's Johnny in *Naked* (Mike Leigh, UK, 1994) who, while not technically bisexual, are equally seductive to both men and women.

42. See Anna Marie Smith, 'Resisting the Erasure of Lesbian Sexuality', in Ken Plummer (ed.), *Modern Homosexualities* (London: Routledge, 1992).

9

The Androgynous Self:
Höch and Cahun

Sharon Morris

Introduction

The artists Hannah Höch and Claude Cahun were contemporaries: Höch lived and worked in Berlin during the Weimar years and throughout the war, Cahun lived in Paris until her exile to the island of Jersey in 1937.

Höch first exhibited as a member of the Berlin Dada group in the first International Dada-Fair, 1920, while Cahun formed an active association with the French Surrealists. The overlap in their subject matter and technique owes much to these particular cultural movements, but their ability to both reflect and expose contradictions in the representation of women makes their work unique. The categorical split of 'man' and 'woman' is challenged through Höch's collages and Cahun's self-portraits which exhibit both 'masculine' and 'feminine' signifying codes. Their work is transgressive during a period when the personal and social boundaries of gender difference were questioned but also simultaneously brutally instantiated.

The recent monographs *Cut with a Kitchen Knife: The Photomontages of Hannah Höch* by Maude Lavin[1] and *Claude Cahun: l'écart et la métamorphose* by François Leperlier[2] raise the question of how art by women may be conceptualized within an art-historical framework drawing on psychoanalysis. Specific implications follow the conflation of artwork with the psyche of the artist depending upon the psychoanalytic theory employed. Terms such as *narcissism, immaturity, sexual ambivalence* or *ambiguity* imply particular attitudes toward sexuality and assumptions about sexual difference which may diffuse the politics of Höch and Cahun.

This chapter lays out the possibility of a bisexual viewing and reading of their work using the psychoanalytic concept of identification, with special attention to how Höch and Cahun represent their self-ideals and carry the viewer's idealism.

The first question raised by these monographs is whether the concept 'narcissism' adequately accounts for the deconstruction of the stereotype *woman* by Höch or describes the complexity of sexual position and gender raised by Cahun's self-portraiture.

Narcissism[3] and identification[4] are terms introduced early in Freud's career as a neurophysiologist working with Breuer, and therefore predate psychoanalysis as such. In the 1915 paper 'On Narcissism: An Introduction'[5] Freud writes that the concept of narcissism became necessary as a result of his clinical work with homosexual clients, 'those who have taken as a model not their mother but their own selves'.[6] The paradox of the narcissistic object-choice is that the choice of object is made on the basis of identification with the other: however, the ego is itself formed through the internalization of identifications. The ego is therefore a structural inheritance of such residues of attachment. This narcissistic object-choice may be based on: (1) what he himself is (self-love), (2) what he himself was (a lost ideal-ego), (3) what he himself would like to be (ego-ideal), or (4) someone who was once part of himself (mother or primary carer).

All of the above refer to ideals of the self, but, before taking up the function of ideals in identification, it is necessary to refer to Freud's early work on sexuality and in particular the importance of his concept of bisexuality.

The first part of the paper 'Three Essays on the Theory of Sexuality'[7] lays out a concept of bisexuality firmly grounded in biology, taking hermaphroditism as paradigmatic. As far as Freud was concerned, the contemporary work on inversion and the concept of the 'Third Sex' developed by Gley, Krafft-Ebing, Weininger and others was a mistaken development. In the same paper Freud writes that some men's homosexual relations with boys were based on the youths' 'physical resemblance to woman', and 'their feminine mental qualities'. In a later footnote, Freud writes that this object-choice 'is a kind of reflection of the subject's own bisexual nature'.[8]

There are contradictions in Freud's theory of sexuality, particularly in his description of the basic source of sexual energy, or libido, which Freud terms the *drive*. For example in 1905 he uses the term 'inverted impulses'[9] and again in 1914 he refers to 'libido of an essentially homosexual kind',[10] implying the existence of distinct homosexual drives.

However, the 'Three Essays on Sexuality' also equate all 'active' sexuality with 'phallic' sexuality, which by Freud's definition is also male. This conflation of the active with phallic underpins his later account of female masturbation,[11] in which Freud concludes that continuation of active clitoral activity amounts to a refusal of femininity. It also lends itself to the argument that there is only phallic desire, since all active sexuality is phallic: the object of desire is passive and therefore non-phallic and therefore feminine.

Freud's term *bisexual* thus emerges with differing connotations, even in his early writing. Is the anatomical body bisexual, that is hermaphroditic; or does the term refer to psychic structure, the 'nature' of the subject? Is bisexuality the conjunction of feminine and masculine mental characteristics or signifiers of gender? Does bisexuality reside in the object or does it lie in the subject, as a conjunction of heterosexual and homosexual drives? Is the ego itself gendered or does the ego reflect lost identifications irrespective of gender?

The concept of bisexuality is of central importance to the radical argument put forward in Freud's 1923 paper 'The Ego and the Id',[12] which postulates the existence of the total Oedipus complex, that which includes both the positive and negative routes. The positive route is that by which love for the parent of opposite gender leads to a heterosexual object choice, resulting in identification with the parent of the same gender. The negative route is the contrary process entailing a homosexual outcome.

This resolution of the Oedipus complex results in the confirmation of social norms and ideals under the direction of the super-ego. The super-ego is an unconscious structure which operates as an internalization of the parents' unconscious ideals. In this sense social and familial structures are inherited and enforced through the unspoken taboos of Oedipal law. Freud's classical explanation for this rite of passage accords with the myth of Oedipus, who unknowingly kills his rivalrous father in order to gain the love of his mother.

However in this 1923 paper, Freud writes the following: 'it may be that the ambivalence displayed in the relations to the parents should be attributed entirely to bisexuality and that it is not (as I have represented above) developed out of identifications in consequence of rivalry.'[13] Bisexual desire therefore constitutes a dramatic critique of the very existence of the Oedipus complex. Freud's conclusion that the outcome of the Oedipus complex may consist in identifications with both parents is at odds with the previously outlined theory of Oedipal resolution which takes desire for the parent of the opposite gender as the necessary correlate of identification with the parent of the same gender.

The study on lesbianism and psychoanalysis by O'Connor and Ryan, *Wild Desires and Mistaken Identities*,[14] brings together writings by analysts from different orientations. These include those analysts who take the dichotomy between desire and identification as an opposition between what one would like to have and what one would like to become. The collapse of desire to identification is then understood as regression to the pre-Oedipal stage. In suspecting this categorical division O'Connor and Ryan base their criticism on contradictions in Freud but also on the impossibility of a philosophical split between subject and object.

Freud's 1923 formulation clearly implies that identification with and desire for a particular object-choice need not be mutually exclusive, thus opening up the possibility of human relationships less categorically differentiated into those whom we love or desire versus those with whom we identify.

Integral to the process of identification is the role of self-ideals. The post-Freudian psychoanalyst Jacques Lacan[15] makes a distinction between the 'Ich-ideal' or 'ego-ideal' and the 'Ideal-ich' or 'ideal-ego' following Freud's terminology of 1914. The ideal-ego marks the reappearance of the subject's narcissism and is therefore an idealization of an earlier self. Lacan theorizes that the birth of the ego takes place at the 'mirror stage', chronologically the period between six and eighteen months when the infant both recognizes and identifies with her/his reflection. It is simultaneously the point of alienation when the infant gazes at her/himself from the point of view of another. This crisis precipitates the child from the mode of being dominated by fantasy and fascination which Lacan calls the Imaginary, into the social order of patriarchy which Lacan terms the Symbolic.[16]

In Lacan's metaphysics the ideal-ego is Imaginary, based on illusion and phantasy, free from the Symbolic strictures of Oedipal law. The Symbolic ego-ideal, however, presents the values of this law as an ideal: the ideal of sexual difference organized around the phallus. It is the action of the super-ego, the echo of the parents' unconscious ideals which in exerting its ruthless demands and prohibitions enforces social morality.

Freud's reformulation of the Oedipus complex also explains the footnote to 'Three Essays on the Theory of Sexuality'[17] in which Freud states that 'all human beings are capable of making a homosexual object choice and have in fact made one in their unconscious'. The resolution of the Oedipus complex therefore entails negation of an object choice through repression or unconscious forgetting. The energy of that forbidden desire is therefore available to form new relationships, for creative work or other 'sublimations'.

The contemporary theorist Judith Butler[18] takes up the point that sexual identity requires that other sexualities be negated or prohibited, emphasizing the fragility of heterosexuality. In Butler's theory the gendered body has no ontological status; there is only an idealization of an interior psychic life with an ideal of fixed gender and sexual position. The instantiation of sexual difference in Butler's account rests entirely on prohibition through social and juridical law. This must be visibly enacted, thus heterosexuality depends upon a continual act of performance through the codes of dress and the display of those characteristics used to signify 'male' and 'female', termed the 'masquerade'.

Butler's use of the masquerade derives from the psychoanalyst Joan Riviere's introduction of the concept in her 1929 paper 'On Womanliness as Masquerade'.[19] The masquerade is the clothing of the ego, which on the basis of Freud's theory of identification is the construction of the woman's ego in response to male desire and male ideals. The act of 'dressing up' is therefore inseparable from the development of the ego and identical with becoming woman as opposed to man.

Höch's and Cahun's work is performative in Butler's sense in that both artists expose the fragility of the masquerade of heterosexuality. The next section looks at the images presented by Höch and Cahun, the representation of ideals of the self and the possibility of the viewer's bisexual identification and interpretation.

Höch (1889-1978)

Hannah Höch studied design and graphics in Berlin, where she first met artist and writer Raoul Hausmann, the founder of the Dada circle in 1917.

Visions of the Neue Frau edited by Meskimmon and Shearer-West[20] describes the complexity of the feminist context in which Höch worked. Ninety per cent of women voted in the first Weimar election after gaining suffrage in 1919. Women constituted over a third of the working population of Weimar Germany, that is over one and a half million. Their economic position appeared to be more powerful than ever before, and changes to the laws on abortion and rights to childcare were high on the agenda of women's rights organizations.

The main organization of feminist liberation, the Bund Deutscher Frauenverein (BDF) was ideologically opposed by both the Federation of Housewives Association and the Federation for the Protection of Mothers and Sexual Reform. After gaining the unifying goal of suffrage, the spectrum of feminism within the BDF failed to encompass the more 'radical' feminist politics of liberation and the ideology of the 'Neue Frau', the 'New Woman'. With a history of nationalism and class divisions, the BDF moved further to the right during the 1920s, explicitly supporting the National Socialists through the journal *Die Frau*. As the economic crisis deepened, so the BDF voted in favour of removing housewives from the labour force on the grounds that they were double-earners.[21]

Dorothy Rowe's essay 'Desiring Berlin: Gender and Modernity in Weimar Germany'[22] elucidates the social context for the single woman. The dichotomy of sexuality was split into the private domain of marriage, where patriarchal and conjugal laws were rigorously enforced, and the domain of the public, which accommodated transgression only within specific limits. The freedom of the single 'New Woman' for the majority of those under twenty-five was actually confined to those brief years of work in the labour force prior to marriage, when independence meant a meagre income as a typist living in the family home.

The repeal of censorship laws in 1919 facilitated the flourishing growth of cabaret, film, theatre and the extension of night-life. The modernism which came to Europe through American ideology – the Tiller girls, an androgynous appearance and the dynamic 'Bubikopf' hairstyle – became fashionable but also the object of satire and ridicule.

Two opposing ideologies thus became distinctly visible: modernity versus a return to the home and family. The fascination with sexual transgression was accompanied by deep fear, hatred and misogyny. The real achievements of German feminism also produced a backlash: the growth of women's ego carried the blame for the increase in prostitution, marital breakdown and the number of abortions. As Klaus Theweleit exposes in his study entitled *Male Fantasies*,[23] this hatred culminated in the dark fantasies of violence against women which formed an intrinsic part of Nazi ideology and were endemic in the Freikorps.

Höch collected these contradictory representations of contemporary culture in 'scrapbooks' cut out from the new journals, *BIZ, Berliner Illustrierte Zeitung, Die Dame* and *Uhu*. These early illustrated periodicals carried images of new fashion, contemporary cultural codes of dress, pictures of the body emphasizing health and fitness: the new social ideals of modernity. The renascence of the Greek aesthetic ideal reappeared through an American standard, requiring the readers of these magazines to measure their bodies against a template of beauty. The 'New Women' of Weimar are depicted joining previously designated male professions as members of parliament, aviators, writers and artists.

One of her best-known early Dada collages, *Dada-Ernst*,[24] represents an alliance of sexuality and money. A woman athlete poised at the starting line gazes directly at the viewer. An eye is placed in the crotch of the lower half of a woman, an eye which confronts the spectator at the point of desire. It is an unnerving dislocated image of woman as sex object, juxtaposed to other stereotypes of femininity, typical of Höch's ambiguous representations of the modern woman.

In 1922 Höch severed her connection with Hausmann, and within four years moved to the Hague as the partner of female Dutch writer Til Brugman. During the intervening years Höch produced a series of collages depicting the fashion for androgyny which became increasingly acid in their critique of gender divisions. The integrity of the body is broken in the process of creating a representation of indeterminate gender.

The series of three collages dealing with coquetry exemplify this ironic exposure of the codes of heterosexuality. In *The Coquette I*[25] male desire is represented by a man's head on the body of a dog; another dog in begging position makes an offering to the woman; the woman is represented as a set of phallicized legs, her head displaced by a masculinized mask.

It is not known if Höch considered herself to be lesbian or bisexual. Concluding a letter to Til Brugman she writes, 'To be closely connected with another woman for me is totally new, since it means being taken by the spirit of my own spirit, confronted by a close relative.'[26] They were accepted as a couple by close family and friends but only Brugman became politically active in a homosexual organization.

The montages of 1926–35 concentrate on themes of love, sexuality and marriage, taking apart the idealization of romantic love and the Symbolic social ideals of the institution of marriage by depicting figures formed through combining male and female parts of the body.

Apart from being fashionable, androgyny signalled a declaration of the 'New Woman's' self-assertion and presented a challenge to the social role of gender division without implying an ambiguity of sexual desire or object choice. However the 'manly woman', valued only for her masculine characteristics, prescribed a role for woman which did nothing to further the cause of feminism. Competing theories of homosexuality were split between those like Ulrichs and Weininger, who believed in the existence of a third sex, and Freud, who placed bisexuality as the fundamental condition of the psyche. Those who wore badges identifying themselves as 'Uranians' following Ulrichs

H. Höch, *The Coquette I* (1923–5), 18.5 × 20.5 cm, photomontage,
Institut für Auslandsbeziehungen, Stuttgart, © DACS, London

did so in the hope of strengthening their political position by anchoring their sexuality to the biological.[27]

Lesbianism in the Weimar Republic, as opposed to male homosexuality, was not a criminal offence, and was accorded limited visibility, for example the publication of the paper *The Girlfriend: Weekly for the Ideal Friendship*; the novel *The Scorpion* (1919) by Anna Weirauch and the film *Mädchen in Uniform* (1931) by Leontine Sagan. Contemporary reviews of the film focused on the anti-authoritarian implications of a sexual relationship between teacher and student as opposed to the social significance of the representation of a lesbian relationship.

Representation of active female desire on film was also delineated by the male prerogative. Marlene Dietrich's appearance in *The Blue Angel* (1930) by Joseph von Sternberg, based on a play by Heinrich Mann, appears to legitimize the representation of active female sexual desire. But in characterizing Lola as the seductive adulterer it could be argued that Mann continued to uphold the view that female sexuality is dangerous and destructive to vulnerable men.

Höch's collage *Marlene*[28] dissembles the contradictory image of Marlene Dietrich; 'Marlene', who carefully controlled her own representation as lesbian icon, was known also as bisexual. The men depicted in the collage gaze at the inverted woman's legs, dismembered, stockinged, wearing high-heeled shoes, elevated on to a plinth. The red lips, clichéd in their seductive appeal, tantalize the viewer from the top right hand corner. It is only the graphology of Marlene's signature which suggests the personal, the subject who speaks.

A current reading of this image cannot be completely divorced from the historical importance of the cultural phenomenon 'Marlene', valued for her status as an actress and singer, and also an icon of woman representing her own sexual desires. For the female viewer the question of identification in reading the collage *Marlene* becomes critical. Does she identify with the depicted male gaze, or does she form an identification with the fragmented and objectified body of Marlene? Or is she placed in the position of the lesbian gaze of desire?

It is hard to avoid the reference to the phallus in these elongated structures; high-heeled shoes, classical column, lengthened legs which reappear later in the collage *Der Schuss*.[29] Höch may be commenting on Weimar sexual theories which divorce desire from the masculine or feminine characteristics of mind, desire irrespective of gender.[30] Alternatively perhaps Höch may be referring to the Freudian interpretation of lesbian desire as necessarily phallic on the basis that all active desire is phallic. Female clitoral activity must be relinquished according to Freud in order that passive femininity prevails and heterosexual relations follow.

Höch may also be making a critique of all forms of sexual objectification irrespective of sexual desire or object-choice. The three collages *The Coquette I, II, and III* (1925)[31] and *Made for a Party*[32] depict flirtation with bitter

H. Höch, *Marlene* (1930), 36.7 × 24.2 cm , photomontage, Dakis
Joannou, Athens, © DACS, London

irony. *Marlene*, idolized here for her phallic attributes, appears to uphold the heterosexual masquerade of femininity, but the viewer's knowledge of her ambiguous sexual status integral to the reading of the image undercuts the masquerade.

'Marlene' as lesbian icon represents an idealized object of lesbian desire, a narcissistic ideal through identification and an ideal for a particular group identity. As previously discussed, Freud's paper 'The Ego and the Id'[33] rewrites the Oedipal scenario of conflict in terms of a fundamental bisexuality, which finds resolution in both identification with and desire for the same parent. The interpretation of Höch's collage *Marlene* therefore brings into question unconscious bisexual identification and desire irrespective of the sexuality of the spectator.

Lavin writes of *The Strong Men*[34] that this collage requires a shift in interpretation from 'androgyny' to 'bisexuality'. The depicted silhouette is that of the boxer Max Schmeling, whose upper body reinforces masculinity while the lower half of the body is denied. In the centre a seamless collage of a male and female face is combined to form one gaze which looks directly at the spectator. Lavin concludes that via this disturbing alliance, which oscillates between masculinity and femininity, a bisexual relationship to the object is established.

> *The Strong Men* is not only a representation of androgyny but a deliberate destabilising of the viewer's gaze. It institutes an oscillation between polarised positions of masculinity and femininity, establishes a bisexual relationship to the object of desire, and shifts between disavowal and recognition of that bisexuality. All of these responses can be described as fundamental conditions of female spectatorship. In the case of Höch's *The Strong Men* both male and female viewers are put in the feminine position.[35]

A bisexual reading based on bisexual identification and bisexual desire is assimilated to the feminine position by Lavin's analysis. Although Lavin introduces the discussion of this image in terms of bisexuality as opposed to androgyny, her interpretation of bisexuality in terms of feminine and masculine characteristics, as adopted traits or signifiers, does not reflect the psychic structure of bisexual desire or identification. There is a distinct difference between an interpretation based on androgyny understood as a denial of gender and sexual position, 'neither male nor female', and bisexuality as affirmative of 'both male and female' sexualities.

The Strong Men addresses the spectator through the representation of ideals. The representation of the ideal-ego, in Lacan's terminology the Imaginary, marks the reappearance of the subject's narcissism which in this case may reflect a bisexual subject. The collage brings into play bisexual desire through representing an ideal bisexual object-choice. As Freud writes in 'Group Psychology and the Analysis of the Ego',[36] individuals may identify with each other through processes of unconscious identification by setting

H. Höch, *The Strong Men* (1931), 24.5 × 13.5 cm, photomontage, Institut für Auslandsbeziehungen, Stuttgart, © DACS, London

up the same object in place of the ideal ego. *The Strong Men* represents the possibility of identification with other bisexual subjects and group alliance under an ideal identity.

The operation of such bisexual ideals is therefore in opposition to the apolitical fashion for androgyny, where androgyny conceals rather than reveals sexual position.

Cahun (1894–1954)

Born as Lucy Schwob, Claude Cahun lived in Paris with her life-long partner and collaborator, the graphic artist Suzanne Moore, until their exile to Jersey in 1937. Cahun's public output consisted of a number of publications involving poetry and prose, punctuated by complex photo-collages produced in conjunction with Moore. Throughout her life Cahun photographed herself, although only one of these self-portraits was published in her lifetime.

Absent from histories of French Surrealism, Cahun's contribution has only recently been given recognition by the art historian François Leperlier. His thoroughly researched monograph[37] and catalogue[38] bring to light the innovative quality of Cahun's oeuvre, ranging from the imaginative metaphors of her poetry and prose to the complex irony of the photo-collages.

The self-portraits record the various conditions of the feminine masquerade, parodies of coquetry and female cross-dressing, traversing the boundaries of gender. Dressed as marionette and pierrot, Cahun exemplifies the asexuality which she refers to explicitly in her early writings on the angel and conversely Satan. Asexuality as the denial of sexuality returns to the idealism of an impossible innocence, a pre-Freudian sexuality, a deliberate denial of Cahun's sophisticated readings on sexuality which included Freud and Havelock Ellis.

Vues et Visions,[39] Cahun's first publication, appeared under the pseudonym Claude Courlis. This is an autobiographical work dealing with Cahun's childhood and family difficulties in which she blames her mother for the breakdown in the relationship between herself and her father. Leperlier cites this text as narcissistic, demonstrating how Cahun rejects her own femininity, clings to childhood and shows herself to be both self-torturing and immature. Narcissism in this interpretation is linked to regression and is in accord with a reading of Freud which ascribes heterosexuality to the resolution of the Oedipus complex and homosexuality to a pre-Oedipal stage of development.

The twenty-five paragraphs in *Vues et Visions* are doubled and laid out according to the logic of symmetry, comparison, transposition and inversion.[40] In each section the same metaphors and adjectives are applied to different nouns and subjects with the stated aim of maintaining an equivalence of sensation. Leperlier interprets these formal relations of doubling and reflection as evidence of narcissism at the mirror stage according to Lacan. The relation between the infant and others at the mirror stage is transitive, obeying the symmetry of reflection. There is at this time a tenuous distinction between myself' and 'another' which produces a tendency to confuse 'my hand' with your hand'.

The series of self-portraits dated 1928 explicitly employ mirror relations, either by staging photographs in front of a mirror or through manipulating the image in processing. The double exposure of the photomontage *Que me veux-tu?*[41] shows Cahun looking at herself posing the question 'what do you want of me?', or perhaps 'how do you desire me?'. This is a questioning sexuality, difficult to attach to a specific gender or sexual position and therefore problematic for the viewer to identify with. Apart from the visual reflection, Cahun's question introduces the sliding spoken relation of 'I' to 'you' as 'other'. The moment referred to here is poised between the illusory formations of narcissism and the patriarchal symbolic relations of speech. It is the desire of that 'other', the 'you' in the mirror which becomes paramount in dictating the formation of the subject.

Cahun declared her own sexual position as 'polymorphous' in an unfinished text, *Jeux Uraniens (l'ami et l'aimé, le Maître et l'amant)*.[42] Although the text refers to Uranianism, Cahun's stated aim was to nullify sexual difference through polymorphism. The political position of the female homosexual, prepared to follow Ulrich's theory that homosexuality was congenital, is denied by Cahun's return to polymorphism. Here Cahun uses terminology derived from Freud's writings on sexuality, the polymorphous perverse being an infantile state of plural desires and partial drives; indifferent to sex and gender and unknowing of genital difference. In 1918 Cahun engaged with the demand of politics, abandoned the cover of polymorphism and made an overt political statement on the equality of homosexuality and heterosexuality in terms of the rights of the individual.[43]

Two articles with the title 'Héroïnes' appeared in 1925,[44] exploring the history of the mythic muse through the female ideal: Judith, Margaret, Salomé, Hélène and Sappho. These cultural ideals, which serve simultaneously male fantasy, female identification and lesbian desire, are explored from a psychological perspective. This included a study of Andromeda and the myth of the androgynous Argonauts.

Androgyny as masquerade was as fashionable in Paris as in Höch's Germany. Cahun's self-portraits from 1919 to 1930, however, present a less populist image. Using distortion Cahun produced a series of disturbing representations throwing into doubt the sexuality of the object and making uncomfortable the viewer's desire.[45] One of these photographs of her elongated shaven head and stark open-eyed gaze, suggests emaciation or manipulation of the body. In another which appeared in the photographic magazine *Bifur*[46] Cahun twists her head so that the front and back view are confused.

These images are interpreted by Leperlier as depicting ambivalence of sexuality, implying that Cahun suffered from an inability to make a choice around the poles of gender as a result of regression. The self-portraits exhibit a sustained engagement in contemporary representations of the masquerade, using masks and costumes taken directly from theatre. Cahun's collaboration

173

with Diaghilev and Albert-Birot provided the backdrop for her persona performances in front of the camera generating a series of self-portrait appropriating the male dress code of the 'dandy'.[47]

Leperlier describes Cahun and Moore's life together as 'theatrical'. They would often walk around Montparnasse dressed in the fashionable clothing of modernity, the ethnic and the exotic. The exhibitions which Cahun and Moore held at their home, no. 70 bis rue Notre-des-Champs, were attended by distinguished artists and intellectuals of their generation, Albert-Birot, Sylvia Beach, André Breton, Jacques Lipchitz, Tristan Tzara and Jacques Lacan. The possible link with American expatriate modernist writers is indicated by the publisher Sylvia Beach but the culture of the Paris Salons provided a forum which was public yet also closed and exclusive to particular élites.

Aveux non avenus,[48] Cahun's most ambitious and complex work, appeared in 1930. This publication consisted of accounts of dreams, extracts of correspondence, polemical and speculative statements, in the form of fragments from an intimate journal, satires, poems and maxims. The text was interspersed with photocollages which resemble the work of Höch, cutting and dissembling the ideal representations of women as objects of sexual display. *Photocollage no. IV*[49] repeats and doubles the self-images of *Que me veux-tu?* to make a formal pattern broken by two smaller images of female classical Greek statues. As in her earlier work the thematics of personal confession, self-representation and the deconstruction of the representation of the female ideal remained her central concern.

During the 1930s the political situation in Europe and Russia necessitated a change in the direction of modernism; the emphasis on the interiority of the psychic life of the individual was replaced with the demand for writers and artists to align themselves in relation to the opposing factions, 'communism' or 'fascism'.[50] Within the Surrealist milieu Cahun drew such criticism from the Stalinist Aragon, who accused her of being concerned with art for art's sake, fulfilling the demands of the bourgeois individual at the expense of serving class struggle. In 1932 both Cahun and Moore joined the the Association des Ecrivains Artistes Révolutionaires (AEAR), an organization of artists and writers who expressed solidarity with the idealism of the Soviet revolution. In reaction to Stalinism both Cahun and Moore severed their alliance by 1935, to become members of the Trotskyist organization Brunet, a group which provided Cahun with the necessary platform for her ideas on eroticism, art and politics.

It is in the continual act of self-portraiture that Cahun best articulated the relation between the masquerade of representation and the body. Returning to the self-portrait of 1927, *I Am in Training, Don't Kiss Me*, the tension of the image derives from a teasing eroticism which is simultaneously presented and denied.[51] The mask invites the gaze; the written text prohibits; the body confronts. Irrespective of the sexual position of the viewer, the situation is recognizable as seductive. In Lacan's terminology the appeal to the viewer is to enter into the Imaginary seduction, which is prohibited in

C. Cahun, *Self-portrait* (1928),
© Jersey Museums Service

C. Cahun, *Self-portrait with Dumb-Bells*: 'I Am in Training, Don't Kiss Me'
(1927), © Jersey Museums Service

the Symbolic by the text written across the chest: the real sex of the bod remains concealed.

Cahun's performance poses the conditional 'as if' into the domain o 'reality': the performance of art becomes indistinct from the performance o life, a condition which may be termed perverse. As Cahun herself speaks o the angel, 'the angel, as the demon of perversity',[52] the denial of heterosexualit may also be placed within the domain of perversion. Throughout the rang of Cahun's self-portraits, the viewer's identification with Cahun either a represented or with the camera position produces a conflict of desire. T identify with Cahun is to identify with an unknown sexual position, raisin the possibility of a bisexual identification. The precise structure of Cahun' masquerade in relation to the camera remains unknown: for whose gaze doe she present herself? To identify with the desire of the camera is equall problematic as the structure of desire is here deducible only from th masquerade of the object. As in the analysis of Höch's *Marlene* and *Th Strong Men*, the repressed bisexual identification becomes unavoidable i reading these images.

Because of their politics and Cahun's Jewish ancestry, Cahun and Moor in 1937 escaped from France to the island of Jersey, where they became activ members of the resistance. After the Nazi invasion of the Channel Island they proceeded to carry out a daily regime of Surrealist actions designed t disturb and distract the Nazis. These took the form of 'playful' actions, such as pushing all the requisitioned cars into the sea or writing anti-fascist slogans One of these actions included sailing a boat in front of the Nazi headquarters bearing the following slogan in German: 'Jesus is great – but Hitler is greater Jesus died for the people – but the people die for Hitler'.[53]

The ideals and values by which Cahun lived her life led her to oppose fascism, National Socialism and the duplicity of Vichy France. Her capacity for self-reflection drew on her ability to articulate unconscious fantasy through dream, writing and images. This rigorous exploration of her own subjectivity, augmented by her engagement in political debates around art, life and sexuality, necessitated that her narcissism be exceeded in the search for her own symbolic ego-ideals. Cahun's flaunting and denial of the masquerade of heterosexuality brought her into particular political alliances and group identifications non-complaisant with the normalization of fascism.

Conclusion

Höch and Cahun exemplify different strategies in reworking the psychic systems of ideals. Lacan's differentiation between the different metaphysical registers of the Imaginary, based on illusion at the mirror stage of the birth of the ego, and the Symbolic restructuring of the subject according to the values of the Oedipal ordered society through language clarifies the distinction between the ideals. To recap, the ideal-ego based around narcissism at the mirror stage brings about identifications on a different basis to the symbolic values of the ego-ideal operating under the direction and coercion of the inherited parental super-ego.

Höch and Cahun use particular strategies to articulate this gap between the Imaginary and Symbolic ideals of the female self. The representations of the Imaginary ideal-ego restore a necessary narcissism to women otherwise determined by the demands of male fantasies and ideals. The ideal-ego is therefore exemplified by the image of the 'New Woman' according to the modernist ideology of the women's liberation.

The presence of the Symbolic ego-ideal determined by the Oedipal super-ego continues to push woman into a binary sexual position, lacking the phallus. In Lacan's phallic theory of sexual difference[54] woman is defined as being the phallus for the man, the man in this patriarchal order possessing the phallus only in relation to the feminine other. As Lacan points out, this role of 'being the phallus' entails adopting the masquerade of femininity. It is this which Höch parodies through dissembling and literally cutting up the Symbolic codes of the phallus. Deconstructing the feminine masquerade exposes the juxtaposition of two registers of the ideal: the Imaginary narcissistic ideal and the oedipal Symbolic ego-ideal obeying the prevailing social norm.

Cahun's strategy is different: a representation of herself as an object of fascination, admiration and glamour, both for her own gaze and for the gaze of others. This self-conscious performance of her own life presents a carapace of the narcissistic Imaginary ideal-ego.

The Symbolic ego-ideal raises her spectra through the negation of the male fantasy of woman and lesbian. As Butler points out, heterosexuality demands that the phallic law defines its other through forms of negation, denial, repression or foreclosure, in order to determine its own existence.[55] The stability of heterosexuality depends upon the phallic law of difference being seen to be maintained at the expense of all other sexualities. Thus the lesbian in an Oedipal ordered society is represented in male fantasy in the negative as lawless, anti-social, unhappy, unstable, cruel and theatrical, with a tenuous grasp on reality etc. Cahun reclaims authorship of the image of the non-heterosexual at the level of the ideal-ego and also through her presentation of an ego-ideal that refuses the phallic differential of Lacan's Symbolic.

The symbolic identifications of Cahun's ego-ideal operate not in conformism with Oedipal law and its ethical code but according to a morality based on identifications free from the parental super-ego: a new ethics. As revealed in the account of her life, Cahun made a series of identifications with political groups and movements which opposed fascism.

Viewers and readers of Höch and Cahun are required to experience the differences between their own Imaginary and Symbolic identifications. The invitation to form identifications with the represented objects necessitates that the viewers confront the contents of their denied object-choice and excluded sexuality. To return to the quotation from Freud previously cited, 'all human beings are capable of making a homosexual object choice and have in fact made one in their unconscious'⁵⁶ and vice versa. In this sense of integrating the contents of the unconscious, bisexual identification takes place irrespective of the sexuality of the viewer and reader.

On this basis another question emerges of how are we to form group identifications not bound to Symbolic phallic law, through either its instantiation or its negation? With the retrieval of repressed object-choices and desire, comes the demise of the moralizing force of the patriarchal oedipal super-ego. The consequent emergence of different symbolic ideals and other values gives rise to new questions of ethics.

A rereading and revisioning of the life-work of Höch and Cahun may allow us to perceive the ethical demands of their work and enable us to ask the question, 'Who carries our ideals?'

Notes

1. M. Lavin, *Cut with a Kitchen Knife: The Photomontages of Hannah Höch* (New Haven and London: Yale University Press, 1993).
2. F. Leperlier, *Claude Cahun: l'écart et la métamorphose* (Paris: Jean Michel Place, 1992).
3. The concept of narcissism first appeared in Freud's letters to his friend and colleague the physician Fliess, with whom he corresponded during the 1890s. Freud held the theory, stemming from his work as a neurophysiologist, that the structure of the psyche was based on networks of neurones, from which the ego is formed as a differentiation of that structure ('Project for a Scientific Psychology' (1895), in *The Origins of Psychoanalysis*, ed. E. Kris, M. Bonaparte and A. Freud (London: Imago, 1954). In Freud's first topological theory the ego is that part of the psyche capable of directed consciousness and logical thought processes; it is the location of the speaking 'I' as opposed to the unconsious psychic systems organized according to the processes of dream.
4. The concept of identification evolves in Freud's writings from his earliest theory of hysterical identification with another's symptoms to identification as literally becoming another person through introjecting or swallowing of that other. 'Mourning and Melancholia' (1917) (*The Standard Edition of the Complete Works of Freud* (*S.E.*), trans. and ed. by James Strachey (London: Hogarth Press, 1955), vol. XIV, reprinted as Penguin Freud Library (*P.F.L.*) (London: Penguin Books, 1984), vol. 11) describes how the loss of identifications, as a result of death or any other reason, leads the ego to set up the other as a part of her/himself in a vain attempt to keep the relationship alive. The depression associated with mourning is therefore explicable as the anger with this lost other, now being directed at the indistinguishable other within oneself.
5. Freud, 'On Narcissism: An Introduction' (1914), (*S.E.*, vol. XIV), *P.F.L.*, vol. 11.
6. *Ibid.*, p. 81.
7. Freud, 'Three Essays on Sexuality' (1905), (*S.E.*, vol. VII), *P.F.L.*, vol. 7.
8. *Ibid.*, p. 56.
9. *Ibid.*, p. 80.
10. Freud, 'On Narcissism', p. 90.
11. Freud, 'Female Sexuality' (1931), (*S.E.*, vol. XXI), *P.F.L.*, vol. 7.
12. Freud, 'The Ego and the Id' (1923), (*S.E.*, vol. IX), *P.F.L.*, vol. 11.
13. *Ibid.*, pp. 372–3.
14. N. O'Connor and J. Ryan, *Wild Desires and Mistaken Identities: Lesbianism and Psychoanalysis* (London: Virago, 1993), pp. 238–41.
15. Lacan, (1953–4) *The Seminar of Jacques Lacan, I*, ed. J.-A. Miller, trans. by J. Forrester (Cambridge: Cambridge University Press, 1988), pp. 129–42.
16. Lacan, 'The Mirror Stage as Formative of the Function of the I, as Revealed in Psychoanalytic Experience' (1936), in *Ecrits: A Selection*, trans. A. Sheridan (London: Routledge, 1980), pp. 1–7.

17. Freud, 'Three Essays', p. 56.
18. J. Butler, *Gender Trouble* (London and New York: Routledge, 1990).
19. J. Riviere, 'Womanliness as a Masquerade', *International Journal of Psychoanalysis*, X (1929), pp. 303–13.
20. Meskimmon and Shearer-West, *Visions of the Neue Frau* (Aldershot: Scolar Press, 1995), introduction by West, pp. 1–6. Further statistical information is available in Ute Frevert's chapter 'The Weimar Years', in U. Frevert, *Women in German History* (New York and Oxford: Berg, 1989), pp. 168–204, which gives a concise account of the politics of the women's movement during the Weimar years.
21. Meskimmon and Shearer-West, *Visions of the Neue Frau*, p. 5. For a history and analysis of the complex political groupings within the alliance of the BDF, the expulsion of radical feminists during the 1920s, the shift to the right and consequent support for National Socialism, see Richard Evans, *The Feminist Movement in Germany 1914-1933* (London: Sage, 1976), pp. 209–56.
22. Meskimmon and Shearer-West, *Visions of the Neue Frau*, pp. 143–64. For an analysis of the impact of German population control over women's bodies via the medicalization of maternity, abortion, sexuality and contraception, see C. Usborne, *The Politics of the Body in Weimar Germany* (London: Macmillan, 1992).
23. K. Theweleit, *Male Fantasies* (Cambridge: Polity Press, 1987), vol. 1.
24. *Dada-Ernst*, 1920–1. Lavin, *Cut with a Kitchen Knife*, plate 1.
25. *The Coquette I*, ibid., p. 139.
26. *Ibid.*, p. 189.
27. Meskimmon and Shearer-West, *Visions of the Neue Frau*, p. 6.
28. *Marlene* 1930. Lavin, *Cut with a Kitchen Knife*, plate 18.
29. *Ibid.*, p. 143.
30. Anna Rueling speaking as an Uranian, 'What Interest Does the Women's Movement Have in the Homosexual Question?' (1904), in L. Faderman and B. Erikson, *Lesbians in Germany: 1890's–1920's* (Tallahassee: Naiad Press, 1990), makes a clear distinction between absolute and merely psychological homosexuality. The latter refers to personality traits as opposed to desire or object-choice.
31. *The Coquette, I, II , III*, 1925. Lavin, *Cut with a Kitchen Knife*, pp. 139, 140.
32. *Made for a Party*, 1936. G. Adriani, *Hannah Höch 1889-1978 Collages*, trans. E. Martin (Stuttgart: Institute for Foreign Cultural Relations, 1985), p.115.
33. Freud, 'The Ego and the Id'.
34. *The Strong Men*, 1931. Lavin, *Cut with a Kitchen Knife*, p. 196.
35. *Ibid.*, p. 197.
36. Freud, 'Group Psychology and the Analysis of the Ego', (*S.E.*, vol. XVIII), *P.F.L.*, vol. 12.
37. Leperlier, *Claude Cahun: l'écart*.
38. Leperlier, *Claude Cahun, 1894–1954. Musée d'Art Moderne de la Ville de Paris* (Paris: Jean Michel Place, 1995).
39. Cahun, 'Vues et Visions' (1914), *Mercure de France*, 406 (16 May) and *L'Amitié*, 45 (April 1925).
40. Leperlier, *Claude Cahun, l'écart*, p. 33.
41. *Que me veux-tu?* (1928). Leperlier, *Claude Cahun, 1894–1954*, p. 61.
42. Leperlier, *Claude Cahun, l'écart*, p. 37.
43. *Ibid.*, p. 37.
44. Cahun, 'Héroïnes', *Mercure de France*, 639 (1 February 1925).
45. Leperlier, *Claude Cahun, l'écart*, p. 112.
46. *Bifur*, 5 (April 1930); Leperlier, *Claude Cahun: l'écart*, p. 113.
47. See S. Benstock, *Women of the Left Bank Paris, 1900–1940* (London: Virago, 1987), p. 48, for a discussion on the functions of cross-dressing as an appropriation of the heterosexual masquerade, as 'passing' as heterosexual and cross-dressing as a flouting of convention.
48. Cahun, *Aveux et avenus* (Paris: Carrefour, 1930).
49. Leperlier, *Claude Cahun: l'écart*, frontispiece.
50. Benstock, *Women of the Left Bank*, pp. 396–441.

51. Leperlier, *Claude Cahun: l'écart*, pp. 44–5, 48.
52. *Ibid.*, p. 235.
53. Leperlier, *Claude Cahun: l'écart*, p. 278.
54. Lacan, 'The Meaning of the Phallus' (1958), in *Feminine Sexuality: Jacques Lacan and the École Freudienne*, ed. J. Mitchell and J. Rose, trans. J. Rose (London: Macmillan, 1982), pp. 83–5.
55. Butler, *Gender Trouble*, p. 65.
56. Freud, 'Three Essays', p. 56.

Sometimes It's Hard to Be a Woman

Stephanie Device

Being a successful femme

means making a butch desire you

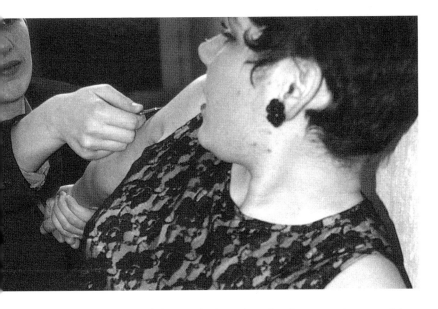

and then enduring when that lust turns into suspicion.

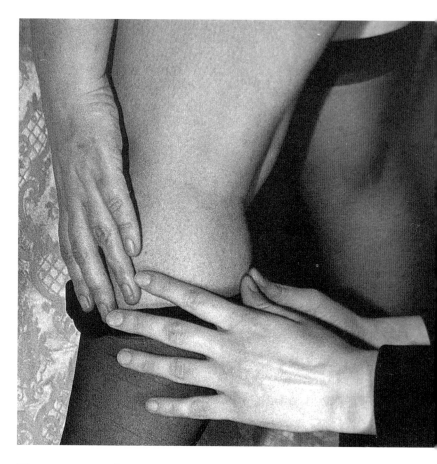

'If you want me,' she sneers,

'you must really want a man.'

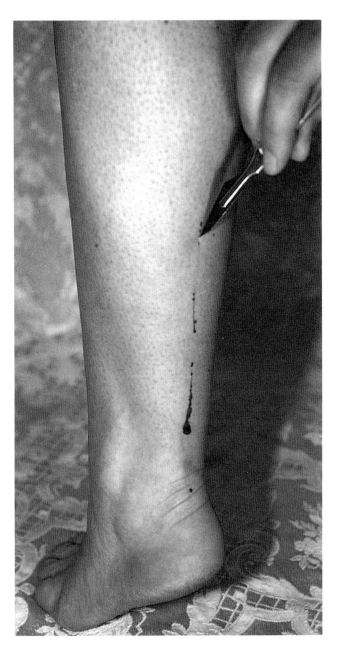

Nobody knows how much it hurts

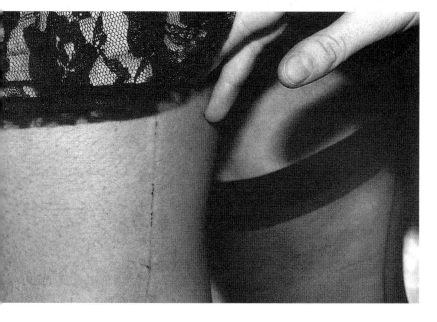

when you go out in the street and straight men tell you the same damned thing.

domestic violence 1

domestic violence 2

silenced 1   missing

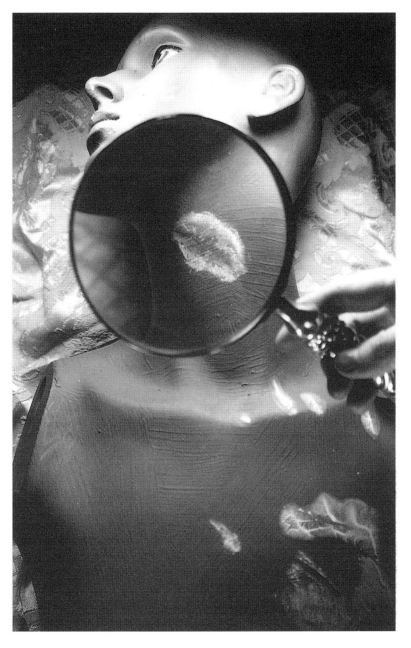

silenced 2   jealousy

Caught in the Act

Stephanie Device

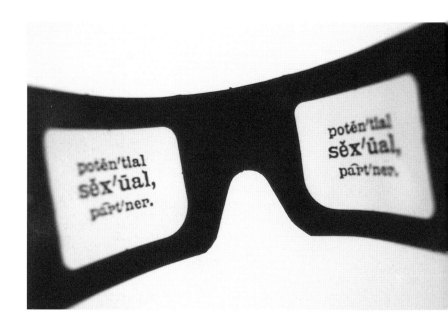

insatiability   props of bisexuality 1:1

insatiability

props of bisexuality 1:2

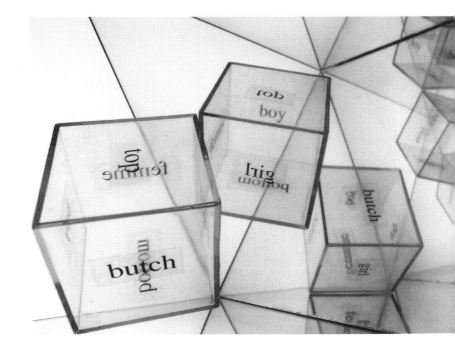

indecision

props of bisexuality 2

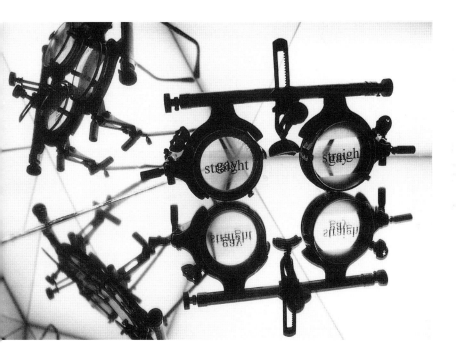

double vision   props of bisexuality 3

Etiquette for Ladies: A true gentlewoman should be as natural and unconscious as the very play of the lungs or the beating of the heart.

FOUR

Available Meanings, Divergent Perspectives

11

Editors' Roundtable Discussion: The Bisexual Imaginary

Existing theoretical perspectives on bisexuality are split between those who consider that bisexuality contributes to and perpetuates sex/gender binaries, and those who believe that bisexuality goes beyond those binaries. For example, Eve Sedgwick posted to the Queer Studies e-mail list in 1994 that while bisexuality disrupts lesbian and gay assumptions that sexuality is fixed by one gender of object-choice it simultaneously fixes the assumption that there are two genders from which to choose. For Sedgwick, it is not bisexuality but queer that is most effective in making that challenge to the 'decisiveness of gender-of-object-choice'.[1] Linked to Sedgwick's view are ideas of bisexuality as 'a western luxury. . . . [a] false-monist polarized word . . . which derives from splitting or division'.[2] The second understanding of bisexuality as transgressive of sex/gender binaries is expressed by, for example, Mark Pritchard, a bisexual man, who says that '[w]hen I have sex I turn into a human being, I am more generous, patient and accepting of myself and others. I forget I'm getting fat, I forget to feel anxious, I feel beautiful and loved. I am liberated from the commerce and conformity of the world.'[3] Pritchard's view that bisexuality turns us all into human beings, moves us beyond gender, beyond commerce, beyond ordinary social concerns stands in direct opposition to the queer view.

How is it possible that bisexuality is understood within sexual politics so oppositionally? This roundtable discussion aims to explore that question by charting the different, sometimes competing meanings of bisexuality that are frequently assumed rather than stated, or critiqued, and to provide a context for reading the articles in this volume.

This volume focuses entirely on theorizing bisexuality, or theorizing bisexually. As many readers will be unfamiliar with this emerging perspective, or may understand bisexuality solely in terns of the above 'deadlock', we thought it was important to try and bring together in the roundtable what may appear to be disparate bisexual imaginaries in the articles. We want, here, to map out the terrain that they (un)cover, and to present and discuss the dominant bisexal imaginaries that these articles engage with or assume. We also hope that some alternatives to the 'deadlock' visions may emerge. This roundtable format was envisaged as an informal way of highlighting the coherence of this volume as well as the differences contained within it, and to give the interrogations here a history.

CH: Kate, in her chapter for this book, mentions what she perceives as the emergence in the 1990s of a politically and theoretically confident discourse of bisexuality. Can we begin by exploring what that emergent discourse is? How does this book develop that discourse of bisexuality?

MS: Up until now the standard move in bisexual writings has been to say that bisexuality means sexual attraction towards members of both sexes, followed by a pitch to separate it from androgyny or hermaphroditism, which produces an ahistorical and idealized notion of bisexuality. For example, Sue George does this in *Women and Bisexuality* when she says that it's a 'confusion' or 'misidentification' to conflate bisexuality with androgyny, as if giving the word the meaning of 'androgyny' were simply a mistake. But the point is that for a good hundred years that's what bisexuality *did* mean – it meant the simultaneous existence of two sexes. A number of chapters in this book distinguish between those meanings – in particular Sharon's and Clare's articles – highlighting also that the resonances of those other meanings are still there, that we can't just erase them. I think we need to look at the role that the past plays in producing current understandings of bisexuality.

JE: And yet those conflations are precisely what have lead to bisexuality being seen as maintaining the status quo, which is why we *do* need to separate them out. It's assumed that, by claiming a bisexual identity, we're resolidifying gender and sex binaries: that the 'bi' in bisexual shows that we believe in two complementary sexes and genders, and is therefore a fundamentally heterosexist concept. Which is why those hostile to us insist on writing it with a hyphen.

CH: And why they tend to ask the very loaded question, 'What does bisexuality mean?' It anticipates an answer that confirms the worst fears of the questioner. If you are unable to answer, then bisexuality must mean nothing, can't exist as a viable sexual identity. If you do answer, in all likelihood in terms of desire for more than one gender of object-choice, or in terms of identity rather than behaviour, bisexuality is seen as resolidifying gender as binary and oppressive. You can't win.

AK: But is there no point to *us* asking that question 'What does bisexuality mean'? Especially since that vexed question of meaning has motivated most of the work on bisexuality, even if there is no single answer.

CH: And since most of the work on bisexuality is undertaken by self-identified bisexuals, who clearly have a sense of themselves as bisexual, even if they can't define absolutely what that means. Addressing that question of meaning is a central way of theorizing bisexuality.

JE: So if we rephrase the question as, 'What does bisexuality mean for this collection?', what would the answer be then?

CH: To begin by just picking out a few of the meanings in this book, bisexuality means sexual desire for more than one sex, means androgyny, means pre-Oedipal potential, as you might expect. But it also means a structural base for dominance of heterosexuality in Nick's and Merl's and my articles, and for racialization of sexuality as well in Merl's; a body without inhering subjectivity in Mariam's; a trope for something else, like greed or Americanism in Nick's and Jo's pieces, as well as lack of boundaries in Jo's; an identity mapped on to and inseparable from lesbianism in Ann's piece and mine; something which is displaced or erased in Phoebe's; a challenge to temporality of sexual identity in Phoebe's or Ann's; and a way of thinking through historical and political effects of sexual representation, as in Kate's piece.

AK: So even at a cursory glance, bisexuality obviously means more than the sexual or gender explanations commonly ascribed to it, or understood as producing it. The chapters in this book *connect* disparate strands of feminism, capitalism, psychoanalysis, colonialism, literature and art, amongst other things, through the sometimes notional figure of 'the bisexual'. Sharon's article, for example, links the psychoanalytic concept of identification with the artistic work of Höch and Cahun, through the idea of a 'bisexual viewing'.

MS: And one very important perspective which these chapters share, is that without taking account of bisexuality scholarship cannot make these fundamental connections.

JE: Yes! That's very much the impetus for my work: to show how the figure of the bisexual is absolutely necessary in the films I look at, how it holds together meanings of greed, instability and consumption. Without the presence of 'the bisexual' these texts simply would not work.

MS: For my work bisexuality is important not just for its own sake but also because of what it can reveal about the constitutive role of 'race' in the history of sexuality. I think you can only see that by looking at the centrality of bisexuality for those early sexological texts.

AK: I'd like to stress here that these various meanings we're picking out all have very different political implications. Bisexuality certainly *means* different things, but the effect that those meanings have *do* different things as well – they can enable or disenable positive adult bisexual desires and identities.

PD: Let's take an example from psychoanalytical approaches. There's a tendency for bisexuality to be split into heterosexuality and homosexuality. The analyst splits fantasy and reality and then, if the client is in a relationship, that relationship is taken as the 'real' sexuality. Or, as for Anna Freud, fantasy is seen as the determinant of that sexuality. So clients who might term themselves 'bisexual' are seen as *either* heterosexual *or* homosexual. I mean, on that very basic individual level, bisexuality is split, uncomfortable contradictions are split between fantasy and reality, between heterosexuality and homosexuality.

JE: So here is an understanding of bisexuality which translates into a set of structures that the analyst may impose on the client. It's not just psychoanalysis but all sorts of helping professions – telephone helplines, local support groups – which have an imaginary notion of what bisexuality is, and to which potential clients or callers are expected to conform if they are going to have access to these resources.

PD: So somebody might ring up and say 'I fancy a man, but I'm sleeping with a woman' and the person on the other end of the phone fits them into preconceived ideas of how sexuality works and what it is. More often than not, bisexuality is not acknowledged at all. *Either* the person they are sleeping with *or* the person they fancy tends to be seen as indicative of their 'true' sexuality.

AK: Of course, I wouldn't want to suggest that bisexuality is wholly constrained. Bisexuality is also *constraining*, it's imposed upon people and used as a grid for making sense of their desires. For example, psychoanalytic understandings of bisexuality-as-potential are used as a way of dismissing lesbian and gay desires and identities. If 'we are all bisexual really', bisexuality is seen as the reason lesbians and gay men can be 'cured', the reason they can be forced back into heterosexuality. Bisexuality can be a vehicle for 'compulsory heterosexuality'. Potential lesbians and gay men may also misrecognize *themselves* as bisexual for similar reasons.

JE: I'd like to emphasize that we're not saying there are some 'real' understandings of bisexuality and some other 'imaginary' ones. Ideas about sexuality are always culturally current groupings of images, ways of thinking about sexuality that are specific to particular political movements, professions or theoretical positions.

AK: Perhaps, then, we should look at some of the available meanings of bisexuality which have the most influence currently?

PD: It's most often thought of as a universal potential which has been repressed and which, if released, is liberating. To believe that sexuality is liberating *per se* flows into a Reichian argument that imagined sexual freedoms will emerge and liberate us without the need for any other political context or effort. Nick's article could be seen as a direct critique of that Reichian view. He argues that the sexuality expressed in Ginsberg's poetics is not liberatory or revolutionary but a mythopoetic defined by American commodity capitalism in the 1950s. Sexuality has been defined by capitalism – there is nothing intrinsically revolutionary about it.

AK: It's really strange because a lot of the arguments about sexuality as liberating in the 1960s, even though they often came from straight men and appeared to shore up heterosexuality, were frequently *acted out* in ways which *were* quite liberating for some of us on the 'outside' –

straight women, lesbians and bi women, gay men. Something about the time did create new spaces for all kinds of behaviour. So I'd go along with Angela Carter when she claims the 1960s as a decadent, radical *and* liberating time. It *was* a time which challenged notions of gender and sexual orientation, and the relationships between bodies, genders and sexualities. For example, I identified strongly with the 'feminine men', the hippy guys: I wanted to *be* Neil Young. I wanted to play with meanings of femininity and womanness, and my (female) body was only one variable in all this.

JE: Your experience in the 1960s, Ann, also has echoes in the emergence of similar ideas more recently. There's been an emergence of a youth culture in which androgyny is often more central than gender division. And with that comes the idea that anyone could be your sexual partner, because you can't make easy gender distinctions. Ecstasy, which encourages a non-gender-specific sensual love for those around you, is a drug that could only have taken off in such a climate.

AK: Did anyone else hear Sadie Plant on Radio four recently, when she said that those adolescents who've experienced the sheer pleasures that 'E' provides are not going to settle for conventional boring 'straight' sex?

CH: I wish I could believe that! But I'm not sure the idea of androgyny as sexually radical really gets us very far. Look at Garber's book, *Vice Versa*, which re-presents these views of bisexuality as androgynous, repressed, and therefore liberatory. And nobody appears to be critical of it. I'd like to point out that this is actually a wholesale bisexual investment in Freud, who states that bisexuality is the pre-Oedipal base on which we build our sexuality. For Freud that repression is necessary for us to function in society; for Garber – as for Reich, and also Marcuse – repression is rewritten as a denial of a true bisexual self.

MS: And not just Garber. June Jordan, in her essay 'A New Politics of Sexuality', talks about bisexuality as liberating, as all about freedom, and uses the phrase 'an honest human body'. It's a fabulously powerful piece of rhetoric, but it still buys into that Freudian notion of bisexuality as the 'honest' thing which has been repressed by 'society'.

JE: To play devil's advocate for a moment, though. What's actually *wrong* with rewriting Freud, with trying to 'unrepress' our bisexual potential?

PD: Well, even if it could theoretically be 'released', its meaning as a universal human potential only stems from the Freudian notion of repression. The pre-Oedipal notion of bisexuality precludes the possibility of its being fully understood as an adult sexual identity – adult heterosexuality is assumed to be the developmental norm. You can't divorce the idea of bisexual potential from its oppressive structure.

CH: Whenever we say 'we're all bisexual really', we're really saying we'll all grow up to be straight!

JE: But this notion of bisexuality does, at the same time, provide ways, however contradictory, of affirming bisexuality.

AK: I liked what your mum said to you, Clare.

CH: Well, when I came out as bisexual to my mum at the age of fifteen, I said, with a bit of preamble, 'Mum, I'm bisexual.' She replied, with no preamble, 'Yes darling, of course you are: we all are.' On the one hand that was incredibly validating for me to hear – no recriminations, no disgust – and enabled me to continue having sex with women and men without denial, to her or to myself. On the other hand our two understandings of bisexuality could be said to be in direct opposition. I want acknowledgment for my adult sexual *desire*; she endorses the sense of bisexuality as potential that actually *precludes* that adult desire from being taken seriously, that endorses heterosexual privilege.

JE: Though isn't it far preferable to have someone say 'Yes darling' than to have them say 'Get out of my house'? And yet, while that might be a positive response for a child to receive from a parent, it's also the way that straight people handle bisexuality more generally, recuperating us back by insisting that because of this imagined universal bisexuality we're no different from them.

AK: But there are a lot of people who have non-het sexuality who enjoy that feeling of being outside: it feels glamorous and radical.

CH: These days I'm more likely to want to be called a pervert and less likely to want to be understood as pre-Oedipal.

JE: That dichotomy between benign tolerance and outright rejection exemplifies the position of bisexuals in the lesbian and gay community. Although Lesbian and Gay Pride in the UK is now Lesbian, Gay, Bisexual and Transgender Pride, I'm not at all convinced that all bisexuals will be welcome. Boy–boy and girl–girl couples will probably feel at home, but what sort of response will girl–boy couples, or swingers get?

CH: Yes, and I'm sure the same will be true for transsexuals. A number of people in the gay press have been making it clear that while gay drag queens will be welcomed at Pride, straight passing transsexuals won't. It's also worth pointing out that transsexuality has commonly been figured within feminist, lesbian and gay, and queer politics and theories in similar ways to bisexuality – as either the height of transgression or the depths of conservatism. I think that tracing the parallels between transsexual and bisexual relationships to feminist, lesbian and gay, and queer communities can be very fruitful as a way of challenging those assumptions and discussing alternative subjectivities.

MS: This issue of exclusion is also extremely pertinent for the bisexual community, which likes to pride itself on its diversity. For example, the 1996 International Bisexual Symposium in Berlin is called: 'Diversity: The Many Faces of Bisexuality'. Claims for 'diversity' can be nothing more than a condescending gesture of inclusion that doesn't amount to much more than an assimilation of those who already fit.

AK: Swingers, and *married* 'opposite-sex' couples, for example, often find little more acceptance within the bisexual community than they do at

Pride. I think that may be because in the last ten years or so bisexuals have tended to emphasize their contribution to lesbian and gay communities and have insisted on inclusion within those communities. The desire for lesbian and gay acceptance has resulted in *some* bisexual practices and identifications being downplayed or marginalized.

JE: So it could be seen as kind of paradoxical that one dominant model for bisexuality is that of coalition and harmony: for example, for many years the national bisexual newsletter was called *Bifrost – The Rainbow Bridge,* as if we could forget the fact that we are caught up in *conflicts* of class, gender and 'race'. But it would be a mistake to assume that when bisexuals talk about diversity it's always a hollow claim. Since there are virtually no exclusively bisexual spaces it could be argued – as Ann and Clare do in their chapters – that bisexual identities are often patched up or pieced together from a range of different places. Out of this comes a sense of a bisexual hybridity pulled together out of all sorts of locations which are mostly either gay or straight.

AK: I think the fact that a lot of bi theorists use the word 'hybrid' is really interesting. That's such a dominant trope in theories of sexuality and culture right now. It's a kind of sexual multiculturalism. There are lots of explicit comparisons in *Bisexual Horizons,* for example, of bisexuality with multiculturalism, or claims that the bisexual movement is a multicultural one, and that's presented as an unproblematically good thing in a very liberal way. There's no acknowledgment that there's any kind of radical or feminist critique of the notion of multiculturalism.

MS: In Australia, for example, where the Labor government made really big, self-conscious attempts at multiculturalism and at presenting Australia as a multicultural society, feminists and Aboriginal activists have been criticizing it as something still based on liberal models of toleration which do nothing to dislodge white hegemony, which is basically racist. I guess part of the problem too is that 'multiculturalism' means quite different things in different contexts – 'mutliculturalism' means something quite different in the Australian context than it would in western Europe, say, or the US – whereas forms of bisexual politics that invoke 'multiculturalism' do so in ways which presume that it's self-evident and transparent, that we all know what it is and that it's always a good and progressive thing.

AK: I want to say something here, though, about the importance of hybridity for me for thinking about bisexuality. Like many of us, when I first started to theorize bisexuality there was very little around that related to how I experienced or thought about my sexuality. Until I read Elizabeth Däumer's article, the pieces which worked most for me were Hélène Cixous's thoughts on a bisexuality which 'stirred up differences', Donna Haraway's cyborg stuff and Gloria Anzaldúa's theorizing around the *mestiza* figure. None of these are 'about' bisexuality, but they are ways of thinking about the self as a hotch-potch of processes and understandings. I found Anzaldúa's work particularly useful as her thinking is focused around a hybridity which has 'real' material consequences and so doesn't lose itself in the idealism of a lot of white 'borderlands' thinking.

JE: I also think that capitalism is a key context for understanding the status of 'diversity' rather than hybridity. The goal of diversity is to offer people as many choices for their identity as possible – as if by having more choices one necessarily had better choices, or even any real freedom of choice. It's the logic of the free market, where profound constraint is passed off as liberation.

CH: In relation to Pride, you could see the addition of 'Bisexual and Transgender' either in terms of political acknowledgement and inclusion of differences, or, you know, as identifying a new group to spend the Pink Pound. As Mariam illustrates so beautifully in her article, visibility is taken as the proof of the authenticity of an identity. We are all required to legitimate our identities with the purchase of T-shirts, badges and books: I have to go and buy the 'Nobody Knows I'm Bisexual' T-shirt. We are included in part because we constitute a new market.

JE: More than that even, sexual identity is thought through the logic of the commodity: it is a leisure product in itself, that you can possess, wear out and exchange for next year's model. Which is one reason why bisexuality is so popular at the moment, and why transgender is rapidly becoming equally embraced: what will it be next year, I wonder?

MS: And yet, as we see from Pritchard's quote that we opened the roundtable with, bisexuality is frequently thought of as a way out of such commodification. It's such a fantasized state – 'I'm divorced from the commerce of the world', as if sex were never commercial.

PD: I mean, you only have to look in the pages of the *Pink Paper* or *Boyz*.

JE: You only have to go and look in the newsagent's window.

MS: You've only got to look in Ann's handbag!

CH: I like the way that Nick's article demonstrates this mutually beneficial relationship between bisexuality and capitalism, highlighting the ways that capitalism welcomes and encourages the notion of bisexuality as freedom of object-choice, *as removing all* restrictions on a person's sexual behaviour.

JE: Yes, but his article also emphasizes the way that bisexuality enables a more fluid mode of desire, which isn't confined to binary structures. Perhaps bisexuality is even enabled by capitalism in a liberating way rather than simply being its reproduction.

MS: Bisexuality is talked about in that way a lot. The way it is presented is that the straight/gay division is binary and belongs to the logic of non-diversity. Bisexuality supposedly goes *beyond* or deconstructs that binary, simply by virtue of not being gay or straight. One of the problems here is the idea that by introducing bisexuality as a third option 'the binary' supposedly ceases to exist. But since 'the binary' is a conceptual form not a numerical tally there is no reason why three – or more – choice shouldn't be contained within that form. For example, the apparent diversity of choices represented by bisexual/lesbian/gay/straight has simply been reformulated into a new binary: monosexual/bisexual. And it's bisexuals who've done that!

JE: Another objection would be that power does not only – or even primarily – operate through binaries. Nineteenth-century sexology, for instance, uses a taxonomy of innumerable sexual types, not solely organized around a gay/straight division. And yet clearly, as Foucault has documented, this structure serves to pathologize and control those subjects it produces.

MS: It has even been proposed that by evading one binary, bisexuality enables an escape from every other binary structure. Hence Paula Rust's assertion that bisexuality is somehow going to undermine the basic fundamental structure of western thought. That kind of bisexual consciousness has led to claims that bisexuality paves the way for solving the problems of all binaries, without any need to interrogate the power relations inherent in those structures – as if, for example, 'race' was something we could just voluntaristically forget, or dissolve by 'going beyond' black and white.

AK: OK, but just because there is a tendency to assume that since bisexuals 'go beyond' one binary they also go beyond others such as 'black/ white' doesn't mean that there aren't ways of working with ideas of 'racial' hybridity. In fact, I think it's very important that, since bisexual theory is still predominantly white, we *do* work from theories of black women and women of colour, that we think about the links between sexual hybridity and racial hybridity without substituting one for the other, in critical and self-conscious ways, as I suggested earlier.

CH: This 'going beyond the binary' has been assumed to be the primary bisexual theoretical and political insight – and not just by bisexuals either. It's further argued that, by refusing to choose between heterosexual and homosexual, you're also refusing to choose between masculine and feminine, between male and female. This is how bisexuals are able to claim that not only does bisexuality go beyond the sexual binary, but that bisexuals themselves are not binary-formed, are themselves androgynous and innocent of gender.

JE: Which is why bisexuals are also supposed to be the switches in the SM community, rather than tops or bottoms. Again, the assumption is that bisexuals go beyond every rigid binary category. That's why butch/femme is not supposed to work for bisexuals.

CH: It works just fine for me! But you're right, it's extremely difficult to convince people – and not just bisexuals – that it is possible to be a bisexual femme or butch, that bisexuals *don't* necessarily 'combine genders' in an androgynous way. In fact many bisexuals gain a sense of identity through gendered roles and object-choices. I'd also go so far as to say that those bisexuals who say that they do not see bodies or genders, but only people, are lying – *of course* it's bodies which we desire, bodies which are always gendered.

AK: Part of the difficulty is also that within the lesbian community, where butch and femme have most currency, femmes have had to spend a long time arguing that they are *not* 'really straight', that they are just as lesbian as butches are. Given the myth that lesbian femmes will eventually leave their butches for men, there is an understandable unwillingness to acknowledge bisexual femmes, who really *might* do it – as indeed they have every right to.

MS: Stephanie's photo-essay looks at what happens when that myth becomes a real possibility. Her images of femme–butch and drag narratives explore how femininity can be understood and negotiated as bisexual.

JE: The photos are a good example of bisexuality working entirely comfortably within a binary.

MS: Yes! Normally in a bisexual collection you'd expect a 'happy ending' with the butch and femme having changed clothes!

JE: Part of the subversive power of her photographs is that, by using images that wouldn't be read as bisexual in any other context, they raise the question of which other images could also be read as bisexual. After all, while some images could clearly *never* be read as lesbian, or *never* be read as straight, no image could *never* be read as bisexual.

AK: If an image assumed to be lasbian could be bisexual in a different context, surely the reverse must also sometimes be true. This raises interesting questions for me about the differences between bisexual women and postmodern lesbians. In my own work I find these differences difficult to negotiate. Both groups attempt to destabilize dominant meanings of bodies and gender and sexuality; and, for both, identity is both relevant and extremely problematic. I think I'd be hard pushed to distinguish between a bisexual woman's imaginary which is concerned with sexual attraction, androgyny and hermaphroditism, and a postmodern lesbian imaginary which is playing around with desire, gender and fleshy bodies. Both are – dare I say – a particularly *feminine* way of inhabiting the sexed and sexy body. And no, I don't know what 'feminine' means – though I was intrigued by Kate's attempt in this book to tease out the differences between a 'feminine' and a 'masculine' bisexual desire.

MS: Perhaps we don't need to resolve all these differences. One thing that comes across very clearly in this collection is the positive value of theorizing women's bisexuality in relation to lesbianism.

CH: Certainly my, Ann's and Mariam's chapters all seem consciously unwilling to separate, and positively desirous of teasing out, the links between bisexual women and lesbians. The two positions are contingent upon, rather than separate from, each other.

JE: They may be contingent upon one another – and yet for most peopl
a sense of psychic wholeness is important, and is achieved by constitutin
oneself as separate and different from others. This is why I think
Lacanian notion of the Imaginary is useful, because it defines a momen
in our psychic development, which then becomes a structure that w
live and with which enables us to think ourselves as individuals. If w
extend that to a notion of a collective cultural imaginary, by whic
different communities maintain a sense of integrity and separatenes
we can see why particular figures are so contested. If the icon whic
once defined me now defines someone different, does that mean I hav
become the same as them? The fear of the loss of an icon is the fear c
a loss of self.

MS: Take the example of Oscar Wilde, who has been imagined for a lon
time as a gay icon. Now some bisexuals are saying: 'He was marriec
he had relationships with women, he's not a gay icon at all. He wa
bisexual all along, he's ours and gay culture stole him from us.' That
less a rediscovery of the truth about Oscar Wilde than it is an act whic
constitutes bisexuality as something different from gayness. Wha
constitutes a bisexual position in the debate about Wilde is the act c
complaining that he has been taken away from us. It's that complain
that allows us to imagine ourselves as a separate, autonomous, bisexua
collectivity at all.

CH: Do we really have to choose? A particular figure can be important i
the constitution of a bisexual imaginary *and* a gay imaginary, surely.

JE: This is definitely true of Robert Mapplethorpe. Although he behave
bisexually it would be disastrous to deny, in the name of a bisexua
separate imaginary, the centrality of a tradition of (racist?) gay mal
iconography in his representation of the black male body. His bisexualit
does not take him *outside* a gay tradition. But also, keeping him insid
an *exclusively* gay tradition ignores the bisexual elements in his work
I'm tired of the insistence on his photographs of flowers bein
unproblematically phallic, when they in fact cross and fuse images o
male and female genitals in what we might see as a very 'bisexual' way

CH: It's clear from our discussion how inseparable bisexuality is from othe
identities, and yet what also emerges very strongly from this book i
the usefulness of a distinctive bisexual theoretical position. For instance
I'm struck in Jo's reference to Mapplethorpe that one of the things tha
makes bisexual theorizing so vibrant is its sense of partiality. Bisexual
are constituted by their sense of being made up from their experience
in other places, which are radically incompatible, but between which
we cannot choose.

AK: I think that's why we can legitimately say that bisexuals are in a positio
to hold those tensions, to be conscious of the oscillation between multipl
identifications. For example, I think it's extremely interesting that i
Bisexual Horizons several contributors end their articles on bisexuality

with the statement that their sexual identity has changed since writing, and that this is seen as positive.

PD: Maybe that's a productive effect of bisexual temporality, which recognizes that in a lifetime a person's experiences may change and with them their identity. Those changes don't just take the person from one finished identity to another, but exemplify the rifts within any identity which make identity *un*finished.

JE: In that way bisexuality makes visible what's true about all desire: its mobility. How can sexual identities, founded on desires which are never stable, try to be stable themselves?

CH: A bisexual perspective can afford to focus on – is in fact dependent upon – those very rifts which other identities may gain more from avoiding. So, for instance, in personal accounts or narratives of sexual identity generally we tend to find retrospective rewriting of past experiences to make sense of one's whole life as leading to, and as proof of, what one is now. Of course, bisexual 'coming-out' narratives repeat that retrospective gesture, insisting that the bisexual subject has always been bisexual, and that previous identities – such as lesbian, straight or gay – were mistaken. But that's not true for everyone. Some of us previously identified quite happily as lesbian, for example, and don't believe that that needs to be rewritten as repression of a 'true' bisexual self. If we are interested in theorizing bisexuality in ways that acknowledge how that identity is always – and, I am suggesting, *primarily* – 'patched up' from different places, as Jo said earlier, and as I argued in my chapter, we need to be critical of bisexual stories that mimic the temporal narratives of other identities.

JE: This is why many of us feel anxious about moves to create a distinct and separate bisexual community – or, in academia, towards creating 'Bisexual Studies' – which would feel the need to make itself whole by smoothing over those very cracks that are so productive. Fortunately that kind of integrity is an impossibility, given that bisexuals will remain invested in experiences from outside that community – for example, Mapplethorpe's nudes, camp or rough trade.

MS: That move towards historical 'integrity' is one of my main criticisms of Garber, and one of the main pleasures in reading her too. On the one hand, Garber acknowledges that she can't theoretically justify ascribing bisexuality either to those who precede the historical arrival of the bisexual identity or to those who, for whatever reason, refused that label. On the other hand, she attempts to create that vision of the ahistoric bisexual figure, a figure with an undifferentiated, whole, complete sexuality. And yet – I loved that bit in Garber about Errol Flynn and Truman Capote being bisexual! As a reader I was doing exactly the same thing as Garber: I couldn't allow myself to believe that those people were really bisexual, yet I really enjoyed the illusion that they were. Or at least, giving myself permission to entertain the fantasy that they were.

CH: The pleasure is in seeing yourself reflected in, for example, Frida Kahlo. It gives your identity a sense of wholeness over time: the very wholeness we've been critiquing! And yet we rely on that wholeness, because without it, how could we see ourselves as bisexual?

AK: But you two are doing it in an ironic way, aren't you ? You believe it and disbelieve it simultaneously.

MS/CH: No!

MS: No. The pleasure is not ironic. The pleasure of reading the book and thinking, 'Georgia O'Keefe? I didn't know that' – that's not an ironic pleasure.

JE: So is the problem with Garber that what she recognizes in those images is not what we recognize?

MS: I think that the difference is that she's locating them in a bisexual imaginary which has closure. She has a vision of bisexuality as an undifferentiated, whole, complete sexuality. Whereas we might recognize ouselves in the images, or misrecognize ourselves more correctly, and take pleasure in the misrecognition, we also want to go on to say that we *know* it's a misrecognition and we're not willing to settle for the closure. So yeah, at a particular moment I can look up at my picture of Byron and think, you know, Byron: bisexual, fat, walked with a limp, that's me. But actually at another moment I will disidentify since Byron was a nineteenth-century male poet, and I'm not.

CH: Well, I have to say that I feel like my experience of the pleasure *is* closed down. It's not as if we inhabit a different bisexual imaginary from Garber. I look at a picture of Frida Kahlo: bisexual meets bisexual. Even though I'm not an early twentieth-century Mexican artist, and I never had an affair with Leon Trotsky. It's the sameness not the differences that I identify with.

JE: This is typical of the tensions we have discussed in relation to bisexual theorizing: however much we want to recognize our complicity with power, our dislocation, *and* the fluidity that comes with a bisexual temporality, at the end of the day, our bisexuality draws us back to investing in the imaginaries we have described.

CH: Perhaps a good way of ending this discussion, then, is to suggest that one very concrete way in which this collection resists the notion of a 'discrete bisexual integrity' is that the contributors to this volume are not all bisexual, though they do all share a commitment to exploring the uses of theorizing bisexuality. It has been important for us that this book – in as many ways as possible – embodies the contingency, partiality and connection to other identities that we are suggesting typifies bisexual theorizing and bisexual identity now, as well as presenting alternative visions that might accompany a bisexual perspective.

Notes

1. Eve Kosofsky Sedgwick, 'Bi', Qstudy-l <qstudy-l@uvbm.cc.buffalo.edu>, Wed, August 17, 15:49:34-0400 EST.
2. Anon., letter to Clare Hemmings, 2 April 1996. Other theorists who consider bisexuality to be the epitome of non-transgression include: Elizabeth Wilson, in 'Is Transgression Transgressive?', in Joseph Bristow and Angelia R. Wilson (eds), *Activating Theory: Lesbian, Gay, Bisexual Politics* (London: Lawrence & Wishart, 1993), pp. 107–17; Elizabeth Grosz, cited in Steven Angelides, 'Rethinking the Political: Poststructuralism and the Economy of (Hetero)sexuality', *Melbourne Historical Journal*, 23 (1995), pp. 39–58; and Mary McIntosh, as cited by Merl Storr in this volume.
3. Mark Pritchard, 'Liberating Pornography', in Naomi Tucker (ed.), *Bisexual Politics: Theories, Queries, and Visions* (New York: Harrington Park Press, 1995), p. 177.

Related Bibliography

Anzaldúa, Gloria, *Borderlands/La Frontera: The New Mestiza* (San Francisco: Spinsters/Aunt Lute, 1987).

Carter, Angela, in Sara Maitland (ed.), *Very Heaven: Looking Back at the 1960s* (London: Virago, 1988).

Cixous, Hélène, 'Sorties . . .', in Hélène Cixous and Catherine Clement, *The Newly Born Woman*, trans. Betsy Wing (Manchester: Manchester University Press, 1987).

Däumer, Elizabeth, 'Queer Ethics, or the Challenge of Bisexuality to Lesbian Ethics', *Hypatia*, Special Issue, Lesbian Philosophy, 7, 4 (fall 1992), pp. 91–105.

Foucault, Michel, *The History of Sexuality: Volume 1: An Introduction* (London: Penguin, 1978).

Freud, Anna, *Problems of Psychoanalytical Training: Diagnosis and Techniques of Therapy* (London: International University Press, 1971).

Freud, Sigmund, 'Three Essays on the Theory of Sexuality' [1905], *On Sexuality* (London: Penguin, 1977).

Garber, Marjorie, *Vice Versa: Bisexuality and the Eroticism of Everyday Life* (New York: Simon & Schuster, 1995).

George, Sue, *Women and Bisexuality* (London: Scarlet Press, 1993).

Haraway, Donna, 'A Manifesto for Cyborgs: Science, Technology, and Socialist Feminism in the 1980s', *Socialist Review*, 80, pp. 65–108.

Jordan, June, 'A New Politics of Sexuality', in Sharon Rose, Cris Stevens *et al.* (eds), *Bisexual Horizons: Politics, Histories, Lives* (London: Lawrence & Wishart, 1996).

Lacan, Jacques, *Ecrits* (Paris: Editions de Seuil, 1966; reprinted, London: Routledge, 1989).

Marcuse, Herbert, *Eros and Civilisation: A Philosophical Inquiry into Freud* [1955] (Boston: Beacon, 1966).

Plant, Sadie, 'Into the Millennium', Radio 4, 13 May 1996.

Reich, Wilhelm, *The Function of the Orgasm* (London: Souvenir Press, 1993).

Rose, Sharon, Stevens, Cris *et al.* (eds), *Bisexual Horizons: Politics, Histories, Lives* (London: Lawrence & Wishart, 1996).

Rust, Paul, *Bisexuality and the Challenge to Lesbian Politics: Sex, Loyalty and Revolution* (New York and London: New York University Press, 1995).

Index